Bob Fine taught at Brooklyn College, City University of New York in the early 1970s and now lectures in sociology at the University of Warwick. He co-edited *Capitalism and the Rule of Law* (1979) and *Policing the Miners Strike* (1975) and has written widely on the police, law, social control and South Africa. He contributes regularly to *Socialist Organiser*.

Bob Fine

# Democracy and the Rule of Law

Liberal ideals and Marxist critiques

Pluto Press

London and Sydney

First published in 1984 by Pluto Press Limited,
The Works, 105a Torriano Avenue, London NW5 2RX
and Pluto Press Australia Limited, PO Box 199, Leichhardt,
New South Wales 2040, Australia

Second impression 1986

Cover designed by Jacque Solomons

Photoset by A.K.M. Associates (U.K.) Ltd.,
Ajmal House, Hayes Road, Southall, Greater London.
Printed in Great Britain by WBC Print
Bound by W. H. Ware & Sons Ltd
Tweed Road, Clevedon, Avon

British Library Cataloguing in Publication Data
Fine, Bob
    Democracy and the rule of law.
    1. Rule of law — Political aspects
    I. Title
    340′.11   K3171

ISBN 0-86104-784-2

# Contents

# Acknowledgements

I wish to thank Glyn Cousin for reading the manuscript at every stage of its production, for her fruitful comments on content and style, for the advice she offered even in the face of the author's stiff resistance and for the clear socialist commitment she brings to all matters. She was also gracious enough to revive her typing skills for which I am most grateful. I wish to thank my colleague from the Law Department at Warwick University, Robert Millar, for going through the text with a fine-tooth comb, for talking through many ideas and for the open way in which he has pursued them in our joint teaching. I wish to thank Simon Clarke of the Sociology Department, Warwick University for his critical and insightful comments, the value of which I have over time learnt to appreciate, and for the honesty with which he expresses his disagreements as well as his support. I wish to thank Martin Thomas of *Socialist Organiser* for the critical, clear-sighted, revolutionary Marxism which he expresses and from which I have tried to learn. I wish to thank Richard Kuper of Pluto Press for being an encouraging, tolerant and sufficiently pressing editor and also for the very wise advice he has given on the structure and content of the book. He has made me aware of the enormous value of Pluto as a socialist publishing house. I wish to thank my good friend, Lawrence Welch for the work which he has put into reading and criticizing the text, for his good sense and for the enduring warmth of his friendship. I wish to thank for their stimulation, advice, ideas and support Simon Frith, Ken Foster, Sol Picciotto, Julio Faundez and other colleagues from the Law and Sociology Departments at Warwick University and from the CSE Law and State Group; my students from Warwick; Sean Matgamana, Bruce Robinson, Nik Barstow and other fellow-contributors to *Socialist Organiser*; Michael Ignatieff, Raff Samuel and others from the History Workshop; and Duncan Innes and Francine de

Clercq from whom I have learnt so much in our joint work on South Africa. Lastly I wish to thank Rossie Fine and Lillian Cousin for the help they generously provided.

# Introduction

My question concerns the relation between Marxist and liberal ideas about private property, law and the state and my starting point is a discontent with two polar versions of Marxism, each of which seems to me to be in its own way equally mistaken. On the one side, Marxism appears as no more than an extension of liberalism, committed to the establishment of the rule of law, parliamentary representation, an impartial police and army, separation of powers between legislature, executive and judiciary and a check on the excesses of private property by state intervention. It is said that liberal ideas about legality and democracy are fully adequate for socialists; it is only a question of defending them against their subversion, of extending them into the economic sphere of capitalist society, or of realizing them fully through the establishment of socialism.

The strength of this approach lies in its appreciation of the achievements of liberal thought, in its recognition of the importance of fighting for or defending the establishment of liberal principles of democracy, the rule of law, civil liberties, etc., and in its efforts to forge a political alliance with liberals on these grounds.

Its weakness lies in its tendency to divorce liberal forms of authority from their class base; its elevation of the rule of law, parliamentary representation, civil liberties, etc., into eternal truths rather than historical accomplishments; its failure to perceive the limited democratic character of these forms and its inability to shake off the shackles which liberal constitutionalism imposes on democratic struggles. The alliance which this sort of Marxism seeks to forge with liberalism is a marriage in which Marxism is subordinated to liberalism and in my view loses its own independent and distinctive identity.

On the other side, Marxism sometimes appears as no more than a negation of liberalism. It presents liberal ideas of freedom and equality before the law, of parliamentary democracy, of impartial administration and policing, etc., as mere frauds which serve as an instrument of class rule, which function to reproduce relations of production based on the expropriation of the majority by the minority, and which obscure the brute realities of oppression and exploitation. Freedom of property appears as little more than freedom to exploit; the law appears little more than an ideological instrument of oppression and the state as essentially authoritarian. From this perspective, it may seem that current attacks by the right on liberal freedoms expose the true – coercive – nature of property and authority in capitalist society, which liberals previously obscured under the veneer of 'rights' and 'law'. The task of socialists appears thus not as one of spreading illusions about liberalism, whose ideals, if they ever could be realized, can no longer; but rather to make a clean break from liberalism and struggle instead in socialist ways for the establishment of socialist forms of authority entirely distinct from those advocated within the liberal tradition.

The strength of this approach lies in its critique of the class basis of liberal thought and in its assertion of the independence of Marxism from liberalism. Its weakness, however, seems to me to lie in its inability to grasp not only the achievements of liberal thought but also to grasp the debt that Marxism has to it. Marxism is not just a rejection of liberalism – this is true of many kinds of radical and reactionary doctrines – but rather a rejection of a definite kind: one that pursues further the principles of democracy and individual liberty which liberalism proclaimed but then inhibited. Thus a Marxist critique of freedom and equality before the law, as opposed to other critiques, does not cynically dismiss these ideals as mere illusions but rather addresses itself to their historical presuppositions and to the restrictive democracy which they express. In securing the independence of Marxism from liberalism, this sort of 'left' Marxism tends to subordinate Marxism to other anti-liberal doctrines akin to anti-authoritarianism, nihilism or to the bureaucratic statism now associated with Stalin's name. While rightly rejecting an alliance in which Marxism is subsumed under liberalism, Marxism may be turned into a sectarian refusal under all circumstances to ally with liberalism, irrespective of the terms of the alliance.

My purpose in writing this book is to develop our understanding of the relation between Marxism and liberalism beyond either of these two unsatisfactory alternatives. To this end I have returned to the classical texts, in order to provide an exposition and critique of the liberal ideas on private property, law and the state which Marx inherited and confronted; of the development of Marx's own critique of jurisprudence; and of three selected attempts to interpret, extend and in one case, 'transcend' Marx's thought in the twentieth century.

The first section looks back to the main currents of liberal thought which preceded Marx – as exemplars of which I have chosen Hobbes, Rousseau, Adam Smith and Hegel – and which together constitute the movement of 'classical jurisprudence'. Classical jurisprudence flowered between the seventeenth and nineteenth centuries in the period of the revolutionary ascendance of the bourgeoisie. Alongside its close companion, classical political economy, it analysed the economic, legal and political requirements of capitalist society: on the one hand attacking the unfreedom, inequalities, economic stagnation and cultural ignorance which characterized the old order; and on the other prefiguring the forms of property and authority appropriate for a new order based on equality, freedom, growth and rational thought. I examine what the liberal proponents of classical jurisprudence meant by private property, law and the state; why they saw these institutions as intimately connected with one another and as the basis of human emancipation, the nature of their critiques of the 'traditional natural law theory' which preceded them; why they should be seen as representatives of a united movement despite the differences between them; and what the significance of these differences was. It was a rich and progressive cultural movement which sought to integrate a form of property based on individual freedom, equality and security with a form of authority based on the consent of the people as a whole. It fell far short of the democratic and social democratic ideas that developed in the nineteenth and twentieth centuries, but it represented a highpoint of liberal jurisprudence, far superior both in its revolutionary ardour and in the quality of its analysis to the 'vulgar' jurisprudence that followed. Its great strength lay in its grasp of the contradictions besetting private property and in its attempts to resolve these contradictions not by going back to the narrow, stagnant and unequal relations of dependency that belonged to the old order but by establishing rational authority based on mutual consent. The attempt by modern right-wing thought to appropriate this tradition for itself in most respects represents a travesty of what classical jurisprudence actually stood for. However, contemporary Marxism has also had difficulties in relating to this tradition: sometimes counterposing one author to another as if they reflected entirely different principles; sometimes opposing their ideas on private property, seen as altogether bad, with their ideas on the rule of law, seen as altogether good; sometimes losing sight of the progressive character of their critique of traditional natural law constraints on property and authority; sometimes artificially elevating one or other classical writer beyond his station, as it were, to the status of a 'Marxist' in all but name; sometimes 'forgetting' the strength of their conceptions of the state.

It was on the basis of an intense study and critique of classical jurisprudence that Marx developed his own ideas on private property, law and the state; thus it is difficult to get to grips with Marx's own theory without this background. Marx affirmed his debt to classical jurisprudence, by emphasizing the 'advances' he thought it had made as well as the limitations of its liberalism. He held up the revolutionary ardour and rational criticism expressed in classical jurisprudence as a yardstick against which to measure the widespread vulgarization of liberal thought among his contemporaries; at the same time, he began to work through its own integral problems. At first, he criticized classical jurisprudence from within, employing its categories but affording to them a more radical, democratic content. His critique of classical jurisprudence was not achieved in one fell swoop but was the result of an intense critical effort, the results of which were not given in advance. Thus in his early writings he retained Hegel's idea of the rational state synthesizing individual liberty and the universal will, but rejected entirely the bureaucratic manner in which Hegel tried to realize this idea. He then began to explore what he saw as the contradiction between the freedom and universality inherent, on the one hand, in the ideal state, and the slavery and egoism inherent, on the other, in civil society, where the pursuit of private interest overrides any social concerns with the whole, leads to the impoverishment of the mass of population for the sake of the few, and subordinates all to the impersonal and uncontrollable power of the market. This critique by the young Marx of classical jurisprudence – the problem he posed and the shortcomings of the solutions he offered – is the subject matter of my second section.

Along with Engels, Marx set off in a new direction, attempting to cut free from his own Hegelian roots in favour of a class theory of law and state. Instead of counterposing the freedom and universality of law and the state to the slavery and egoism of civil society, he now saw law and the state as reflecting the slavery and egoism of civil society. Abandoning the idea of the 'rational state' as a weapon of criticism against the existing state, he now saw alienation and class domination as inherent in the idea of the state. However, his first efforts at developing this new approach, especially in the *German Ideology*, were not surprisingly full of pitfalls and should not be taken as the last word on, or even as the major statement of, Marx's views. It was only in the course of his later theoretical and political writings that he was able to penetrate the contradictory rather than illusory character of the freedom, equality and security associated with the pursuit of private property, the contradictory rather than illusory character of the universality of the state and the connections between private property, law and the state. At this stage, he derived the alien character of the state not from private property but from the division of labour as such; and tended to reduce the universal character of the state to little more than a veil for the enslavement of labour to capital. The achievements and limitations of this approach are the subject of my third section.

Marx never pursued his critique of jurisprudence to the same systematic extent to which he pursued his critique of political economy, though at various times he expressed a desire to do so. However, in his mature writings on economics – the *Grundrisse* and *Capital* – Marx developed a method of critique which can and should be adapted and applied to jurisprudence; he left numerous clues as to how the juridic aspects of capitalist social relations should be addressed; and he offered a substantive analysis of capitalist relations of production which provides a starting point for a critique of their juridic as well as their economic forms of expression. My fourth section seeks to piece together the elements of Marx's theoretical critique of jurisprudence from that of political economy, in order first to reveal the connections linking the juridic categories of private property, law and state, their transitory and historical character, and their derivation from the same relations of production which gave rise to the economic categories of value, money and capital. Economics and jurisprudence are not reducible to each other but are bound together as the twin forms assumed by capitalist relations of production. Just as Marx's critique of political economy was aimed not at replacing one economic theory by another but rather at a social critique of economics in general, and looked forward to the dissolution of the economic sphere in its entirety, this too was the aim of his critique of jurisprudence. Marx revealed the shallow analyses which come from attaching private property, law and the state to the surface of bourgeois society, i.e. commodity exchange, and from abstracting them from the inner content of bourgeois society, i.e. its relations of production. This leads either to a one-sided idealization of liberal notions of freedom, equality and self-interest, or to their equally one-sided repudiation. In this way, Marx traced the roots both of liberal ideals of justice and of the negative critique of liberalism which developed as the obverse side of the same coin. By tracing juridic forms back to production relations, Marx was able to develop a dialectical view of the contradictory elements which run through private property, law and the state.

Marx's political writings reflected and developed this dialectic by analysing the different relations between capital, labour and other classes which develop in capitalist society and the different forms of state which accompany them. Marx criticized existing forms of law and state from the perspective of 'democracy', or, to put the matter in reverse, from the perspective of overcoming the alienation of the state from society. The fact that he saw the state in general as class-based did not mean that he ignored the importance of distinguishing one bourgeois state from another; the state in his view expresses a relation between classes and is not just an instrument of the ruling class. The ruling class does not live in a vacuum. He fought for the democratization of the state, and in so doing applied himself both to the relation between the different elements of the state itself (law, parliament and the executive or bureaucracy) and to the relation between the state and society. He was in favour of maximum possible power for the representative element and minimum possible for the bureaucratic; the independence of the judiciary from the executive but not from parliament. He did not conceive of socialist democracy in a workers' state as a different breed of animal from bourgeois democracy, but rather as the extension of democratic and liberal ideas beyond the point where bourgeois society stopped. He did not see the 'rule of law' as a mere hangover but as a crucial inhibition on bureaucracy and as a crucial guarantor of individual liberty. This followed from his conception of socialist rule not as the subordination of the individual to the collective but as a genuine synthesis of individual freedom and the collective will. His doctrine of the withering away of the state should be seen not merely as 'anti-state' but rather as the extension of the principles of universal will and individual liberty embodied in the liberal idea of the state to the point of the state's own dissolution. The problems that were to confront twentieth-century Marxism – of the growth of the state executive with that of social democracy, the conflict between the democratic form of the socialist state and its class content as a weapon of labour against capital – appeared only at the edges of Marx's writings. However, the progressive and distinctive character of Marx's critique of liberalism, as opposed to other critiques of liberalism, comes out sharply in his political writings and forms the topic of the fifth section.

There are limits to what can be culled from Marx's own comments on jurisprudence. He examined the changing *content* of 'equal right', showing that, while legal equality always entails substantive inequality, the degree and nature of that inequality will differ depending on the relations of production that underlie exchange. Thus the inequalities present in 'equal exchange' between independent petty-commodity producers are quite different from those present in the exchange between labour and capital, which are quite different again from those between labourers and a socialist commune. Marx did not, however, examine theoretically the development of juridic forms, from private property to law, from law to the state, and from the state and law in general to different forms of state and law. In the sixth section I make an exploratory attempt to trace the formal connections between the juridic forms of private property, law and the state on the basis of a close parallel with the economic forms of value, money and capital. My aim is to follow through Marx's critique of the contradictory character of economic relations into a critique of juridic relations, and to show on the one hand the essential connections which link together private property, law and state (against those who dissociate them in one way or another), and on the other the distinctions between these legal forms (against those who reduce them to one and the same legal relation). The bridges linking private property and value, law and money, state and capital are the ones which inform this part of my study.

Finally, in the seventh section, I turn to those twentieth-century attempts to recapture, develop, and in one case to refute Marx's critique of jurisprudence. The first of these is the attempt by the Russian legal theorist Evgeny Pashukanis, writing in the 1920s and 1930s, to develop Marx's theory of law and the state. His great strength lay in his attempt to derive a Marxist theory of law and the state from the method Marx used in his critique of political economy. But I criticize Pashukanis's inability to understand why law and the state should be derived from relations of production, not exchange, why 'private property' and not 'the legal subject' is the elementary category in jurisprudence and why the notion of 'the legal form' as a single entity obscures the distinctions between private property, law and the state. Following from these theoretical weaknesses, I criticize Pashukanis's political failure to understand the democratic character of Marx's critique of bourgeois legality. Pashukanis's ultra-critical view of law was associated with an uncritical view of bureaucracy ('technical control'); it was this combination that made him temporarily useful for the development of Stalinism and exemplifies the dangers besetting 'left' Marxism.

My second case study is that of the contemporary English Marxist historian and activist Edward Thompson. His great strength has been to revive the liberal conception of 'the rule of law' as a weapon against the growth of state authoritarianism; he successfully demolished the right-wing view that the 'rule of law' means unconditional obedience to the state, irrespective of the form and content of the state's commands. The rule of law, in the classical sense which Thompson inherits, represents an inhibition on state power. He also successfully attacked a 'cynical' tendency on the left to dismiss civil liberties as a sham and law as merely a class instrument – a tendency which passes itself off as Marxism but which in reality has little in common with Marx and the liberal tradition out of which he emerged. However, Thompson's subsuming of Marxism to a liberal commitment to the rule of law as an 'unqualified human good' is the target of my critique. Just as Pashukanis's variety of Marxism neglected the democratic element in liberal institutions, Thompson's 'right' Marxism neglected the democratic limits of liberalism.

My final case study is that of the French philosopher and historian Michel Foucault, who presents himself as a 'post-Marxist', transcending distinctions between left and right, materialism and idealism, capitalism and socialism. His theory of 'disciplinary power' underwrote stimulating historical critiques of asylums, prisons, hospitals and the family and has been widely influential, even among some Marxists. His work reveals, however, a rejection of liberalism rooted in Nietzsche and based on entirely different premisses from that of Marxism. His rejection of the juridic categories of private property, law and state in favour of 'power', and his association of despotism with collectivity, lead him down a dangerous road which, I argue, is not only not superior to Marxism but also represents in crucial respects a regression from liberalism.

Such is the outline of my book which, I hope, will provide a clearer understanding both of liberal and Marxist views of jurisprudence; of the relation between them; and of the real phenomena of private property, law and the state. My own views have not remained static in the writing of it and I hope I shall at least stimulate debate. In writing this book, the force of both liberal and Marxist ideas has been vividly impressed upon me; I am aware that both are sometimes turned into lifeless dogmas and the conflict between them into one between two preferred faiths. At the end of this study, I came out more convinced than ever of the relevance of Marxism for contemporary theory and politics, but also of the work which we contemporary Marxists have before us.

# 1. Classical jurisprudence

## Prefiguring the bourgeois revolution

> Every revolution has been preceded by an intense critical effort of cultural penetration . . . The last example and the one closest to us and most similar to our own case, is that of the French Revolution. The preceding cultural period called the Enlightenment, which has been so slandered by the facile critics of theoretical reason . . . was not merely a phenomenon of arid, pedantic intellectualism similar to what we see today . . . It was itself a magnificent revolution whereby . . . an international, spiritual bourgeoisie was formed throughout Europe as a united consciousness aware in all its sections of common sufferings and disgraces. The Enlightenment was the best preparation for the bloody revolt which subsequently took place in France . . . the bayonets of Napoleon's armies found their way already levelled by an invisible army of books and pamphlets . . . which had prepared men and institutions for the necessary renovation . . . The same phenomenon repeats itself today through socialism. (A. Gramsci in P. Cavalcanti, and P. Piccone, Telos 1975, pp. 21, 22)

The disciplinary divisions which now separate law from politics and from economics were not a marked feature of classical thought. Classical jurisprudence arose in close conjunction with studies of the economic foundation of capitalist society conducted by classical political economy. Both kinds of investigation were often authored by the same hand; they did not merely follow parallel tracks but interwove so closely that it is impossible and unfruitful to try to prize them apart. Classical political economy and classical jurisprudence formed the two inseparable wings of a single movement, reflecting the fact that in social life itself these spheres had not yet been fully distinguished. Indeed, one of the aims of classical thought was to perfect what at the time was an incomplete separation between civil society (economics) and the state (politics). This involved the emancipation of private property from political constraints as well as the emancipation of the state from the constraints of private property.

The starting point for classical theories of law was an analysis of the contradictory character of private property. Private property appeared as the rational and natural form in which human beings appropriate the world around them. Why did private property have this special place for classical jurisprudence? In Marxist analysis today private property has been subjected to such thorough criticism that it is hard to recover the spirit of a movement for which the emancipation of private property appeared as an ideal of a free society and as an escape from traditional forms of privilege, personal dependency and stagnation. The protection of private property appeared not as a narrow defence of class interests but as the supreme goal of a universalized justice. In the course of the development of classical jurisprudence, private property was afforded an increasingly sophisticated defence. It was identified with individual freedom: the right to use and abuse one's property as one wishes; to sell and buy at will; to move freely from one area of production and from one place to another; to employ anyone and to sell one's labour to any employer. Private property signified an area of private right, where individual desire, caprice and choice might reign supreme. It was associated with a right to follow the dictates of conscience, to pursue a religion of one's own choice, not to have faith thrust down one's throat. Private property symbolized a sphere of personal right where no external force could tread and which belonged to individuals by virtue of their humanity. Private property was identified with equality in that every property owner was equal to every other, in that none possessed special privilege, rank or status; none had exclusive access to property; all were subject to the same rules not to trespass on the property of another. In exchange or contract, all were equal in that they exchanged like for like, an equal amount for an equal amount, value for value. Finally, classical jurisprudence celebrated the dynamism of private property: the enormous wealth which it set in motion, the improvements in the forces of production, the development of science and the arts, the extension of the market and of the horizons of social life, the cheapening of goods as labour became more productive, the incentives for the individual which it opened up. Private property, it seemed, made possible the break from the stagnation and the narrow boundaries which had hemmed in the old world. Liberty, equality and the wealth of nations – all these were inextricably linked with the emancipation of private property.

Classical jurisprudence did not, however, take an uncritical attitude towards private property. Its theorists were aware of its 'dark side' – the tensions and contradictions with which it was associated. The sphere of private property – which classical theorists referred to as 'civil society' – was a sphere of egoism and self-interest, where people pursue their own aims regardless of the welfare of others and use others simply as a means to their own private welfare. All the theorists of classical jurisprudence were critical of this situation. In different ways, they pointed to the lack of self-sufficiency of civil society; left to itself it would destroy itself through its own rapacity, ending up in a war of all against all or in the despotic rule of the wealthy and powerful. They pointed to the massive inequalities between the rich and the poor that civil society naturally engenders; to the corruption of the moral sentiments of members of civil society caught in a world where self-interest was everything and the interests of the community counted for nothing; to the particular corruption of the rich, who sought to buttress their wealth with political power or paid no heed to the world of politics as long as it did not encroach upon their selfish needs; to the corruption of the poor, whose minds were oppressed by detailed and repetitive labour and lack of education; and to the class antagonisms which were excited between the rich and the poor. They pointed to the one-sidedness of civil society: its development of the individualistic, egotistic side of human nature but its neglect of the social, moral or 'rational' side.

The critical edge with which classical jurisprudence dissected civil society was of the utmost importance for the development of its theories of law and the state. Since, it was argued, civil society left to itself was self-destructive, fraught with internal cracks and tensions and one-sided in its expression of human nature or reason, an authority had to be established outside of civil society which would reconcile the contradictions inherent therein and embody that social, moral or rational aspect of human existence which civil society left out of all consideration. The transformation of the state was to be the solution to the problems of private property.

The ideal form of state was to be one which was based on the consent of the people in general: the state was to become a *public* authority, a *social* form of control, an expression of the *general* will. To base the sovereignty of the state on the will of the people and no longer on divine right, natural right, custom or mere force was the enormous task undertaken by classical jurisprudence. The task faced by classical thought was to analyse what such a state would look like, how it was to come into being and what it needed to do to resolve the contradictions of civil society.

The solution to this problem put forward by classical jurisprudence was that, since civil society was the sphere of private interests, the state – as the sphere of public authority – had to be divorced radically from it. In the old order, what passed for the 'state' was barely distinguished from particular owners of property; the real state was to be distanced as far as possible from private concerns.

It was the search for a solution along these lines which led classical jurisprudence to make the identification of the state and the people formal. The state could not represent the actual will of the people – what men and women in civil society actually thought, felt and wanted – for the actual will was dominated by the principle of self-interest. Rather, the state was to represent the 'rational', or 'general' will of the people: not the real, egotistical consciousness of members of civil society, but their abstract consciousness as rational human beings and citizens of the state. Thus, although the state was to be based on the consent of the public, the formal character of this consent was built into the idea of the state. The state was to represent the people, but it was also to be above the people. To construct a state based on the general will of the rational people but divorced from the particular will of the actual people was the problem classical writers sought to resolve.

Because the identification of the state with the people was formal, it did not mean that it was merely an 'idea of reason' with no practical significance. For classical jurisprudence, the accomplishment of the formal identity required a real transformation of the state, and not merely a redefinition of the source of its sovereignty. The various solutions put forward by the proponents of classical jurisprudence – their analyses of the contradictions of civil society and what was needed to put them right, their theories of what constitutes the rational will of the people, their theories of what was required of the state for popular consent to be presupposed, and their proposals for the constitution of an ideal state – are the subject of the next few sections. Hobbes, Rousseau, Smith and Hegel put forward radically different solutions, even though they faced a common problem and sought to resolve it within the common parameters of private property, law and the state. Some defined 'the people' more narrowly than others, excluding women and the working class; some made popular consent more formal than others, presupposing, for instance, the fiction of a social contract. The standpoint from which Marx was to assess them was the extent to which they allowed 'the democratic element', in its real, bodily form, to enter the state, and the real voice of the people to be heard.

## The defeat of traditional natural law theory

The major theoretical expression of the old forms of property authority that classical jurisprudence confronted was a broad and diverse school of thought known as 'traditional natural law theory'; it dominated the period between the decline of feudalism (around the fourteenth century in England) and the rise to political power of the bourgeoisie. Closely associated with mercantilism and the absolute state, it also provided a framework for their opponents. It was the doctrine which the proponents of classical jurisprudence grew out of and attacked. From their perspective, traditional natural law theory was an archaic doctrine justifying dependence, inequality and despotism. To critics of bourgeois society, traditional natural law theory has sometimes appeared in a much more favourable light because of the moral restraints it imposed on the pursuit of private interest and on the sovereignty of the state. In general, Marx endorsed the classical critique of traditional natural law theory and I shall attempt to show why, in spite of immediate appearances, he was justified in so doing.

Ownership, according to traditional natural law theory, was attached to the performance of definite social functions: owners had neither absolute rights to use and abuse their property according to their will nor exclusive rights under all circumstances to bar others from use of their property. The bourgeois idea of absolute and exclusive property rights was never given full expression. It is in part because traditional natural law theory imposed explicit constraints on property that some critics of private property have sought to reappropriate it.

Paternalist constraints on the rights of private property emerge plainly enough on the question of the poor. All natural law theorists (e.g. Aquinas, Grotius, Pufendorf and Locke) agreed that, at least in the extremities of famine, the needs of the poor must predominate over the rights of ownership. This was not a matter of discretion or good will but one of obligation. They disagreed over the degree of extremity that must be reached before this obligation came into force; they disagreed over the source of this obligation; and they disagreed over what this obligation entailed. But that such an obligation existed and overrode the rights of private property was affirmed within the natural law tradition. Social responsibility was unbilically tied to property. Thomas Aquinas (1225-74) had set the scene for natural law theory with the argument that the world was God's property and was given to the human species as trustees of God's will, its rights limited by God's original intention. While Aquinas argued that 'the individual holding of possession is not contrary to natural law' and that individual property makes possible responsible and productive management of God's estate, individual property rights could in principle be overruled when they proved incompatible with the natural rights everyone possessed to a share in the land. In the extreme case of famine, the poor were entitled to reclaim their original share in the community of goods even against the claims of property:

> When a person is in imminent danger and he cannot be helped in any other way, then a person may legitimately supply his own wants out of another's property.[1]

Grotius (writing in the early seventeenth century) radically revised this Thomist conception of a 'positive' community of goods existing in nature. The land, he argued, was originally common: not in the Thomist sense that its owners are trustees of the community and that everyone has a right not to be excluded from it; but rather in the sense that the world originally belongs to no-one and is open to all to make their own by virtue of first possession. This 'negative' community of goods has been illustrated through Cicero's simile of a theatre: 'Tho' the theatre is common for any body who comes, yet the place that everyone sits in is properly his own.'[2] The people who first take seats have exclusive right to their use; those who are excluded have no right to demand a place. Grotius thus overturned the Thomist conception of common property in order to validate the exclusivity and absolute-ness of private property. Nevertheless, he too posed limits and exceptions to the rights of private property. First, he argued that that which cannot be occupied – like the high seas – cannot be made private (an unsurprising conclusion, since he was arguing on behalf of the Dutch East India Company that Portugal had no right to claim the sea routes to India as its private domain and that therefore the Dutch had the right to capture Portuguese goods in transit!). Second, he argued that in times of necessity the poor retain a right to procure grain and that at all times grain was to be sold at 'a fair price'.

Pufendorf (who wrote his major work on *The Law of Nature and Nations* in 1672) developed the idea of an originally 'negative community' in which the world belonged to no-one but was open to anybody to appropriate as 'his own'. He distinguished between 'preceptive' laws in nature, with their specific injunctions that no-one should take what belongs to another, and 'permissive' laws, which allowed people to divide the land as they thought fit. He made a great advance in seeing exclusive property rights as the outcome of a historical process of development, and justified them as the necessary concomitant of a transition from a society of 'great simplicity' into one where 'improvements' were possible. He grounded private property not merely on possession but on the consent – either 'express' or 'presumptive' – of other people that 'they shall not hinder him in the free use of these conveniences and shall themselves forbear to use them without his consent.' However, this consent, which legitimized exclusive property rights, also limited them: consent could neither be expressed nor presumed if individuals appropriated more than they could use and more than allowed others to 'meet the needs of themselves and their dependants'. If a person 'ranges too far afield and heaps up superfluous wealth by the oppression of others, the rest will not be blamed if, when the opportunity affords they undertake promptly to bring him into line.'[3]

Locke (writing in the late seventeenth century) picked up on this analysis of 'negative community' offered by Grotius and Pufendorf and argued that labour originally set 'the measure of property'. Individuals had the right to own the product of their own labour (and that of their servants and family). In simple societies, before a money economy was introduced, 'no man's labour could appropriate all nor could his enjoyment consume more than a small part'; thus exclusive rights of property owners did not 'entrench on the right of another'. In modern commercial societies, this natural constraint no longer held; the emergence of money in the form of 'a little piece of yellow metal which would keep without wasting or decay', and agreement that it should be 'worth a great piece of flesh or a whole heap of corn', meant that people could now cheat the natural law that they should own only what they can 'enjoy' and 'use'.[4] Locke saw the development of private property as the 'condition of humane life' and welcomed its extension in commercial society; the ensuing inequalities in private property, he said, entailed only the establishment of a government to protect the property of the 'industrious' against the 'rapin and force' of the landless. However, even Locke – as Tully's perhaps exaggerated account clearly shows – placed limits on the rights of private property. Although the notion of 'use' and enjoyment' were extended in a money economy, they did not confer absolute property rights:

> The same law of nature that . . . gives us property does also bound that property too. God has given us all things richly . . . but how far has he given it to us? To enjoy. As much as anyone can make use of to an advantage of life before it spoils, so much he may by his labour fix a property in. Whatever is beyond this is more than his share and belongs to others.[5]

A landowner was not entitled to misuse his land: if, for instance, 'the fruit of his planting perished without gathering, this part of the earth, notwithstanding his inclosure, was still to be looked on as waste and might be the possession of any other.' Though he hedged the rights of the poor to be included in the distribution of the world's goods within narrow limits, and though he offered a firm defence of the rights of property owners to sell their produce wherever the price was highest, Locke echoed the belief that in exceptionally dire circumstances property rights can and should be overridden.

It is not surprising that some commentators have been tempted to draw nostalgic conclusions from the formal ties which linked property to social obligations. They look back to the more ethical days of old when property was neither exclusive nor absolute and paternalist duties imposed their limits upon the pursuit of private gain. The bourgeois defence of absolute and exclusive property rights then appears as a retrograde step alienating the private from the social, substituting unrestrained egoism for public duty. (This too was a view which Marx held in some of his early writings.)

This, however, is only one side of the story. It is true that natural law theory provides a framework for the critique of bourgeois property relations, but such a critique is rooted in the past. The strength of classical jurisprudence was to expose the backward side of the conception of property embodied in natural law doctrines. First, it revealed what lay beneath the surface of traditional natural law theory: that not only did property owners have paternalist duties to the poor, but more important, the poor were subjected to all kinds of personal obligations to the propertied. These obligations expressed relations of personal dependence, servility and bondage. The lifting of these obligations represented a real emancipation. Second, classical jurisprudence did not seek simply to abolish obligations to the poor but rather to relocate them. It transferred the source of such obligations from individual property owners to the state. It saw the attachment of these responsibilities to property owners as opposed to the state as oppressive: for the poor because it reinforced their personal dependence, and for the rich because it imposed upon them arbitrary restrictions. Classical jurisprudence was not, in general, against making demands on the rich to alleviate the conditions of the poor; rather it objected to the *form* in which these demands had traditionally been made – one which reflected and reproduced the discretionary powers of the rich and the personal dependence of the poor. Third, classical jurisprudence sought to demonstrate that the tradtional obligations attached to property served to exclude the majority from new forms of property. Peasants tied by obligations to the land of a particular landowner were barred from access to private property. Certain kinds of property rights – like those to international trade – were reserved as the exclusive privilege of those chartered by the state. The separation of property from obligation was part and parcel of the removal of legal and political bars to the acquisition of property. Lastly, classical jurisprudence sought to demonstrate the stagnant, narrow and backward character of economic relations based on personal obligation. The capacity for technical innovation or cultural development on a local estate where peasants were tied by reciprocal obligations to a particular landlord was, it was argued, very small. It was, in short, in the name of 'man' (women were mainly excluded) – his freedom, equality and material wealth – that the liberal proponents of classical jurisprudence attacked natural law conceptions of property.

With regard to the state, natural law theories attacked the theocratic dogma that the state was a God-given entity derived from 'the divinely ordered harmony of the universal whole'. They agreed that there were certain 'laws' which were transcendent and unchangeable by human hand, but they also made room for a restricted sphere of human initiative. They introduced a principle of human authorship of law, although this principle always remained incomplete.

According to natural law doctrines there are at least two different kinds of law: natural and positive. Natural law was supposed to emanate from God or nature or some other moral authority transcending earthly power, while positive (or civil) law is law posited by human beings. The general idea was that, before the state and its positive laws had come into being, natural law already prevailed as an obligatory collection of rights and duties. It was from natural law that the state was supposed to derive its authority: only those positive laws which accorded with the dictates of natural law were valid; those positive laws which went against natural law were invalid; there was a right to disobey, or even under some circumstances a duty to resist, positive laws which ran counter to those of natural law. The function of the state and its laws was to enforce, defend and extend the laws previously authoritative in nature. As Gierke summed it up, 'whatever statute or act of government contradicted the eternal and immutable principles of natural law was utterly void and would bind no one.'[6] In short, although natural law doctrines allowed some room for the existence of laws made by people, with more or less severity depending on the author they restricted this arena of human action.

Natural law theory limited the field of legislation, since 'the highest power on earth was subject to the rules of natural law.' Even when *new* laws were in fact introduced in order to deal with the new problems connected with the rise of the bourgeois market relations, this took the illusory form not of acts of legislation but of the restoration of natural rights dating back to time immemorial. During the Long Parliament, for instance, new statutes abolishing the prerogatives of the monarch and the rights of private property were presented as interpretations of a fixed and long-established natural code. As Christopher Hill commented:

> Somewhere – in the breasts of judges, in Magna Carta, or in the liberties of parliament – were laws so sacred and so essential to social stability, that no government could override them.[7]

A statute, it seemed, 'declared what law was; it did not create it'. Men like Sir Edward Coke were sent by parliament to search the archives – and sometimes the scriptures – to adapt medieval law to the needs of commercial society. Hill reports how, in 1621, 'a member of parliament could even make the historically absurd claim that the common law did ever allow free trade.' When form and content were in such disharmony, the form was bound perhaps to give way.

Classical jurisprudence was the agent for the abolition of the form of natural law and for presenting law as what it is: a human product in its entirety. It sought to demonstrate that the laws and governments regulating human behaviour are themselves the product of human activity and do not derive from God, nature or any other transcendent moral order. There is no law, they argued, which descends from on high, is fixed for eternity and immune to human intervention. Laws are created by people and can therefore be changed by people.

Natural law theory provided a set of normative limits beyond which the state could not legitimately go. It established a body of natural rights which, if the state violated, the people themselves could uphold. Further, over and beyond such natural rights it was supposed that through a contract among the people themselves (called a *pactum societatis*) the people secured additional conventional rights which also served as a limit on state power. The 'people' appeared as a distinct subject or personality, independent of the sovereign and a counterweight to the sovereign's authority. The contract between the state and the people (called the *pactum subjectionis*) limited the authority of the state within bounds set by the natural and conventional rights of the people.

By doing away with the restrictions of natural law and with the opposition between the people and the state, it appears that classical jurisprudence afforded to the state an awesome power. Thus some critics of the modern state are tempted to look back to natural law theory as a model on which restrictions on state power and the rights of the people can be grounded. But the converse of the natural law doctrine was that not only were the people separate from the state, but the state was separate from the people. The achievement of classical jurisprudence was to identify the state not with a particular interest separate from the rest of society but with the people as a whole. The appearance that this new state was absolutist was illusory; the theory of the absolute state was expressed within the framework of traditional natural law and not that of classical jurisprudence, which had no place for doctrines like that of 'the divine right of kings'. It was not the case that all constraints upon the state were abolished but rather that the character of these constraints was changed. They were no longer to stem from the relation between the 'natural' rights of the 'people' (which meant in effect the privileges of the local princes and the clergy) and the natural rights of the sovereign; rather they were to stem from the requirement that the state become a public authority based on the consent of the people. Classical jurisprudence did not merely abolish the old restrictions on state power; it also sought to establish the state on a new basis.

The limited character of liberal ideas of 'freedom', 'equality' and 'consent' should not blind us to the advance which they represented over their absence in traditional natural law theory. The discovery made by classical jurisprudence, that property, law and the state are social institutions, created by human beings and based on the will of the people as a whole, cannot now be undone by appealing to supposedly 'natural' principles of justice against which to limit them. The problem with classical jurisprudence was not that it broke from the traditonal natural law theory, but rather that it failed to complete the break. It abolished natural law theory in its traditional form, only to resurrect it in a modern form. While it recognized that the distribution of **property, the** content of law and the policies of state are all the products of human activity, it appeared that private property, law and the state themselves were natural forms of human existence. There was in the classical view to be no limit on the laws through which the state rules except that the state must rule through law; no limit on the use and abuse of private property except that private property must be respected; no limit on the authority of the state except that authority must take the form of state authority. The main thrust of Marx's critique was not to return to traditional natural law theory but to complete the break which classical jurisprudence initiated.

## Hobbes's theory of 'public authority'

Thomas Hobbes (1588–1679) was among the earliest of bourgeois theorists to develop a materialist account of law and the state. Drawing inspiration from Galileo's revolution of the natural sciences, he launched an attack on the whole idea of natural law. In nature, he argued, there is no moral order, only the laws of motion governing the movements of material objects: 'all that is real is material and what is not material is not real.' People, he argued, are no exception: material beings, albeit of a special kind that talk, reason and labour. The 'natural law' which governs human behaviour is that people will strive to satisfy their 'appetites' (and call that which gives them pleasure 'good'); and avoid that which gives them pain and call it 'bad'. Reason appeared as no more than the instrument of the passions, working out how pleasure was to be found and pain avoided. There was no room in this materialist universe for eternal moral rules antecedent to those created by human beings. Thus the laws of nature were not properly speaking 'laws' at all but regularities found in nature or 'conclusions or theorems concerning what is conducive to the preservation and defence of men'. By contrast, law properly 'is the word of him that by right hath command over others.'[1]

Hobbes completed his attack on natural law theory by depicting the state of nature as 'a war of all against all'; instead of being a moral order the preservation of which was the task of government, it appeared instead as a state of chaos in which 'life becomes nasty, brutish and short'. Hobbes demolished the idea of natural right by taking it to its limit; by extending it to mean the right of all to everything, natural right perished, in Gierke's phrase, 'by its own abundance'. Hobbes destroyed the traditional idea of natural law theory from within by reducing law to a human relation of power and abolishing the illusion of 'natural' constraints over the laws and government.

Hobbes's second great achievement was to break from natural law conceptions of property. He posited exclusive and absolute private property as a natural relation of people to the world around them. He projected an abstracted image of a society based on private property on to the state of nature, and described its over-riding law of motion as the pursuit of private interest. It was an unsatisfactory theory which later protagonists of classical juris-prudence were to reject for its failure to comprehend the *social* character of private property. But it allowed Hobbes to attack the traditional restrictions, which natural law theory justified, on the freedom to dispose of one's property as one wishes. At the same time, Hobbes ruthlessly traced the destructive consequences of the egoism and competition associated with private property; far from being an uncritical apologist for it, he portrayed the world of private property neither as self-sufficient nor as harmonious but as a world which would, if left to itself, destroy itself by its own rapacity. However, instead of reverting to one or other kind of natural law restriction over private property, Hobbes sought an alternative solution. A new form of authority was to be imposed on property: one that would at once preserve the natural propensity of people to further their own self-interest and at the same time iron out the creases of such a world. He did not reject natural law theory in order to release private property from any and every kind of social obligation, but he transformed the character of such obligations and transposed them on to the state. *Leviathan* was to be his solution to the contradictions of civil society.

Hobbes's third achievement was to attack the idea, common to natural law theory, that the 'people' exist as a subject of rights prior to the establishment of political authority and separate from the state. Apart from the state, Hobbes insisted, the 'people' are merely (to use Gierke's term) 'a disunited multitude'. In Hobbes's world the people came on to the political scene as possessors neither of natural rights nor of further rights acquired through an initial contract or compact. The rights of the people could no longer be counterposed to the authority of the state as if they were two distinct personalities. In place of the two contracts posited by natural law theory – one to set up civil society and the other to set up government – Hobbes substituted a single contract whereby all individuals pledge themselves to submit to a common ruler. No longer could they claim a right of resistance against the positive laws of the state on the ground of their violation of the people's rights, for the laws of the state constituted the people's rights.

Hobbes's opposition to the notion that the 'people' possess natural or acquired rights independently of the state has given rise to the image of him as an 'absolutist'. This is the picture which the liberal commentator Gierke, and, following on from him, the Marxist critic Colletti, have painted of Hobbes. Since the people are bereft of rights, Gierke wrote, 'the sovereignty of the ruler . . . is absolutely unlimited and illimitable, unresponsible and omnipotent, free from all obligation of law and duty.'[2] This interpretation of Hobbes as the protagonist of absolutism can be buttressed by numerous quotations from Hobbes himself. A clear statement appears in *Elements of Law:*

> He that cannot of right be resisted has coercive power over all the rest and thereby can frame and govern their actions at his pleasure, which is absolute sovereignty . . . Secondly, that man or assembly that by their own right . . . may make laws or abrogate them at his or their pleasure, have the sovereignty absolute. For seeing the laws they make are supposed to be made by right, the members of the commonwealth to whom they are made are obliged to obey them and consequently not to resist the execution of them.[3]

Was traditional natural law theory, then, an assertion of popular rights against the state, and Hobbes's revolution in political thought an illiberal regression to a defence of absolute sovereignty, in which the right of the people to disobey or resist the state was annulled? Some critics have tried to rescue Hobbes by arguing that in fact he did not totally abandon the traditional conception of natural right. It has been argued, for instance, that Hobbes retained the idea that people have a natural right to their own self-preservation which the state has no authority to transgress. There are certainly residues in Hobbes of traditional natural law theory; it would be surprising if his break was absolutely clean. But what is important is not this residue, but the new conception of the state which Hobbes put forward (and about which he has been misinterpreted): the state was absolute only as it remained a public authority. As soon as it ceased to be public, it lost its authority. This was the new form of restriction on state power which Hobbes formulated.

Although Hobbes was among the earliest political theorists to base the state on the consent of the people, he had a highly restrictive conception of the 'people'. Tribe has shown that the 'people' included only heads of household and excluded subordinate members (that is, usually, women, children and servants). It also excluded fools and criminals 'who have no use of their reason'. Hobbes was no democrat. His identification of the people with property offered little to those who were deemed incapable of owning it. Hobbes also had a highly formal conception of what constitutes consent to the sovereignty of the state; he based it on an imaginary event, a social contract, which had no empirical substance. From the premiss that in the state of nature self-interest would drive every rational individual to subordinate himself (women being excluded) to a sovereign, Hobbes concluded that the sovereign represented the rational self-interest of every individual. He offered an interpretation of the social contract based on the subordination of the people to the state rather than that of the state to the people. He identified rationality with obedience to the dictates of the sovereign, and opposition to the sovereign with irrationality. The law, he declared, can 'never be against reason'[4] and every member of society 'must acknowledge himself to the author . . . of whatever he that is already their sovereign shall do and judge fit to be done.'[5] The criminal who violates the sovereign's laws suffers from some 'defect of the understanding or some error of reasoning or some sudden force of the passions'.[6] Anyone who complains of injury from the state complains of 'that whereof he himself is the author and therefore not to accuse any man but himself'. In brief, since Hobbes offered no independent basis for assessing rationality other than obedience to the state, his identification of the state with the rational needs of the individual was highly abstract. His initial materialism, which he used to such good effect in his critique of traditional natural law theory, turned into a mystique according to which the state appeared as the embodiment of reason, and subordination to the state as subordination to one's own rational self.

In spite of its formalism, Hobbes's theory of consent was not without practical significance. He was not happy to leave the state as it was and simply declare it public and rational, for he had a definite, if limited, conception of what constitutes a public authority. It was not important, he argued, whether government took the form of monarchy, aristocracy or democracy – or a mixture of all three – but what was crucial was that power should be exercised through the rule of law, whatever form the government took. By the rule of law he meant that the sovereign must rule through law, and that any force that the sovereign wielded outside the law he used as a private person and not by virtue of his sovereignty. Thus, while the state could consist of any form of government, no reform of government was legitimate unless done in accord with legal procedure. The law was to be written, publicized and clearly shown to 'proceed from the will of the sovereign'.[7] An impartial judiciary was to be set up to 'take notice of the law from nothing but the statutes and constitution of the sovereign' and to show 'contempt for unnecessary riches and preferments'.[8] Revenge was to be outlawed, since it proceeds not from 'public authority' but from 'private men'. Punishment inflicted 'without precedent public condemnation', or in excess of that laid down by law, was to be considered 'an act of hostility'. All punishment of innocent citizens was incompatible with state power (though Hobbes was ready to allow 'the infliction of what evil soever on an innocent man that is not a subject, if it be for the benefit of the commonwealth'). In short, there was a 'liberal' side to Hobbes which was not at odds with his 'absolutism' but merely the other side of the same coin. The power of the sovereign could be absolute only so long as it was exercised through the rule of law. Constitutionalism was his solution to the problem of consent.

Politically, Hobbes hedged his bets on the question of monarchy or parliamentarism; but his insistence on the establishment of the rule of law was what distinguished him sharply from absolutism and the old-style monarchy, and identified him equally sharply with the interests of bourgeois private property. His theory of the state reflected accurately the political demands of the bourgeoisie, which were aimed not so much at abolishing monarchy as at making it compatible with the pursuit of their own economic concerns.

Theoretically, Hobbes elevated the rule of law into a natural requirement of any and every social order. He abolished natural law only to render positive law into a natural necessity: 'obedience to the civil law', he wrote, is 'the law of nature'.[9] This naturalization of positive law led to a tension in Hobbes's work between a conception of the rule of law as a necessary condition of social life and a realization that the rule of law was only just coming into existence as part and parcel of the historical rise of the bourgeoisie. How could the rule of law be eternalized as a natural form of authority when it was only just emerging as a new and historically specific form? Hobbes, lacking any historical perspective and probably blinded by contemporary events – i.e. the English civil war – into thinking that the only alternative to the rule of law was anarchy, was unable to resolve this dilemma. It was on this contradictory note that Hobbes laid a groundwork for liberal thought.

## Rousseau's theory of the 'general will'

Jean-Jacques Rousseau, a leading figure of the eighteenth-century French Enlightenment, appears at first sight as a direct opposite to Hobbes: criticizing private property where Hobbes had naturalized it; subordinating the state to the people where Hobbes had subordinated the people to the state; standing for freedom where Hobbes had stood for authority. This is very much the image found, for example, in the essays on Rousseau written by the contemporary Marxist commentator Lucio Colletti. He painted Rousseau as an early critic of civil society and the state and argued that he 'sketched the first and basic chapters of a critique of modern bourgeois society',[1] exposing the ills which flow from private property, prefiguring Marx and Lenin's doctrine of the 'withering away of the state', and anticipating Marx's critique of the 'double life' of modern society split between, on the one hand, bourgeois individuals intent on securing their self-interest and, on the other, communal citizens of the state. I believe this interpretation of Rousseau to be largely wrong: the strengths and limitations of Rousseau's eminently bourgeois understanding of society were shared in common with Hobbes and other proponents of classical jurisprudence, what distinguished them being subordinate to what held them together.

They shared a common commitment to private property, Rousseau's critique of civil society being confined within the limits of classical jurisprudence. Even as he attacked the 'horrors and misfortunes', the 'crimes, wars and murders', which humankind would have been saved from had someone pulled up the stakes or filled up the ditches which mark the boundaries of private property, at the same time he was neither able nor willing to envisage an alternative to private property. His work was not aimed at abolishing but rather at securing its existence and abolishing only its negative side through the establishment of a bourgeois legal order and bourgeois state.

The critical edge of Rousseau's indictment of private property still rings true today. Its curse, he argued, lies primarily in the fact that 'the loss of one man almost always constitutes the prosperity of another';[2] and even more perniciously in that 'public calamities are the objects of the hopes and expectation of innumerable individuals.' Property owners, Rousseau continued, are forced to conceal their endless pursuit of self-interest under 'the superficial appearance of benevolence', the better to gain at another's expense: 'men are forced to caress and destroy one another at the same time . . . they are born enemies by duty and knave by interest.' Massive inequalities grow between the rich and the poor and give rise to a brutal social conflict:

> Usurpations by the rich, robbery by the poor and the unbridled passions of both, suppressed the cries of natural compassion and the still feeble voice of justice and filled men with avarice, ambition and vice.[3]

Rather than dissolve into a Hobbesian war of all against all, the rich consolidate their private advantages by claiming for themselves the legitimacy of law and the protection of government. Beneath an aura of public concern and under the shield of the civil magistrate, private interests feather their own nests all the more efficiently. In this defence of wealth and inequality, Rousseau argued, lay the origins of law and the state which

> bound new fetters on the poor and gave new powers to the rich; which irretrievably destroyed natural liberty, eternally fixed the law of property and inequality, converted clever usurpation into unalterable right and for the advantage of a few ambitious individuals, subjected all mankind to perpetual labour, slavery and wretchedness.[4]

Such was the tenor of Rousseau's penetrating critique of civil society, which went much deeper than Hobbes's. At the same time, however, it appeared to Rousseau that private property is the inescapable basis of society. He was critical of Hobbes for seeing private property as the natural form in which human beings appropriate the world around them; the real object of Hobbes's analysis was not 'the state of nature' but 'civil society'. Rousseau correctly treated private property as a social phenomenon, but he could not conceive of any developed social order that was not based upon it. In the sense that it appeared as an eternal requirement of all society, private property appeared as 'natural' to Rousseau, as it had to Hobbes before him. It was only, Rousseau argued, through the institution of private property that the development of civilization, language, the division of labour, wealth and the 'finer feelings' of humanity, love and justice became possible. Thus Rousseau offered a dialectical view of private property, in the sense that it gives rise to 'the best and the worst . . . both our virtues and our vices, our science and our errors, our conquerors and our philosophers'.[5] Nothing was further from his mind than its abolition:

What then must be done? Must societies be totally abolished? Must 'meum' and 'tuum' [mine and thine, i.e. property] be annihilated and must we return again to the forests to live among bears? This is a deduction in the manner of my adversaries.[6]

The task as Rousseau saw it was not to do away with private property but to construct a form of authority which would do away with its contradictions.

The difficulty Rousseau faced was to discover how an authority could emerge, out of the conditions of civil society, which would genuinely express the 'general will'. The unending quest for private gain makes members of civil society more concerned with their own good than that of the public as a whole. While consciousness of the general will exists in each individual, yet, when civil society encourages pure egoism, 'where is the man', Rousseau asks, 'who can thus separate himself from himself'[7] and subordinate his personal interest to the general will? As for the rich, we have already seen that they are interested only in a state which will serve as a veil and instrument of their own special interests. The mass of the poor appear to Rousseau too uneducated to be relied upon to perform public functions:

> The laws of kindness . . . the social virtues of pure minds . . . all these will never be understood by the multitude. The multitude will always be given gods as stupid as itself, will make slight material sacrifices to them and then honour them by giving itself over to a thousand horrible and destructive passions.[8]

Rousseau's solution to the establishment of an authority which would express the 'general will' of the people was to divorce it as radically as possible from the 'particular will' of private individuals and groups. What was the 'general will'? Rousseau was clear that it could not be equated with the empirical 'will of all'. While the general will, by definition, abstracts from the particular will of actual persons and is 'always upright and always tends to the public advantage'; by contrast 'the actual deliberations of the people do not always have the same rectitude.'[9] The general will is constituted by the general, that is, rational aspects of the will of each individual; so to obey the general will is tantamount to obeying one's own rational, general self: 'so long as the subjects have to submit only to conventions of this sort, they obey no one but their own will.' The general will is an authority 'formed wholly of the individuals who compose it' and thus 'neither has nor can have any interest contrary to theirs.'[10] The conflict between the particular will of individuals and the general will appears to Rousseau as one between one's will 'as a man' and one's will 'as a citizen':

> whoever refuses to obey the general will shall be compelled to do so by the whole body. This means nothing less than he will be forced to be free; for this is the condition which . . . secures him against all personal dependence.[11]

The foundation of the old order was personal dependence, which was manifest both in the suppression of private property rights and in the private appropriation of the state. The establishment of the general will was to break from all the old oppressions.

Gierke and, following on from him, Colletti, have contrasted Rousseau's solution to the problem of civil society and the state to that of Hobbes. They argued that Hobbes and Rousseau both broke radically from natural law doctrines and both rejected the idea of two contracts (see pp. 20–1): Hobbes eliminated the *pactum societatis* and thus subordinated the people entirely to the state; Rousseau eliminated the *pactum subjectionis*, thus, writes Colletti,

> attributing sovereignty wholly and exclusively to the people and transforming the institution of government – which was originally a pact between the people and the sovereign – into a mere commission.[12]

But neither in form nor in content is this distinction as sharp as Colletti wishes to portray it. In form the difference between them is that for Hobbes the rational self-interest of the individual is that which accords with the will of the state, while for Rousseau the state is that which accords with the rational will of the individual. While this distinction is important, it should not be forgotten that in both cases the people appear not in their real flesh and blood but only in formal dress as bearers of reason or general will. Both writers identified the state with the people as a whole, but then turned the 'people' into ghosts of their true selves.

Gierke argued that for Rousseau

> the destruction of the contract of rulership cleared the way for the destruction of every right of the ruler . . . from the permanent and absolute omnipotence of the assemblage of the people, suspending the executive power and the whole jurisdiction of government as soon as it is assembled, he developed his programme of permanent revolution.[13]

Gierke's liberalism was horrified at this prospect. Colletti embraces the analysis and gives to it the positive connotation which was so alien to Gierke; the theory of the social contract, argues Colletti, 'literally constitutes the need for the abolition or "withering away of the state". So far as political theory is concerned', he goes on, 'Marx and Lenin have added nothing to Rousseau.'[14] All that bemuses Colletti is why Marx failed to recognize the obvious debt which he owed to Rousseau.

The real difference between Hobbes and Rousseau, however, was not one between absolutism and revolution but rather between one kind of liberalism and another. For Hobbes, to presuppose consent to the state, it was sufficient that a rule of law be established to restrict the existing monarchical government; for Rousseau it was also necessary that the monarchical form of government itself be turned into a parliamentary one. While the former offered a theory of the 'legal state' that expressed a compromise between the old monarchy and the bourgeoisie, the latter expressed a theory of parliamentary government based on the destruction of the old monarchy. The one represented the English path to bourgeois rule, the other the more radical French path.

The rule of law, for Rousseau as for Hobbes, was the key to the constitution of the general will. He waxed lyrical on the wonders of legality. How can it be, he asked,

> that all should obey, yet nobody take upon him to command, and that all should serve and yet have no masters? . . . These wonders are the work of law. It is to law alone that men owe justice and liberty. It is this salutory organ of the will of all which establishes in civil right the natural equality between men . . . The first of all laws is to respect the laws.[15]

For the rule of law to hold good, the innocent must never be punished; specific privileges must never be conferred on anyone by name; rules must apply to all equally, justice must never be sold for private gain; the discretionary power of government to absolve people from the effects of law or to pardon them for their offences must be limited; the law must 'provide for the security of the least of its members with as much care as for the all the rest'[16] and it must ensure that it protects the poor against 'the tyranny of the rich'.[17] Most important of all, the law must protect private property, for 'the right of property is the most sacred of all rights of citizenship and even more important in some respects than liberty itself.'[18] Private property is the 'true foundation of civil society' and the function of law is not to abolish civil society but to 'guarantee it'.[19] What we find in Rousseau is not a revolutionary critique of the bourgeois character of the rule of law (as we do in Marx and Lenin) but a liberal critique of an old order where privilege and personal discretion have not yet been supplanted by equality and freedom before the law. The defence of private property was at the very heart of this new conception. Just as private property appeared to Rousseau as the natural form of social production, so too the law appeared as the natural form of social regulation. It was the substitution of 'justice for instinct' which seemed to Rousseau to mark the passage from 'a stupid and unimaginative animal' to 'an intelligent being and a man'.[20]

The duty of government, Rousseau argued, is above all to guarantee the law. To this end, it must administer it in such a way that 'it is impossible for anyone to set himself above the law'. It must teach its citizens to love and respect the laws; 'make men', he says, 'if you would command men; if you would have them obedient to the laws, make them love the laws.' Most important of all, the government itself must not abuse the law; it is the mark of 'depotism' when the rules which purportedly 'subject equally the powerful and the weak to the observance of reciprocal obligations' are subverted and used instead by the rich and powerful to put new fetters on the poor. This does not mean, Rousseau adds, that the government 'ought to be afraid to make use of its power', but that 'it ought to make use of it only in a lawful manner',[21] except, that is, in a state of emergency, when the government has the right 'to silence all laws', since 'it is the people's first intention that the state shall not perish.' Such exclusion clauses, introduced with one eye cocked against the latent threat from the 'mob' below, were characteristic of the most radical defences of bourgeois legality.

Rousseau parted radically from Hobbes in his stress on the relationship which should hold between the legislature and the executive. Colletti, however, misreads these passages, which in fact preach the liberal doctrine of the subordination of the executive to the legislature, as a doctrine espousing the dissolution of the state in general. Between these two branches of the state, Rousseau argued, there must be a division of *functions*, for if the same body of individuals executed the laws as made them, the laws would become 'the ministers of their passions ... and their private aims would inevitably mar the sanctity of their work.'[22] Rousseau argued that the executive must be strictly subordinate to parliament; that there can be no 'contract' between them – i.e. no compromise between the old order and the new – for this would imply the legitimacy of executive power autonomous of the laws of parliament. Rousseau himself clarified the verbal difficulties which were none the less to confound Gierke and Colletti:

I call the government or supreme administration the legitimate exercise of executive power, and prince or magistrate the man or body entrusted with that administration ... The government [i.e. the administration] gets from the Sovereign [i.e. the parliament] the orders it gives to the people ... The body of magistrates is simply and solely a commission, an employment, in which the rulers mere officials of the Sovereign, exercise in their own name the power of which it makes them depositaries. This power it can limit, modify or recover at pleasure; for the alienation of such a right is incompatible with the nature of the social body.[23]

This subordination of the executive to the legislature has nothing whatsoever to do with the withering away of the state. In fact Rousseau argued that state officials must be given special powers and privileges distinct from the general population. The 'government' or executive, Rousseau declared, must have a 'true existence and real life distinguishing it from the body of the state';[24] it must possess its own 'particular personality' as a corporate entity, and this implies 'power of deliberation and decision, rights, titles and privileges belonging exclusively to the prince . . . and making the office of magistrate more honourable in proportion as it is more troublesome'.[25] The will of parliament was to constitute the limit of these special powers. The 'prince' or executive has no right to 'usurp the sovereign power' of parliament and parliament has the right to dissolve and replace the existing executive, since 'the depositaries of the executive power are not the people's masters but its officers'[26] (though Rousseau warns that this power should be used sparingly and only as a last resort.) The impartiality of the legislative power, Rousseau argued, 'belongs to the people and belongs to it alone':[27] the people 'being subject to the laws ought to be their author.'[28] But the question which Rousseau posed was how 'a blind multitude which does not know what it wills, because it rarely knows what is good for itself' can 'carry out for itself so great and difficult an enterprise as legislation.'[29] Rousseau's solution, as we have seen, was a constitution based on the supremacy of parliament. There must, he says, be 'no fundamental law that cannot be revoked' by the legislature. As long as it has been lawfully and properly convoked, the legislature can enact or repeal what it will. Majority votes must always be binding on everyone, including those who vote against, for

the citizen gives his consent to all the laws, including those which are passed in spite of his opposition, and even those which punish him when he dares to break any of them . . .

When the opinion which is contrary to mine prevails, this proves neither more nor less than that I was mistaken and that what I thought to be the general will was not so.[30]

Colletti also misread Rousseau's critique of representative democracy: it was based not, as Colletti argued, on a pre-emptive Marxist critique of the limits of parliamentary representation, but rather on the classical model of the city state. Rousseau thought that the legislature must be an assembly of the whole people:

Sovereignty does not admit of representation . . . deputies of the people are not and cannot be its representatives; they are merely its stewards and can carry through no definitive acts. Every law the people has not ratified in person is null and void – is, in fact, no law . . .[31]

Parliament, Rousseau was saying in some of his least auspicious passages, must comprise the whole citizenry! He threw an aside against the populace of England, which 'regards itself as free but is grossly mistaken; it is free only during the election of members of parliament. As soon as they are elected slavery overtakes it.'[32] Does this classical model mean, he asked, that 'the whole nation must be assembled together at every unforeseen event'? No, he replied to his own question. There is no guarantee that if it were assembled 'its decision would be the expression of the general will', and besides it would be 'impracticable.' The best solution, he argued at one point in his *Discourse on Political Economy*, is, 'where the government is well intentioned', to leave it to them to act in accordance with the general will! Rousseau was also well aware that his Greek precedent rested on the enslavement of the mass of the population and that slavery – by freeing citizens from labour – made possible their direct involvement in political affairs. Is liberty, he asks, 'maintained only by the help of slavery? It may be so. Extremes meet.'[33] But this condition was irrelevant for a bourgeoisie which produced on the basis of the exploitation of free labour. Rousseau's dictum also meant that a state had to be tiny enough to permit an assembly of the whole populace: his passages extolling the virtues of smallness were largely irrelevant for a revolutionary bourgeoisie eager to subordinate local principalities and pockets of privilege into new nation states. They reached the

point of absurdity when Rousseau outlined his image of a people
fit to be given laws:

> one that has neither custom nor superstition deeply ingrained
> ... one in which every member may be known by every other
> ... one which can do without other peoples ... There is still in
> Europe one country capable of being given law – Corsica.[34]

In these passages Rousseau expressed the desire of the people as a
whole to be involved in politics, but the naive and sometimes
regressive form in which he expressed it revealed the shortcomings
of even the most radical examples of classical jurisprudence. What
he had to offer was not 'a radical critique [prefigurative of Marxism]
of the representative state or parliamentary government in the
name of "direct democracy" ',[35] as Colletti put it, but a parliamentary republic, based on the rule of law, that none the less fell short
of the principles of representative democracy that democrats and
Marxists were both later to adopt. Rousseau's backwardness from
this standpoint was most marked in his exceedingly conservative
view of the natural subordination of women to men and in his
none-too-flattering image of the actual consciousness of the
masses whose 'stupidity' we have already cited.

Rousseau presented his republic as the solution to the contradictions of civil society. His own unhappiness with his conclusions
can be gauged from his treatment of inequality. He recognized that
civil society breads huge inequalities between rich and poor; he
wanted the state to ameliorate these inequalities and at the same
time not to encroach upon the rights of private property without
the consent of its owners: 'It should be remembered that the
foundation of the social compact is property and its first condition
is that every one should be maintained in the peacefull possession
of what belongs to him.'[36] His solution was progressive taxation
based on the consent of the taxed. Rousseau justified progressive
taxation on the ground that the state 'provides a powerful
protection for the immense possessions of the rich' and 'hardly
leaves the poor man in quiet possession of the cottage he builds
with his own hands.'[37] Since all the advantages are for the rich, the
rich should pay a more than proportionate share in the costs of
public authority. Rousseau believed that if the rich thought
rationally about their situation, they would agree to be taxed up to
the point where their wealth was directly attacked.

Rousseau's moderation was locked in contradiction: on the one hand, he declared that 'the right which each individual has to his own estate is always subordinate to the rights which the community has over all';[38] on the other he assured property owners that 'in taking over the goods of individuals, the community, so far from despoiling them, only assures them legitimate possession and changes usurpation into a true right and enjoyment of proprietorship.'[39] Unable to resolve the contradiction between defence of private property and the collective good, Rousseau kept both options open.

## Adam Smith's theory of 'natural liberty'

At first Adam Smith's theory of property seems to be based on an uncritical defence of self-interest, and his theory of the state to be based on the *laissez-faire* principle of minimum intervention. He is best-known for his doctrine of the 'hidden hand', whereby the mutual pursuit of private interest leads, without conscious planning, to the maximization of the public good. While these themes undoubtedly exist in Smith's writing, they are not the whole story. He also offered an account of the antagonisms associated with private property, and of the interventions required of the state to resolve them, that went beyond Hobbes and Rousseau.

Smith's approach to private property can be read as a response to the moral critiques of egoism which resulted from Rousseau's classicist prejudices. In opposition to Rousseau, Smith argued that the gain of one person does not have to mean a loss for another, since mutual advantage can derive from the egotistical pursuit of self-interest through the exchange of commodities. 'The propensity to exchange' appeared to Smith not as a vice but simply as a natural human characteristic 'common to all men' and 'the necessary consequence of reason and speech'.[1] Unlike other animals, human beings are from the beginning social and 'have almost constant occasion for the help of their brethren'. The manner in which they procure this assistance is by appealing not to the benevolence of others but to their self-interest:

he will be more likely to prevail if he can interest their self-love in his favour and show them that it is for their own advantage to do for him what he requires of them.[2]

The exchange of privately-owned goods is the medium through which this mutually advantageous transaction takes place: one in which 'you give me that which I want and you shall have this which you want.'[3] Smith analysed the mechanisms, which Rousseau was unable to discover, by which a person 'by pursing his own interest' can promote the general development of civilization. First, an exchange of use values is advantageous for both the parties involved, since they alienate that for which they have no use and acquire that which they desire. Second, 'it is the power of exchange that gives occasion to the division of labour',[4] and it is the division of labour which in its turn makes possible 'the greatest improvement in the productive powers of labour'[5] and thus an increase in the general wealth of the nation. In both these ways – statically and dynamically – egoism can be squared with the good of all.

The fundamental law of political economy, that 'the uniform, constant and uninterrupted effort of every man to better his condition . . . is the principle from which public and national as well as private opulence is originally derived',[6] appeared to Smith as eternal and immutable. However, while the nature of the economic laws themselves does not alter, this is not true of the political and legal conditions under which these economic laws operate. Political and legal conditions which restrict the rights of individuals to pursue their own private interests also restrict the mutually beneficial gains which flow from this egoistic pursuit. Thus traditional doctrines of natural law, with their specific inhibitions on private property, appeared to Smith as the theoretical expression of just such a restrictive framework, and he counterposed to them a jurisprudence based on 'an obvious and simple system of natural liberty'. The great advantage, as Smith saw it, of what he called his own 'natural jurisprudence' over traditional natural law theory was that natural jurisprudence supported the independence or liberty of individuals and the general accumulation of wealth from which all would benefit, while personal dependency and economic stagnation constituted the essence of natural law's attachment of social obligations to property. 'Independence', Smith argued, was the creation of commercial society. Feudal landowners had maintained large numbers of retainers who were personally dependent upon their arbitrary power; Smith rightly saw this as a particularly degrading form of bondage in which the retainers relied on the good grace and private expenditures of their masters. The collapse of these feudal arrangements and their replacement by market relations between tenant farmers, merchants and landlords did away with personal dependence: labourers were free to transfer their labour from one master to another and commercial producers sold their wares to any and all who would buy, and thus became dependent on none in particular.

Personal dependency does not only corrupt the soul, it also impedes economic growth. Under slavery or serfdom, workers have no personal stake in the progress of production; where, on the other hand, 'workers are secure of enjoying the fruits of their industry, they naturally exert it to better their condition'. Liberty and economic growth go hand in glove.

The apparently 'hard' side of Smith's opposition to natural law theory and to its tempering of egoism by social duty comes out in his attack on the 'policing' of grain prices according to notions of 'fair price' and 'natural obligation to the poor' (in times of extremity). In his account of eighteenth-century popular struggles over the price of grain and bread, Edward Thompson treats Smith as the arch-representative of the harsh spirit of modern commerce which elevates private gain over the older 'moral economy' of the crowd. But as Holt and Ignatieff have recently pointed out, Smith did not offer this defence of a free market in grain as a dogma for its own sake, but rather argued that a free market would optimize distribution and production. Smith's case for dismantling the Assize of Bread was based on his claim that the Assize kept the price of bread *above* its natural, market price, and he opposed export bounties for the same reason.

The progressive aspect of Smith's opposition to natural law was manifest in his attack on the 'exclusive privileges' which monopolies had won for themselves in mercantilist society. He took a firm stance on the side of popular struggles in the eighteenth-century in his opposition to the Apprenticeship Laws, which were 'a manifest encroachment upon the liberty both of the workman and those who might be disposed to employ him'; to the Laws of Settlement, which violated 'natural liberty' in removing 'a man who has committed no misdemeanour from the parish where he chooses to reside'; to the Excise Laws, which 'our merchants have extorted from the legislature for the support of their own . . absurd and oppressive monopolies' on foreign trade. Smith described the smuggler as:

a person who though no doubt highly blameable for violating the laws of his country is frequently incapable of violating those of natural justice and would have been in every respect an excellent citizen had not the laws of his country made that a crime which nature never meant to be so.[7]

The laws of 'natural justice' were clearly not, in Smith's view, the traditional laws of nature, which never enjoined freedom of trade for all, but the new laws of 'natural liberty' and political economy. Smith's critique of the long-standing Game Laws followed a similar pattern; they set punishments not at all proportionate to the crime for taking things which 'by the rules of common equity' should continue 'in common' and which were enacted on account of 'the great inclination of the great to screw all they can out of the hands of the poor'. Smith added his two-pennyworth to a popular opposition to laws which, dating back to the decline of feudalism, reserved the right to hunt game as a special privilege for landowners of a certain size, thus excluding not only the poor but also smallholders and tenant farmers. Smith saw these barbarous laws, which made violation a capital offence, not only as a denial of liberty but also as an expression of a backward economy in which the unproductive reservation of land for hunting overrode its commercial use for food production.

Smith's defence of the advantages of modern 'natural liberty' over traditional law did not imply that the realm of civil society appeared to him self-sufficient or harmonious. He recognized numerous 'inconveniences' and 'disadvantages' associated with private property. Commercial society splits asunder the moral sentiments, divorcing personal gain from public duty. While Smith saw egoism as no bad thing in itself, he believed that it must be restrained by respect for the rights of others: 'wise and virtuous' persons should, he argued, be ready to subordinate their private interests to those of the general society. In civil society the endless quest for material gain – based on the illusory notion that happiness comes from wealth alone – threatens to overwhelm all other moral sentiments, so that neither virtue nor wisdom can be counted on. Smith sought not to condemn egoism but to marry it with public virtue, and it was this marriage which civil society impeded.

Smith's crucial discovery was that of the class divisions, inequalities and antagonisms which accompany the development of private property. He was among the first to recognize the real division of modern society into 'three gread orders': landowners, manufacturers and labourers. Smith saw these as natural divisions emerging from the very nature of the land, stock and labour, as a form of social organization most conducive to the wealth of the nation as a whole and of *all* its members, including the poor: 'the accommodation of an industrous and frugal peasant exceeds that of many an African king, the absolute master of . . . the lives and liberties of ten thousand naked savages.'[8] At the same time, however, he was well aware that the massive inequalities which these class divisions generate cannot be justified by any standards of natural justice. In a 'civilized society', he wrote:

> the poor provide both for themselves and for the enormous luxury of their superiors. The rent which goes to support the vanity of the slothful landlord is all earned by the industry of the peasant . . . The labourer who bears, as it were, upon his shoulders the whole fabric of human society seems himself to be pressed down below ground by the weight . . . In a society of an hundred thousand families, there will perhaps be one hundred who do not labour at all and who yet, either by violence or by the orderly oppression of law, employ a greater part of the labour of society than any other ten thousand in it . . . Those who labour most get least.[9]

Smith entertained no romantic dreams of returning to a society of smallholders where private property is respected but class divisions are absent. Such a state of affairs, Smith recognized, would immediately regenerate the class divisions which he described. His basic concern was rather to analyse how, out of the competition between private interests and the class inequalities which comprise civil society, a public authority could be established capable of resolving these contradictions.

The problem Smith posed – which Hobbes and Rousseau had neglected – was to identify a class of persons who could be relied on for the performance of public functions. His problem was that none of the three great classes of modern society could be relied on to perform the duties of government. The particular interests of workers, he argued, coincide with those of society in general, since a rise in wages can occur only if there is 'an increase in revenue and stock'. However, labourers were not capable of expressing this social interest because of the corruption of their consciousness. Simple, manual labour rendered those whose lives are limited to it

> as stupid and ignorant as it is possible for a human creature to become. The torpor of his mind renders him not only incapable of relishing or bearing a part in any rational conversation, but of conceiving any generous noble or tender sentiment and consequently of forming any just judgement concerning many even of the ordinary duties of private life. Of the great and extensive interests of his country he is altogether incapable of judging.[10]

The landowning class also had an identity of interest with those of society in general, since 'every improvement in the circumstances of society tends either directly or indirectly to raise the real level of rent of land' and so increase their own wealth. Their consciousness of their own interests was, however, as 'defective' as that of workers:

> That indolence which is the natural effect of the ease and security of their situation renders them too often not only ignorant but incapable of that application of mind which is necessary in order to foresee and understand the consequences of any public regulation.[11]

This leaves the owners of stock: the manufacturers and merchants. While they 'frequently have more acuteness of understanding than the greater part of country gentlemen',[12] the objective interests of this class are too often at variance with those of the public. Smith argued that economic development tends to lead to a fall in the rate of profit; conversely a rise in profit is associated with monopoly and restriction on general development. As a result, this class 'generally have an interest to deceive or even to oppress the public' and 'neither are nor ought to be the rulers of mankind'.

When private property subordinates public concern to private interest and creates three classes, none of which is capable of serving the public interest, how can a 'natural' harmony be established between the equally moral sentiments of egoism and public virtue? This was the question which led Smith to address the theory of law and the state.

Most critics of Smith's theory of the law and the state have focused on his advocacy of *laissez-faire* as a proper basis for state policy. Taking Smith to be an uncritical advocate of the wonders of the 'hidden hand', this interpretation emphasizes his polemic against state intervention in the economy. From this perspective, Smith seems to locate freedom and progress basically in freedom from the state. His theory of the state apprears to be a theory of limits on state activity. This theme certainly exists in Smith's writings and informs those passages where he argued, for instance, that

> all systems of preference or of restraint . . . being thus taken away, the obvious and simple system of natural liberty establishes itself of its own accord. Every man, as long as he does not violate the laws of justice, is left perfectly free to pursue his own interest in his own way and to bring both his industry and capital into competition with those of any other man or order of men.[13]

But this image offers a one-sided view of what Smith's theory of the state was actually about.

The context in which Smith made his anti-interventionist remarks is one of an extended and urgent critique of mercantilism; in this particular instance he has directed his fire against state policies which impede the flow of capital and labour from one area of production to another (from agriculture to manufacture, and vice versa). His objection to all preferences and constraints is specifically directed against government interventions which impede the growth of productivity and free trade by establishing artificial privileges and monopolies for favoured companies and individuals. Smith does not necessarily exclude other forms of state intervention. Indeed, Smith immediately follows this critique of state intervention by detailing the forms of intervention which *are* required of the state: defence, the administration of justice, and 'the duty of erecting and maintaining certain public works and certain public institutions which it can never be for the interest of any individual or small number of individuals to erect and maintain'.[14] It is true that Smith tried to limit the intervention of government, but this must be taken in the context of his critique of mercantilist interventions. Smith also argued that in any society where there are massive inequalities of wealth – and such inequalities he saw as endemic in commercial society – the establishment of a state to protect property is an absolute requirement: commerical society is far too brittle to survive of its own accord:

> It is only under the shelter of the civil magistrate that the owner of that valuable property which is acquired by the labour of many years or perhaps of many successive generations, can sleep a single night in security.[15]

The view that Smith's theory of 'natural liberty' was simply one aimed at imposing limits on the state ignores his extended critique of the 'inconveniences' of commercial society, and the importance of law and the state for their resolution.

In outlining the functions of the state, what was important for Smith was that there are some functions which the state must perform and which must not be left in the hands of private individuals or groups. Thus the problem, as he saw it, with the administration of justice under the old order was that it rested in the hands of bodies which subordinated justice to their own private interests. Where 'fees of court' constituted for the nobility a large proportion of their income, there was no hope of remedy. In eighteenth-century Britain the administration of justice was still tied to private wealth and power. Commercial society, by contrast, made it possible for justice to be separated from private interests and to become the duty of a strictly public authority.

The same theme ran through Smith's discussion of the military. He affirmed the need and right of every nation to defend itself: all the more so in commercial society, since 'an industrious and . . . wealthy nation is of all nations the most likely to be attacked'.[16] At the same time, however, 'the natural habits of the people [in commercial society] render them altogether incapable of defending themselves.' The only solution is for the state to intervene. In all traditional societies war could be, and was, left largely in the hands of private bodies: soldiers supported themselves through their own private means; the expense of arms was relatively small; there was time and motivation for the citizens to practice military skills. In commercial society, by contrast, 'military exercises come to be neglected'; the citizens no longer possessed the time, the money or the inclination to train themselves or to take the field in battle; the expense of an army and navy had become enormous. The state had to step in: to fund and organize primarily a standing army and secondarily a citizens' militia, with safeguards to ensure that it did not become a danger to liberty. Where military functions continued to be borne by private institutions like the chartered monopolies, they were performed badly and abused: to their own narrow interests of buying cheap and selling dear they subordinated the defence of the nation. Far from wishing to limit the state's military role, Smith wished to extend it: to remove the armed forces (like the administration of justice) from the hands of private individuals and groups and to relocate them as the exclusive preserve of the state.

Smith's espousal of state intervention in education provides a further case in point but also shows the limits of his interventionism. 'Ought the public', Smith asks, 'to give no attention to the education of the people?'[17] Whereas in the past the function of education could be left almost entirely in private hands, this was no longer the case. 'In every improved and civilized country', he argued 'some attention of government is necessary in order to prevent the almost entire corruption and degeneracy of the great body of the people':

> The common people . . . have little time for education. Their parents can scarce afford to maintain them even in infancy. As soon as they are able to work, they must apply to some trade by which they can earn their subsistence.[18]

In these circumstances, in which the poor are in any case demoralized by their conditions of work, the government must intervene to provide them with a basic education. The state owes this to the poor for the sake of their own intellectual development, since 'a man without the proper use of the intellectual faculties of a man . . . is mutilated and deformed';[19] and it owes it to itself, since 'an instructed and intelligent people . . . are always more decent and orderly than an ignorant and stupid one'.[20] In a nation, Smith argues, where 'the safety of government rests very much on the favourable judgement which the people may form of its conduct', the education of the public by the state becomes a top priority.

We can see, then, that Smith's theory of the state was not merely a theory of limits on the state. Indeed, his analysis of feudal society points critically to the weakness of the feudal state in relation to the lords, and his analysis of feudal law applauds the first tentative attempts of the state to impose discipline on these lords. The idea of 'order and good government' meant for Smith the legal defence of property: threatened on the one side by the translation of economic into political power by feudal magnates, merchants and foreign powers and on the other by the ignorant mob who fall prey to demagogues.

The strength of Smith's work as a whole was that he did not simply look to the effect of state intervention on commerce but also reversed the question to examine the determination of the state and its laws by commercial society:

> Commerce and manufacture gradually introduced order and good government, and with them, the liberty and security of individuals ... This though it has been the least observed is by far the most important of all their effects.[21]

Rejecting entirely the myth of a social contract, Smith offered a detailed historical account of the relations between different 'modes of subsistence' and the forms of law and state to which they gave rise. 'Property and government', he declared, 'very much depend on one another.' His account was evolutionary, tracing the development of society and its division of labour through hunting, pasturage, agriculture and finally commerce. Thus, in a society of hunters, there is little or no property and consequently 'no regular form of government'. In pastoral societies the growth of inequalities between the rich and the poor 'requires the establishment of civil government' to protect property; but government in this period is the exclusive preserve of the landowners and 'is in reality instituted for the defence of the rich against the poor.' The sovereign exercised judicial authority as a source of private revenue and without the possibility of any redress against corrupt decisions. Agricultural societies took various distinct forms – allodial, feudal and absolutist. The laws and government reflected the personal dependence to which the lords, princes and sovereigns subjected their vast numbers of servants and retainers; government was simply an extension of these relations of dependence without the presence of any clear distinction between the private rights of the lords and their public duties; thus

> not only the highest jurisdiction both civil and criminal but the power of levying troops, of coining money and even that of making bye-laws for the government of their own people, were all rights possessed allodially by the great proprietors of land.[22]

The emergence of absolutism did not fundamentally alter this situation of personal authority and dependence; it simply concentrated authority among a few of the most powerful lords and the monarch. The class inequalities regenerated in commercial society made the persistence of law and government imperative; but – and this was the nub of Smith's lengthy argument – law and government could be dissociated from privilege and dependence. It was the independence of the labourer, the tenant farmer, the tradesman and the artificer from reliance on a particular lord – so that they are 'obliged to all' but 'not absolutely dependent upon anyone'[23] – which provided the foundation for a political 'system of liberty'.

The great advance which Smith made in constructing a historical account of law and the state has been celebrated by Ronald Meek as a direct forerunner of Marx's materialist approach. We should, however, note that it was vitiated by an evolutionary framework which posited history as a succession of phases, culminating in the mature and final phase of commerce as the 'natural' condition of society. Smith also faced a methodological difficulty in relating jurisprudence to economics, which he never solved. Since he considered the 'propensity to exchange' to be a natural and eternal fact of human life, he was able to distinguish different modes of subsistence only by on the one hand the technical development of the division of labour (where it was least developed, there was least opportunity to exchange) and on the other by its laws and government. In the first case, Smith found himself committed to a technological determinism; in the second he was trapped in a circular argument, explaining law and the state by a mode of subsistence which was itself determined by law and the state. The technical determinism of the one was as unsatisfactory as the circularity of the other; Smith never resolved this problem.

The major shortcoming of Smith's historical account lay in his equation of commercial society with a society organized according to the laws of nature. His attempt to portray this product of history as the fulfilment of human nature turned his 'historical materialism' into a 'historicism' that attributed a natural goal to historical development. Smith was right to reject social contract theory in favour of materialism, but his materialism — rooted in a naturalistic account of human sentiments – was abstract. He no longer based the state on the abstract consent of the people (as expressed in social contract theory); but he identified it with the equally abstract idea of the natural sentiments of the people.

The crucial link, he argued, between the egoistic and the social individual is human sympathy for the passions of other people. This appeared to Smith as a natural human trait. Sympathy leads us to assess the 'propriety' of people's conduct on the basis of how others feel about it. Thus, if one person harms another, we feel a 'sympathetic resentment' at the injury done and look to the punishment of the wrongdoer.

The particular twist which Smith gave to this theory – which he inherited from Hume – was to abstract the idea of 'sympathy' from the *actual* feelings of men and women. First, he meant by it a capacity to share in the passions which other people *should* feel in a given situation, irrespective of whether or not they actually feel them: 'sympathy does not arise so much from the view of the passions as from that of the situation which excites it.'[24] One may sympathize with the affliction of an idiot, who may be happy or unaware of his or her affliction, or of a dead person who feels no passion at all. We put ourselves in their shoes even if they cannot respond appropriately. Second, Smith meant by sympathy the feeling that someone *ought to* have watching a particular situation rather than that which he or she actually has. Sympathy becomes the attribute not of concrete persons but of a 'well-informed and impartial spectator'.

Justice is based on the sympathies felt by this impartial spectator for what ought to be the passions of those who have been injured. People soon discover that they are the objects of evaluation by other people and begin to judge themselves as others judge them – or rather, as an impartial spectator would judge them. The impartial spectator within us becomes 'reason, conscience, principle, the inhabitant of the breast, the man within, the great judge and arbiter of our conduct'.[25] The sense of 'propriety' on which impartial spectators base their assessments is dependent on particular situations: it changes with place and time; but in any given situation there exists a definite judgement which the impartial spectator holds.

The problem Smith saw as facing civil society was the divorce between the actual sentiments of real people and the ideal sentiments of impartial observers. The egoism associated with private property, while good in itself, tended to block out sympathy for others. His solution in part reflected Hobbes's and Rousseau's formalism: it lay in the establishment of an external authority, which would embody and where necessary enforce the sentiments of the impartial observer and which individuals could look to as the expression of their own 'inner voice'.

The state was to be based, not on the real sentiments of real people, but on the 'proper' sentiments of ideal spectators. The result was at times a rather arbitrary indentification by Smith of those laws and constitutional arrangements which he supported with the impartial spectator's mark of approval, and conversely those he did not support with an imaginary scowl of disapproval.

When people fail to have a clear view of justice in cases where their own interests are involved – where, for instance, 'every man revenges himself at his own hand whenever he fancied himself injured' – the state must, in Smith's view, intervene lest civil society become 'a scene of bloodshed and disorder.' Smith's specific contribution was to address the conditions necessary to bring the actual sentiments of the people nearer the ideal sentiments of the impartial observer. He hoped that society would develop in such a way that the two would become the same – especially if everyone had a sufficiently wide circle of acquaintances and broad education – and that reason would thus prevail without state intervention. At the same time, state intervention – for example, in the form of education and law – was needed to transform these social conditions. While Smith resolved his ambivalence generally in favour of minimum intervention, later writers were to develop programmes of far more extensive social economic legislation without violating any of Smith's basic assumptions.

Smith's constitutional conclusions were built on the foundations of the liberal state already laid by Hobbes and Rousseau. At the centre of his 'system' of natural liberty' was the impartial administration of justice: the rules of law should be general, determinate, apply to all equally, and admit of 'no exceptions or modifications'. The biggest threat to the rule of law he saw as deriving from 'the interests of the government' as a corporate body (i.e. the state executive) or from 'the interests of particular orders of men who tyrannize the government and warp the positive laws of the country from what natural justice would prescribe'. The danger was that the executive would absorb 'every other power in the state' and assume for itself 'the management of every branch of revenue which is destined for any public purpose'. To prevent this, the right of imposing taxes was to be reserved for the 'assembly of the representatives of the people'; ministers were to be impeachable, habeas corpus was to insure against arbitrary imprisonment. The independence of the judiciary was essential, by which he meant independence not just from private interests but also from executive power:

> In order to make every individual feel himself perfectly secure in the possession of every right which belongs to him, it is not only necessary that the judicial should be separated from the executive power but that it should be rendered as much as possible independent of that power. The judge should not be liable to be removed from office according to the caprice of that power. The regular payment of his salary should not depend upon the good will or even the good company of that power.[26]

Smith was unclear how this independence was to be secured in fact (should judges be paid salaries, or be men of independent means, or be paid a market fee in such a way as to block off the possibility of corruption?) and he played around with a number of possibilities. He was, however, clear that judicial independence meant freedom from bureaucratic pressures and not from legislative direction; the right of judges to vet executive decisions but not to vet parliament. Smith shared Rousseau's fears about the despotic character of state bureaucracy but appreciated, on the basis of British experience, that bureaucracy was not a hangover from absolutism but a new and dangerous principle which threatened liberty as much as did the private interests of merchants. Smith's ideal of the rule of law was intended not as a ratification of state power – it did not convey an unconditional obligation to obey the laws of the state whatever their form or their content – but rather as an expression of what Edward Thompson has called 'a cultural tradition of bloody-mindedness towards the intrusion of authority'.[27]

### Hegel's theory of the 'rational state'

The political consequence of this principle [of the 'infinitely free personality'] is the modern European state, whose task it is to reconcile the principle of the *polis* – substantive generality – with the principle of Christian religion – subjective individuality. In this dialectical harmonization of two opposing powers Hegel sees not the peculiar weakness but rather the strength of modern states! The generality of the *polis* is of no value without the particular willing and knowing of the individuals, and the individuals are of no value when they do not themselves will the general will of the state . . . Hegel considered this synthesis not only possible but actually accomplished in the contemporary Prussian state![1]

Karl Löwith summed up the central problem faced by Hegel: how to reconcile individual freedom and the general will, private property and the state, the principle of 'particularity' and that of 'universality'. the problem was on the one hand philosophical: to create a synthesis between the classical ideal of the *polis* (city state), in which the will of the community as a whole predominates at the expense of subjective freedom, and the bourgeois ideal of individualism, in which the rights of individuals to pursue their own interests predominate at the expense of public authority. It was also a historical problem. Bourgeois society brought with it the rights associated with private property and in their name attacked – and in the case of the French Revolution demolished – those states which no longer corresponded with its idea of freedom. All this was, as far as Hegel was concerned, to the good. But bourgeois society brought with it the danger that subjective freedom would turn into mere egoism and that particularism would overwhelm universalism. It was not enough to demolish the old state: a new state had to be established in its place. The principle of the new state was to fuse the satisfaction of private desires, caprices, interests and needs with obedience to an external authority which represented the social whole.

Hegel sought a solution in the form of a 'rational state', at once dissociated from the private interests which comprise civil society and premised on their preservation. This involved him in a twofold attack. On the one hand, he opposed feudal critics of the modern state – see, for example, his polemic against von Haller – who based the state on the rule of the strong over the weak and denied any association between the state and individual rights. Such a conception, far from dissociating the state from private interests, turned the state into a private interest and, far from preserving the sphere of private interests, threatened it at every point. On the other hand, he opposed 'subjectivist' critics of the modern state – witness his polemics against Fries and the student radicals – who rejected all external authority in the name of moral subjectivism. Hegel attacked their belief that the only right is what one feels to be right; he argued that such an ethos allows people to do as they will and justify whatever they do on the basis of good intentions. As a result of such a philosophy, 'all the trouble of rational insight and knowledge is of course saved': any crime may be justified by reference to subjective meaning, any law may be condemned as a shackle on one's inner feelings. For Hegel, criticism of existing positive laws was to be drawn from the standpoint of 'rational law'; the repudiation of all law from the viewpoint of subjective conviction merely elevates the egoism of civil society into an absolute principle at the expense of any external authority. The task as Hegel saw it was not to do away with external authority – in which case self-interest and self-conceit are given full rein – but to make it rational.

In contrast to absolutism and subjectivism, Hegel saw Hobbes, Rousseau and Smith as having made great advances in the formation of a rational state, but he saw their accomplishments as incomplete. To some extent Hegel simply translated their concerns into the language of speculative philosophy, inheriting their identification of private property with freedom and the state with reason. However, he took their ideas ultimately down a quite different path. Private property seemed to him to represent the triumph of 'free mind' over external nature. He argued that the distinguishing mark of human freedom is that humans, unlike animals, are not restricted to natural instincts and fixed ways of satisfying them; rather, through the mediation of labour, humans transform nature to make it useful to themselves and in the same process transform their needs and their means of satisfying them. Hegel associated humanity with the conquest of nature, not subjection to it, and criticized the romantic identification of freedom with nature, reflected in Rousseau's rhetorical quip that 'man was born free but is everywhere in chains'.[2]

While labour initiates the process of human transcendence over nature, Hegel saw the institution of private property as giving a form adequate to this process: one in which a person exercises 'the right of putting his will into any and everything and thereby making it his'. What is essential in private property is the 'will': the natural characteristics of the thing become no more than the accidental form in which people objectify their will. Hegel argued that private property implies recognition by others of oneself as a free human being. When others respect your property by not trespassing on it, they respect you as a human being. The establishment of private property represents a mutual recognition of people as free and rational beings, expressed in the form of the contract whereby 'the parties entering it recognize each other as persons and property owners' and recognize each other's right to buy and sell as they choose without constraint.

Private property expressed for Hegel the subjective freedom of the individual. Owners of private property can do as they wish with their property: use it, abuse it, exchange it, keep it: it is a matter reserved for their discretion, their caprice, their arbitrary desire. He identified the individual freedom of property owners to do as they pleased with more general individualistic values like 'love, romanticism, the quest for the eternal salvation of the individual, moral convictions, conscience etc.'. The product of self-interest appeared to Hegel as mutual satisfaction, Smith's 'hidden hand' being translated into the dialectic of reason.

As with Smith, it is the division of labour and exchange which 'makes necessary everywhere the dependence of men on one another and their reciprocal relation in the satisfaction of their other needs'. One person's gain becomes – through the division of labour and exchange – not another's loss but another's means of self-satisfaction. It is thus that Hegel discovered 'in the sphere of needs this show of rationality'.

Hegel's critique of Smith was aimed at the merely contingent character of the link he formed between freedom and private property. Smith justified private property as a means of satisfying human desires; but for Hegel private property was no longer a *means* of satisfying needs but 'the first embodiment of freedom and therefore a substantial end in itself'; it was presented by Hegel as the essential embodiment of free will and human personality. For Smith, freedom derives empirically from the existence of private property; for Hegel, private property derives logically from the idea of freedom. Subject and predicate are inverted: the march of freedom becomes the subject of history, while private property becomes freedom's predicate at a certain stage of its historical progress. Free will appears as the foundation of private property rather than private property as the basis of free will.

Though Hegel made absolute the connections between private property and freedom, he did not abandon classical critiques of the contradictions inherent in civil society. Since civil society is the sphere of 'universal egoism', the pursuit of unrestrained self-interest threatens to pull it apart from within: 'by means of its own dialectic the civil society is driven beyond its own limits as a definite and self-complete society.' The inherent tendency of private property is to turn freedom into licence: what results is a spectacle of excess, misery and physical and social corruption'. Poverty is the inescapable by-product of civil society: while Smith may be right that the modern peasant is better off than the old tribal chief, poverty is relative and should be measured against the new needs generated by society. On the one side of civil society lies the massive accumulation of wealth, on the other impoverishment:

> when the standard of living of a large mass of people falls below a certain level of subsistence . . . and when there is a consequent loss of the sense of right and wrong, of honesty and self-respect . . . the result is the creation of a rabble of paupers.[3]

The contrast between wealth and poverty fills the poor with 'inner indignation and hatred', making them incapable of leading a public life or of acting 'in the spirit of the whole'. As for the wealthy business class, they sink into their own private concerns, interested only in their own prosperity at the expense of all else. As they become preoccupied with their private affairs, public life becomes an alien power remote from their own interests and left to social forces – the monarch, the estates – who are themselves no more than private interests. They have no regard for the whole; private property is turned 'into an absolute'. The agricultural class, tied to a patriarchal way of life and to the natural products of the soil, have a mode of subsistence that owes little to intelligence or independence of thought. While they are more suited to public affairs by virtue of being free from immediate pressures of the market and of possessing independent means, they are too unreflective, simple, subservient for a public role.

Hegel perceived the negative side of Smith's 'hidden hand'. The market is an 'alien power' over which the producer has no control; this dependence is illustrated when 'whole branches of industry which supported a large class of people suddenly fold up because of a change of fashion or because the value of their product falls due to new inventions in other countries'.[4] The key to the problem of civil society is that a free society should be the conscious subject of its own development; in civil society the integration of separate private interests into a general line of development is the product not of free rational decisions but of chance and necessity. The question Hegel faced was whether, out of the particularism that characterizes civil society, it is possible for the principle of universality to arise as a real social force. Hegel's critique of Hobbes, Rousseau and Smith was directed both at their belief that it is possible and at the specific solutions which they proposed. In Hegel's view, the contradictions present in the 'universal egoism' of civil society were too irreconcilable for a public spirit to emerge out of them. Rather than derive the universal state from the particular interests of civil society, the state had to be established in its own right and imposed on civil society.

The classical theorists had never fully broken from the perspective of members of civil society according to which the state appeared as no more than a guarantee of their self-interest: a means for the protection of private property rather than as a self-sufficient principle which transcends private property. It would be difficult, for example (Hegel argued) to justify taxation on the basis of rational self-interest, or even more difficult to justify military service. Each of these is a duty which goes beyond the interest of the citizen as a private person. Civil society is a 'system of needs' in which individuals see others as no more than means for securing their own private ends; classical writers reproduce the vantage point of civil society when they treat the state as no more than a means of satisfying egoism.

The divorce of the state from civil society, initiated by classical jurisprudence, had to be completed. Because it is ruled by blind market forces, civil society cannot be a sphere of 'objective' freedom; whereas the state, because it embodies the self-conscious will of the people as a whole, is the sphere of objective freedom. So,

Hegel concluded, Hobbes was right: civil society must be sub-ordinated to the state rather than the state being surbordinated to civil society.

It was this reversal of the relation between civil society and the state that has given rise to the impression of Hegel as an absolutist. His commitment to the 'absolute authority' of the state has been interpreted as marking a shift in bourgeois thought away from its radical phase, when it counterposed natural right to established authority, to its authoritarian maturation, when it demanded unconditional obedience to a state, now in bourgeois hands. It seemed that Hegel's subordination of individual rights to the collective will weakened the foundation for the protection of civil liberties. It also gives rise to the impression of Hegel as a proto-revolutionary, putting community before property, the general good before private interest, conscious planning before blind market forces. Hegel's ideal state was no longer a servant of private property but the autonomous embodiment of the will of the community. Neither version, however, captures the real significance of Hegel's reversal of the relation between civil society and the state. On the one hand, as a counter to absolutism, he argued that the rational state must generate a sphere of individual freedom; on the other, as a counter to revolutionism, he argued that the state must guarantee private property. The state, in other words, had to 'posit' civil society as a 'moment' in its own formation.

Hegel pursued this philosophical revision of the relation between civil society and the state into his analysis of law, welcoming the attack on traditional natural law theory initiated by Hobbes, Rousseau and Smith. All law, he declared, is 'positive', that is, posited by human beings; natural law is the illusory form which law takes before human beings become conscious of their freedom to make laws as they choose. Hegel was scathing in his critique of the 'old rights' enjoined by natural law theory:

'Old rights' are such fine grand words that is sounds impious to contemplate robbing a people of it rights. But age has nothing to do with what 'old rights' . . . mean or whether they are good or bad. Even the abolition of human sacrifice, slavery, feudal despotism and countless other infamies was in every case the cancellation of something that was an 'old right.'[5]

Law must represent freedom in its content (and so cannot justify slavery, serfdom or personal dependence) and in its form (and thus cannot take the form of natural law). The idea of 'rational law', Hegel argued, is premissed on free will in both form and content: that is, on the freedom to posit law without natural constraint and on the freedom of private property under law.

Hegel's correct critique of Hobbes, Rousseau and Smith was that in one way or another they all resurrected natural law theory in the form of a natural right to private property. For Hegel, the authority of positive law was to encounter no such 'natural' barriers. The connection between private property and the law was not an external one of protection or preservation, but an imminent one of form. The idea of a legal subject, that is, of one who possesses rights, implies ownerships of private property; or, to put the matter in reverse, private property is the external form taken by the concept of 'right': 'Right is . . . the immediate embodiment which freedom gives itself as an immediate way, i.e. possession which is property ownership.'[6] The connection between law and private property, in other words, is not contingent but essential, not a matter of content but of form. Law should not be analysed in terms of the protection of private property but as its embodiment.

The rationality of law, Hegel argued, lies in its 'universality'. It treats everyone alike; each owner of property is equal to every other; none has privileges and none may be barred from ownership. The right of ownership is implicit in the human personality as such. Everyone is free because at the very least they own their own 'mental endowments' or capacity to labour. This was the quality of law that previous classical writers idealized. Hegel, by contrast, pointed out that the universality of law was purely 'abstract': what and how much a person owns is 'a matter of indifference as far as rights are concerned', for law is concerned only with 'the equality of abstract persons as such' and not with differences like the amount of property they happen to possess. Thus, short of alienating one's whole personality as in slavery or serfdom by selling 'the entire time of one's concrete labour', the real dependence of one individual on another – manifest in the relation between worker and capitalist – is outside the sphere of right and compatible with legal freedom and equality.

From the fact that the universal character of law is only formal, Hegel did not conclude that it was therefore meaningless or illusory but rather that it was limited. Freedom and equality before the law, Hegel argued, provide a minimum of freedom and equality and must accordingly not be discarded; however, by themselves they are not sufficient to embody the universal will. Far from rejecting equal right as a myth, Hegel sought to translate it into a legal system based on definite formal standards. Laws must be made universally known, for only the tyrant would 'hang laws so high that no citizen could read them';[7] laws must be general, applying to all equally and referring to none by name; laws must be determinate in order that their application to particular cases be not arbitrary; retroactive legislation must be ruled out. Trials must be conducted by a 'public authority' and no longer be 'optional acts of grace or favour on the part of monarchs and governments'; they must be held in public, since 'the right at issue . . . affects the interests of everybody';[8] they must be held before lay juries, since 'knowledge of the facts of the case . . . involves no pronouncement on points of law', and juries must comprise the peers of the accused, since confidence in them is based 'primarily on the similarity between them and the parties in respect to their particularity, i.e. their social position'.[9] Judges should have some discretion in applying universal laws to particular instances, since it is a matter of contingency whether, for example, 'justice requires for an offence . . . corporal punishment of forty lashes or thirty-nine',[10] and since the important point for Hegel was the practical requirement that 'something be actually done . . . no matter how'.[11] Laws should be codified, either in statute or in case law, since the 'just systematization' of law is what 'our time is pressing for'.[12] (Hegel was critical of what he saw – wrongly perhaps – as the principle of English common law that judges are themselves the 'repositories of the unwritten law' and so become in effect legislators exempt from the authority of their predecessors.) Legislation may pertain only to that which is in principle 'external' and not – as was the case in ancient society – to ' the field of inner life' (love, feelings, integrity, etc.).[13] Right must be determined by formal legal procedures; since in spite of widespread antipathy to legal formalities, they are the means by which 'the validity of my will . . . should be recognized by others.'[14] Forms of punishment are a matter of contingency related to the conditions of particular societies; where societies are stable, punishments may be mild and where societies are weak, they may for the same offence be severe in order to set an example. What was important was only that punishments be legal and that no crimes be left unpunished. The rule of law was, in Hegel's terms, the ideal legal system which realized the concept of right and marked the victory of freedom over despotism: 'despotism means any state of affairs where law has disappeared and where the particular will as such, whether of a monarch or a mob, counts as law or rather takes the place of law'.[15]

The formal character of equal right means, however, that under the rule of law alone blind market forces will not be subordinated to conscious direction, inequalities between the rich and the poor will not be overcome, relations based on exchange of property will not be replaced by 'true association', and the subjective will of the individual will not be meshed into the rational will of the whole. Even an ideal legal system will not be the final point of integration of civil society, since its universality pertains only to the abstract rights of private property and not to the needs of real individuals. The solution, in Hegel's view, was not to get rid of the restricted amount of freedom and equality which the rule of law provided but to supplement the rule of law with a force capable of governing the 'particular' aspects of people's lives. Following on from Smith and others, Hegel called this the 'police' and defined its role as providing welfare for the poor, a fair balance between the interests of producers and consumers, public health care, public building works, a public education system and the planning of various aspects of private production; in short, as creating a balance, which Hegel never specified, between freedom of trade and the general good. The problem Hegel faced was how to construct a 'police' without resurrecting the spectre of despotism. Since the law was an aspect of civil society, Hegel's solution lay in the formation of a state more radically divorced from civil society than the doctrine of the 'legal state' made possible.

The key to the rational state, in Hegel's view, was that the people themselves should enter government only in their 'rational form'; their influence on government, in other words, must be mediated in order that it be a rational influence and not merely a reflex of the passions of the 'rabble'. Unmediated, public opinion comprises no more than 'a hotch-potch of truth and endless error';[16] the point of mediation is to sift the true from the false, the rational from the irrational. Nothing could be worse, in Hegel's view, than for the people to run the state by other than 'legal and orderly means'; for if such means are lacking 'the voice of the masses is always for violence'.[17] Hegel shrank from the prospect of the 'democratic element' coming into 'the organism of the state without any rational form'; as for instance in Rousseau's proposal that

> every single person should share in deliberating and deciding on political matters of general concern on the grounds that all individuals are members of the state, that its concerns are their concerns, and that it is their right that what is done should be done with their knowledge and volition.[18]

Hegel saw in this a recipe for disaster. For the rational will of the people to predominate, first, the rational part of the population, centred around the middle classes, was to be separated off from the irrational part, 'women and children at least', and the latter excluded from participation in the state, thus Hegel called the people the 'many' rather than the 'all'. Second, a system of mediations had to be established to serve as a kind of filter through which reason might pass and unreason be kept out.

Hegel's first mediation was the constitution itself. In the constitution, he argued, is expressed the rational will of all. It embodies the unity of the state: the three functions of government – executive, legislative and monarchic – are but the organs of the constitution working in harmony with one another. For Hegel, prefiguring later developments in legal positivism, it appeared meaningless to ask where a constitution came from, since a people by definition, as opposed to a 'formless mass', must have a constitution. The existence of a constitution is thus turned into a premiss rather than a product of organized social life:

> it is absolutely essential that the constitution should be regarded as something made, even though it has come into being in time . . . It must be treated rather as something existent in and by itself, as divine therefore and constant and so as exalted above the sphere of things that are made.[19]

The will of the people had to be constitutional to be rational: this did not rule out innovation but restricted rational innovation to that which is constitutionally legitimate. Hegel thought that real advances in the constitution were often 'imperceptible' and 'tranquil in appearance': over a long period of time a constitution maintains its own outward appearance but gradually turns into 'something quite different from what it originally was'.[20] While gradual, constitutional change appeared to Hegel, in passages such as these, as the only rational means of reform, there was an ambivalence in his thought resulting from his immediate awareness that the modern Prussian constitution, of which he approved so warmly, had been imposed by Napoleon in a manner that was neither constitutional nor gradual.

Hegel's next mediation was the system of representation. The deputy in parliament was to represent the means by which truth was to be culled from the field of conflicting prejudices that make up public opinion:

> Since deputies are elected to deliberate and decide on public affairs, the point about their election is that it is a choice of individuals on the strength of the confidence felt in them, i.e., a choice of such individuals as have a better understanding of these affairs than their electors have and such also as essentially vindicate the universal interest, not the particular interest of a society or corporation.[21]

Thus the relation between electors and their representatives was not to be one of 'agents with a commission or specific instructions', but one of 'trust' in which representatives were mandated to make their own decisions, on the basis of their own greater knowledge and expertise in public affairs and on the basis of debates within the assembly, since it was there that all the members 'deliberate together and reciprocally instruct and convince each other'.[22]

A more archaic mediation was to be secured through the establishment of 'estates'. Hegel argued that in civil society people do not appear as 'a mere indiscriminate multitude' nor as 'an aggregate dispersed into atoms'; they appear, rather, organized into classes. These classes, Hegel suggested, mirroring a traditional form of argument, should be given political significance as 'estates'; that is, people should vote for their representatives not on the basis of universal suffrage of individuals, but as members of these 'estates'. Where people vote as individuals it leads to 'electoral indifference', since a single vote 'is of no significance where there is a multitude of electors';[23] this in turn leads to the concentration of power in fact into 'the hands of a few, a caucus'. The decisive reason Hegel puts forward for election to be based on estates is that at no point should the people appear as 'an unorganized aggregate'; for in this case they are 'a formless mass whose commotions and activity could . . . only be elementary, irrational, barbarous and frightful'.[24] This also informs Hegel's analysis of 'corporations', which are meant to organize particular interests within civil society and represent them to the state, while remaining themselves 'under the surveillance of the public authority.'[25] Hegel had an intense distrust of 'unorganized' masses: not only, he said, should voting be organized around the representation of estates, but the assembly should be divided into two houses, the upper one of which should be reserved for the landowning estate. Hegel justified this unelected upper house on the grounds that the landowning class were naturally suited to political position, since their fixed ownership of land allowed them independence of the market, the executive and the 'mob'. The great advantage of this arrangement, in Hegel's view, was that it acts as 'a surer guarantee of ripeness of decision' and that it means that 'there is less chance of the Estates being in direct opposition to the executive'. Thus Hegel did not only purport to derive a particular kind of representation form the idea of the 'universal', he also derived from it a hereditary upper chamber! Further, as a form of mediation, Hegel confined representation to the sphere of the legislature, that organ of the state whose power is to 'determine and establish the universal'. The specific object of legislation was the enactment of determinate and universal laws; 'the ways and means of enforcing them', however, were generally a matter for the executive, which was not to be subject to election of any kind. In other words, representation was, first, to be based on trust rather than commission; second, it was to be based on estates and a separate House of Lords; third, it was to be limited to the sphere of legislation and excluded from the sphere of the executive. This for Hegel was the specific form which representation was to take in order to impose the 'general will' over 'the will of all'.

Hegel defined the executive as 'the power to subsume single cases and spheres of particularity under the universal'. In this case the mediation between civil society and the state was not through representation but through the construction of a specific class whose interests were said to be divorced from those of civil society and identified instead with the universal interests of the state as a whole. This was the class of civil servants, or the bureaucracy. By being paid salaries as state employees they were to be relieved of having to supply their own personal needs through labour in civil society or through corruption; they were to be appointed on merit, based on the passing of public examinations; their positions were to be open to all citizens; their offices were to be neither saleable nor transferable by gift or inheritance (Hegel, for instance, criticized the practice which still survived in England of purchasing commissions in the army); they were to have tenure so long as they performed their duties and were to be subject to hierarchical controls from above and pressures from below by the representatives of the estates to insure against the abuse of their powers. Through the establishment of a rational bureaucracy, Hegel believed that he had found the solution to the problem which had plagued classical jurisprudence: the formation of a class of people whose interests were identified with those of society in general and who were conscious of this indentity. 'What the state really requires', Hegel wrote, 'is that men shall forgo the selfish and capricious satisfaction of their subjective ends and by this very sacrifice acquire the right to find their satisfaction in, but only in, the dutiful discharge of their public function.'[26] Hegel believed that a rational bureaucracy met this requirement; especially as most civil servants were middle-class, 'the class in which consciousness of right and the developed intelligence of the man of the people is found'.[27] Believing that 'the highest civil servants necessarily have a deeper and more comprehensive insight into the nature of the state's organization and requirements'[28] than the people, Hegel reformulated the relationship between the executive and the legislature, no longer as one of subordination of the one to the other, but as one of two complementary wings of a unified state. He described as 'a most dangerous prejudice' the view of a division of powers which sets the assembly in opposition to the executive. 'To regard the will of the executive as bad', he argued, 'is a presupposition characteristic of the rabble.' Montesquieu's general doctrine concerning the 'division of powers' made the 'fundamental error' of supposing that independent powers are merely a 'check' on one another; such independence, Hegel concluded, 'destroys the unity of the state and unity is the chief of all desiderata'.[29] As regards the subordination of the executive to the judiciary, Hegel displayed his opposition by abolishing altogether their separation and including the judiciary under the rubric of the executive. The bureaucracy was now elevated as the major partner among the organs of the state.

The third element in Hegel's division of powers and the third form of mediation was the crown or monarch: 'the power of subjectivity, as the will with the power of ultimate decision'.[30] It was a constitutional monarchy which Hegel had in mind; one on which substantive decisions were taken according to the principles laid down in the constitution but then given a formal ratification by the monarch in order to count as valid decisions of the state. Since this is all the monarch has to do, Hegel argues that it matters not what his or her personal attributes are; all that does matter is the stability of the monarchy, because of its symbolic importance in representing in one person the will of the people. Under these circumstances the most appropriate means of selection is primogeniture, which leaves the private character of the monarch to chance but insures the stability of the throne. This works well because 'in a well organized monarchy, the objective aspect belongs to the law alone and the monarch's part is merely to set to the law the subjective "I will".' If the deputy was raised above the particular interests of civil society by means of representation and the bureaucrat by means of hierarchy and the like, the monarch is thus elevated by virtue of his or her natural, and not social, being. Every society must have a leader: 'there must always be individuals at the head . . . everything is brought to completion by the single decisive act of a leader'.[31]

These, then, were the mediations through which Hegel hoped to subordinate the real will of flesh-and-blood individuals to the rational will of the whole: the rule of law, the 'police', the constitution, monarchy, representation and bureaucracy. Hegel's attempted synthesis between the private will of individuals in civil society and the rational will of the state turned out, however, to be an unhappy marriage: in effect he idealized the state as the embodiment of reason and the bureaucracy as the embodiment of the state. In Hegel's succinct terminology, the mind which 'knows and wills itself' is the state mind.

Hegel's formal identification of 'external authority' with 'immanent reason' was clearly revealed in his comments on crime and punishment. Crime appeared not merely as a violation of the positive laws of the state, but for this reason as a violation of one's own rational consciousness. Punishment appeared as a right established within the criminal himself . . . Punishment is regarded as containing the criminal's right and hence by being punished he is honoured as a rational being.[32] It seemed that punishment, rather than being an act of force by one person or set of persons against another, is the criminal's self-retribution.

Hegel took the formal identity between the state and the people to its limit: on the one hand establishing an *identity* between the state and the people by locating the 'real' will of the individual in the state; on the other, establishing a *chasm* between the state and the people, by abstracting the state from the real will of individuals in society and elevating it as a special power alienated from the people. The fetishism of the state which to varying degrees was present throughout classical jurisprudence – the idea that the external authority of the state *is* the rational will of the individual – finds in Hegel's idealism its ultimate expression. While his project – that of creating a synthesis between individual freedom and collective authority – represented a high point in the liberal tradition, his solution was both mystificatory and authoritarian. It was from this contradictory heritage that Marx took off.

# 2. Marx's critique of classical jurisprudence

## Democratizing the rational state

Taken as a whole, theorists of classical jurisprudence demolished traditional conceptions of natural law but in their place naturalized positive law. They demonstrated the human origins of law, but concluded that it is in the nature of humans to 'posit' law. They subjected all traditional institutions to the test of reason, but presented bourgeois private property, law and state as the embodiment of reason. They attacked the isolation of reason from human history, but projected the achievements of human history as the realization of reason.

Marx began from here. He applauded the 'advance' made by classical jurisprudence, but saw it as incomplete. In his criticism of classical jurisprudence, Marx did not seek to return to the dogmas of traditional natural law theory – though occasionally he slipped back into this mode – but rather to radicalize the break already achieved by classical jurisprudence. Marx's own critique of liberalism did not come about in a flash of inspiration but as the organic outcome of a lifetime's theoretical and political activities: on the one hand there was no 'fundamental rupture' between early and late Marx, nor, on the other, did Marx have everything worked out in his early works. Both of these 'extreme' versions (put forward by Althusser and Colletti respectively) have won considerable attention, but both obscure the dynamic character of Marx's confrontation with liberalism and the deepening of his critique as time went on: the former tears Marx away from his liberal roots, while the latter dissolves Marx into radical liberalism. Marx's point of departure was classical jurisprudence and his journey away from it was accomplished only in stages, without a preconceived destination.

At first Marx accepted Hegel's notion of the 'rational state' as an ideal against which to measure existing states. The task of the rational state appeared to Marx in the same way as it did to Hegel, as 'the realization of natural freedom', the synthesis of the universal will of the whole and the particular will of every individual. But he parted from Hegel's way of embodying the rational state. The nub of his criticism was that the Prussian constitutional monarchy – which appeared in Hegel's eyes to be close to the real embodiment of the rational state – failed entirely so to do.

In his critique of the censorship laws (1842) Marx argued that they made the bureaucracy – to which was granted the power to censor – too powerful, the result being that 'not so much the whole state, as part of the state, the "government", carries on a real political life.' How can the people be free when 'freedom of the press is the privilege of a few people' rather than 'the privilege of the human mind'? The free press is the medium through which the 'public spirit' may express itself. Censorship is the means by which the government substitutes its own private will for the universal will of the people; in place of the public spirit it creates an 'oligarchy of the spirit'; in place of freedom it is 'a preventative measure of the police against freedom'. It asks 'unlimited trust in the officialdom' but flows from 'unlimited distrust of all non-officials'. It means that the government 'hears only its own voice', which it mistakes for the voice of the people, while the actual voice of the people is suppressed by officialdom. It justifies itself by pointing to the imperfection of human beings, whom the state needs to save from themselves; but its solution is to fall on one's knees before certain privileged individuals. For Marx it is only the aggregate, and not a privileged official, that can remedy the imperfection of the individual: 'true censorship', he argues, 'is criticism', while offical censorship is 'criticism as a government monopoly'. The rational state, in short, must guarantee the right of the free press, if the private will of the 'government' is not to masquerade as the universal will of the body politic as a whole. Marx's practical alternative at this stage is the rule of law. A censorship law he describes as an 'impossiblity', since what is legal must be free. While a law can punish me only for my acts, the censor punishes me for my opinions; while a law is based on objective norms, the discretion of the censor is of indefinite scope; while the law is open and public, the censor works secretly and in the dark. In opposition to the power of the bureaucracy, Marx pointed to the rule of law as the embodiment of the rational state. The worst thing about a censorship law is that people begin to think that 'what is lawless is free' and that 'what is legal is unfree'.[1]

Similar themes ran through Marx's critique of the laws concerning the theft of wood (1843). These laws turned the 'traditional rights' of the poor to gather dead wood from forests into serious criminal offences and were passed at the behest of the landowners. Marx attacked these laws as an invasion by private interests into the universal sphere of the state. They turned the forest owner into the representative of the state – his warden was at once policeman, prosecutor, judge and punisher – and hence the state into an instrument of landed property.

These theft laws corrupt the 'state idea' itself by subordinating the general interest to the particular and elevating the freedom of the landowner over the freedom of all others. Marx formulated his indictment in terms of the ideals of rational law: 'private interest', he declared, 'has overruled right', while rational law 'is the conscious expression of the will of the people and therefore is made with the will of the people and by it.'[2]

In these early writings Marx used a Hegelian framework to break from Hegel and to offer a far more democratic rendering of what constitutes rational law and the rational state. The target of his critique was on the one hand the corruption of the universal will of the people by private interests, and on the other the substitution of the will of the government for the universal will of the people. In his critique of Hegel's *Philosophy of Right*, Marx followed through on these ideas in a more systematic way, attacking the methodological basis on which Hegel drew his conclusions.

## Against Hegel's image of the rational state

Marx argued that Hegel's deduction of the Prussian constitutional monarchy from the idea of the universal was spurious. What he really did, Marx said, was to describe a particular state of affairs (like hereditary monarchy, a reformed bureaucracy, a bicameral parliament, the incorporation of the judiciary within the executive) and assign to it the logical attributes of universality. In this way Hegel idealized empirical reality, turning the existing state into the embodiment of the universal: 'empirical reality is accepted as it is; it is even declared to be rational.' The deception practised by Hegel's idealism was to invert the relationship between subject and predicate. Instead of saying that the rational state is universal, Hegel says that universality expresses itself in the form of the state. The universal becomes the subject, while the actual state appears as its mere predicate. Marx reinstated the true relation between subject and predicate:

> Hegel makes the predicates autonomous but hides this by separating them from their real autonomy, viz, their subjects. The real subject subsequently appears as a result whereas the correct approach would be to start with the real subject and then consider its objectification. The mystical substance therefore becomes the real subject, while the actual subject appears as something else, namely as a moment of the mystical substance.[3]

The point of departure, Marx argued, should not be the idea of universality but the actual state. The critical task is to investigate how universal are the specific forms of organization of the existing state; Hegel's sole concern, by contrast, 'is simply to rediscover "the idea" in every sphere of the state that he depicted'.[4] Hegel's method was uncritical: 'it is very easy to fasten on what lies nearest at hand and prove that it is an actual moment of the idea.' For example, from the general need for an executive power to apply universal norms to particular cases, Hegel purports to deduce the rationality of the particular Prussian bureaucracy. But the deduction is false, since it proves nothing about the appropriateness of the latter: just as there is more than one way of skinning a cat, so too there is more than one way of exercising executive power: 'an explanation which fails to supply the differentia is no explanation at all . . . Hegel uncritically accepts this inappropriate form [the bureaucracy] as a fully adequate reality.' Granted that some means must be found for applying general rules to particular circumstances, the question that Marx raises is the adequacy of the particular means employed in Hegel's version of the Prussian state. The same argument applied to Hegel's idealization of existing forms of representation, of parliament, of law and of monarchy: in each case the point is to begin with the real institution and assess its universality, not to begin with the idea of universality and spuriously deduce these institutions from it.

The question Marx pursued in his *Critique of the Philosophy of Right* was how universal the actual state was; it was not yet how the actual state as it was had come into being: the actual state was still a starting point for him rather than something to be explained. His method allowed him to criticize the Prussian state's claim – as voiced by Hegel – to embody the universal, but not to explain the emergence of the Prussian state itself. He retained Hegel's idea that the 'essence' of the state lay in its universality and separation from particular interests and criticized only the identification of the Prussian state with the essence of the state. This way the meaning of his comment that Hegel ought not to be blamed 'because he describes the essence of the modern state as it is but rather because he presents what is as the essence of the state.'[5] In other words Marx was still struggling with Hegel, impatient with his conservativism, which projected Prussian authority as the essence of the state, but committed none the less to the notion that the essence of the state lies in its universality. The point for Marx was to create a genuinely universal state and not pass off the shoddy material of the Prussian state as if it were the genuine article.

The core of Marx's critique was twofold: he attacked the intrusion of private interest into the running of the state, which Hegel sanctified under the illusion that it was the state that was intruding into private interests; and he attacked the alienation of the state from the actual will of actual people, which Hegel sanctified as the realization of the rational will of rational people. Either way, through the subordination of the state to private interests or through the elevation of the state as a special power above the people, the universality of the state was corrupted. Hegel's ideal state showed symptoms of both.

With respect to the intrusion of private interests into the state, Marx tore into the privileged political status which Hegel reserved for landed property, especially in the form of an unelected Upper House which was to comprise members of this estate alone and to create 'a surer guarantee of ripeness of decision' and 'less chance of the Estate being in opposition to the executive'. What this privilege really meant, Marx argued, was not the power of the state over private property but the power of 'true' private property – i.e. 'landed property' – over the state. Further, the selection of the monarch from the landed estate by means of primogeniture meant that landed property wielded its private power at the very apex of the state. How, Marx asks, can this blatant instance of class privilege be rationally justified as the embodiment of the universal will? How indeed? This is what Marx referred to when he wrote that 'the political constitution at its highest summit is then the constitution of private property. The highest political opinion is the opinion of private property.'[6] For Hegel, he said, 'independent private property', which means to say landed property, was 'not only the support of the constitution but the constitution itself'. This was Marx's way, not of demonstrating that bourgeois private property is the foundation of a state bereft of privileges, but of attacking a state which still rested on the privileges of landed property. At this stage of his development, Marx made no effort to incorporate an overall critique of private property into his critique of the state.

It was class *privilege* which Marx objected to here, not the existence of class itself; monarchy and a House of Lords were the direct expression of such privilege:

> The chamber of deputies and the chamber of peers . . . are not different manifestations of the same principle. Instead they spring from two essentially different principles and social conditions. The chamber of deputies is the political constitution of civil society in the modern sense while the chamber of peers belongs to a constitution in the sense of the old estates.[7]

The 'old estates' refer to the traditional order, when the private power of landlords was fused with their political power as agents of the state. Hegel's insertion of a House of Lords into his rational state was a guarantee against the lower chamber 'as the political existence of empirical universality'. It was not parliament as such to which Marx objected but to its specific bicameral form in Hegel's system and in the Prussian state.

The other wing of Marx's attack was directed against the independence of Hegel's ideal state from the will of the people as a whole, and thus the corruption of the state as a private interest of its own. The separation of the state from the people was built into Hegel's theory, since it appeared that the interest of the state *was* the public interest: 'the abstract reality of the state consists in the fact that its end is the universal interest as such.' The 'formalism' of the state lies in the semblance that the general will is embodied in the state whether or not the state accords with the particular 'will of all'. In Hegel and in the modern state, everything appears upside down: empirical consciousness – what people really think, feel and what – is subordinated to rational consciousness, i.e. what they would think, feel and want if they were rational. The state acts in the public interest but keeps the actual public at arm's length:

> As long as the state-mind mystically haunted the ante-chambers, it was treated with obsequious courtesy. Where we meet it in person, it is scarcely heeded . . . 'matters of universal concern' already exist as the business of the state; they exist without really being matters of *universal* concern; they are in fact anything but that for they are of no concern to *civil society* . . . If they now really enter public consciousness and achieve 'empirical universality', this is purely formal . . . The truth of the matter is that the *implicit* 'matters of universal concern; are *not really universal* and the real, empirical matters of universal concern are purely formal . . . The matters of universal concern are now complete without having become the real concern of the people. The real affairs of the people have sprung into being without the interference of the people.[8]

(One may be reminded by these striking passages of a police mentality which declares that it serves the 'public interest' but which fears nothing worse than that the public should appear in person to assert its interests practically rather than formally: by holding the police accountable to themselves or by appropriating the functions of the police. This formalism may be taken to absurdity when the police suppress the empirical will of the real public in order to serve the rational will of the formal public.)

The alienation of Hegel's ideal state from the real will of the people, and its emergence as a particular private interest among other private interests, appear concretely in Hegel's constitutional proposals. The constitution itself, Marx argued, should not be treated apart from its human origins: it is 'not the constitution that creates the people but the people that create the constitution'. Just as the people create one constitution, so too they can dismantle and replace it: 'a constitution produced by past consciousness can become an oppressive shackle for a consciousness which has progressed.' History reveals the emergence of new constitutions – including the Prussian one – based not on the gradual transformation of old constitutions by constitutional means (though this is not excluded) but on revolution. Hegel's category of 'gradual transition' first of all is historically false, and secondly fails to explain from where the constitution arises. Hegel explicitly elevated the constitution over the men who made it; for Marx, by contrast, 'man is the principle of the constitution.' It is a 'practical illusion' to suppose that the constitution always serves as the real expression of the will of the people. To the question – does the people have the right to make a new constitution? – Marx answers definitely yes.

Marx's polemic against Hegel's monarchism was based not only on his refutation of hereditary rule but also on his rejection of the notion that the will of the state can be embodied in one person. In Hegel's eyes sovereignty of the people and sovereignty of the monarch were not opposed principles; rather it was through the monarch that the people acquired their being and organization. Marx rejected this identity as a mystique: 'sovereignty of the monarch or sovereignty of the people, that is the question'. Here were 'two completely opposed concepts of sovereignty', while the idea of constitutional monarchy is 'a hybrid thing which is thoroughly self-contradictory'. The constitution purports to reconcile the general interests of the community with the particular interests of the individual; monarchy turns the universal interest into the private property of an individual and subordinates the particular interests of all others to itself. Marx's conclusion is to do away with constitutional monarchy – which is but the expression of a compromise between the old order and the new – and so to abolish monarchy in all its forms.

The bureaucracy passes itself off as the universal class whose end is the end of the state, and this is the image which Hegel mirrors. In reality, Marx argues, 'the identity of the state interest and the particular private aim is established in such a way that the state interest becomes a particular aim opposed to the other private aims.' The bureaucracy identifies its own interests with those of the state as a whole but is in fact based on a definite kind of private property, one which is 'the essence of the state itself'. The bureaucracy 'holds the state in thrall as its private property'; it appears to itself 'as the ultimate purpose of the state' while 'the

purposes of the state are transformed into purposes of offices'.[9]
Beneath the surface of its pretensions, the bureaucracy isolates
itself from the real will of the people. It covers its actions in a cloak
of secrecy far from the public gaze:

> The universal spirit of bureaucracy is secrecy; it is a mystery
> preserved within itself by means of hierarchy and appearing
> to the outside world as a self-contained corporation.[10]

Power is exercised not by the people from the bottom up but from
the top down, breeding an ethos of 'passive obedience', 'worship
of authority', and 'rigid principles, views and traditions'.

Hierarchical authority relations, which are intended to prevent
individual abuse of power, are themselves the principle abuse:

> The few personal sins of the official are as nothing compared
> to their necessary hierarchical sins. The hierarchy punishes
> the official when he sins against the hierarchy or commits a
> sin which is superfluous from the hierarchy's point of view,
> but it will come to his defence as soon as the hierarchy sins
> through him.[11]

As for the individual bureaucrat, his commitment 'to the purpose
of the state' soon turns into 'a private purpose, a hunt for
promotion, careerism'.[12] Opening the opportunity to join the civil
service to every citizen creates an identity between it and the public
only in the sense of an 'identity of two hostile armies in which every
soldier has the opportunity to join the hostile army'.[13] What
protection, Marx asks, is left for private citizens against the alien
power of the bureaucracy? Hegel resorts to the moral uprightness
of officials, selected for their character and educated in ethical
conduct. But what guarantees do these qualities offer, when the
bureaucrats' office provides them with their daily bread; when
selection is organized by the hierarchy itself through an examination
system that is like a 'masonic initiation'; and when education is
organized by the hierarchy itself?

The idea that the state bureaucracy is a universal class is a
mirage: its essence lies in its alienation from the people; its solution
lies in its 'abolition'; but Marx's alternative was still obscure:

> in a true state it is not a question of the possibility of every
> citizen devoting himself to the universal class as a particular

class but of the capacity of the universal class to be really universal, that is the class of every citizen.

Not too much should be read into this philosophical conclusion, but waiting within it is the idea – which Marx developed later – not that public functions would disappear (e.g. the function of policing would still be necessary) but that they should be performed by the people themselves rather than by an alien force separate from the people.

Marx's critique of representation – that is, of the election of deputies to a popular assembly – differed substantially from that offered by Rousseau. Rousseau attacked the whole idea of representation in the name of the ancient Greek ideal of direct participation by all free members of the state; Marx, by contrast, saw the necessity for representation arising in part out of the size of the modern state and in part out of the abolition of the classical distinction between citizen and slave. Rousseau's observation that 'all as individuals should wish to share in the legislature' proves that 'it is the will of all to be real active members of the state or . . . to give reality to their existence as something political.'[14] Quite right too, Marx echoes. But, first, 'the question of quantity is not without importance'; the whole population cannot be squeezed into an assembly. Second, participation in the assembly is not the only way that one can participate in the state; to take part in the 'general concerns' of the people in any way is to participate in the state. It is only from 'the abstract view of the political state' that the legislature appears as the 'totality of the state'. It is when matters of general concern are alienated from the people in civil society, and when 'this single activity of legislation is the only political activity of civil society' that 'everyone both wishes and ought to share in it at once'.[15] The true state is the body politic as a whole, comprising both the political state and civil society. The problem with Hegel's account was that 'the state exists only as a political state'; in fact political concerns are not limited to the sphere of the political state. Parliament does not possess a monopoly on matters of universal concern.

The real question with respect to Hegel concerned the limits which he imposed on popular representation. What was crucial, Marx argued, 'is the extension and the greatest possible universalization of the vote, i.e. of both active and passive suffrage'. The problem with the form of representation embodied in the Prussian state and reflected in Hegel's system was how far short it fell from unrestricted active and passive suffrage.

The core of Marx's critique of Hegel's theory of representation was that it elevated deputies over the people who elected them and turned them into an elite insulated from public pressure. Instead of deputies being the servants of the people, mechanisms were instituted to turn them into masters. 'Parliamentary freedom' came to signify the freedom of parliament from the people rather than the freedom of the people through parliament; it was a form of representation whereby deputies, as soon as they are voted into office, are freed from dependence on their electors. Instead of being deputies of civil society, linked to their electors by an instruction, commission or mandate, they become alienated from their electors and responsible only to parliament. Instead of their being accountable to their electors, their representation is grounded 'on trust'. What Hegel presented as a guarantee required by the electors – that deputies be guardians of the general interest rather than representatives of particular interests – 'has been imperceptibly transformed into a *guarantee against* the electors'.[16] Worst of all, the bureaucracy becomes the power which determines the general interest and vets the 'thoughts and opinions' of the deputies to ensure that they are '*its* thoughts and opinions'. In this regard Hegel shows how 'thoroughly contaminated by the wretched arrogance of Prussian officialdom' he has become: in effect subordinating the legislature to the executive and identifying the executive with the political state in general. While the political convictions of civil society appear as mere 'opinion' and 'caprice', the deputies are supposed to have 'a better understanding of public affairs'; to have 'knowledge, skill and temperament'; and to have the capacity to reach universal decisions through parliamentary debate. Parliament appears as the people, while the real people outside appear as nothing but a formless mass. In this form of representation Marx finds two basic contradictions: a 'formal' one, in that the deputies of civil society 'should be *deputies* [i.e. tied to their electors by a 'commission'] but they are *not*'; and a 'material' one, in that deputies have authority as representatives of public affairs, 'whereas in reality they represent particular interests'. The elitism inherent in Hegel's conception – which is the fundamental conception of modern parliamentarism – drove Marx to an understandable despair: 'God help us all' was his final, unanalytic comment before the manuscript broke off.

It is quite misleading to speak of Marx as offering a 'critique of representation'; his attack was aimed not at representation as such but at Hegel's restrictive form of representation. Marx sought, first, to create universal suffrage and an end to all privileges of the landowners; second, to create an 'active suffrage' in which deputies would be accountable to their electorate; and, third, to elevate the assembly – as the sphere of representation – into the totality of the political state. Far from attacking representation, Marx attacked the exclusion of the bureaucracy from representation. It was the narrowness of the sphere to which suffrage applied – legislative but not executive – that Marx found fault with and not the institution of suffrage itself.

The vantage point from which Marx directed his critique of Hegel was that of democracy: democracy was 'the essence of *every* state constitution', the 'resolved mystery of *all* constitutions'. By this Marx meant that all forms of law and the state rest not on God, nature, reason or any other alien force above the people, but on the people themselves. If this is the essence of every state, this essence is realized only when democracy in fact becomes the empirical form of state. Democracy is 'the true unity of the universal and the particular'. While Hegel was thus right – in the manner of classical jurisprudence as a whole – to identify the state and the people, he 'proceeds from the state and conceives of man as the subjectivized state'. True democracy 'proceeds from man and conceives the state as objectified man'. In the one 'man exists for the sake of the law' while in the other 'the law exists for the sake of man'. In Hegel, the democratic element is introduced in a form mediated by the abstraction of the rational individual; in true democracy, 'the constitution is founded on its true ground: real human beings and real people'.[17]

What was the 'true democracy' which Marx counterposed to Hegel's idealization of the Prussian state? It seems to me that Marx was far less clear on his positive alternative for the future than on his critique of what already existed. Indeed, he was soon to justify this approach in his critiques of utopian communism. In answer to the question 'what is your new world going to look like?', Marx argued for a 'new direction', not another blueprint for a perfectly democratic society but an analysis of that which already exists: 'we do not dogmatically anticipate the world but rather want to find the new world through criticism of the old.'[18] In his critique of Hegel, however, Marx did not leave the cupboard of the future entirely bare.

Colletti has argued that in his critique of the *Philosophy of Right*, Marx's conception of true democracy meant the withering away of the state in its entirety. There are passages which give this impression, but in general Marx's idea of democracy at this stage presupposed a state. 'Democracy' meant that on the one hand the political state must become a genuine expression of the will of the people, and on the other that it must become 'only . . . a particular form of existence of the people'; that is, it will take care of *some* matters of universal concern, but not *all* matters. The people will mediate some of its public affairs through the state but not all; the state will disappear only 'in so far as the political state as such, the constitution, is no longer *equivalent to the whole*.'[19]

Marx did not yet challenge Hegel's and his own identification of the rule of law as the embodiment of universal freedom. Accordingly, he identified the legislature – the body whose function it is to make universal, determinate and public laws – as the 'rational core' of the political state and wrote of it with great approval:

> The legislature made the French Revolution; in fact, whenever it has emerged as the dominant factor it has brought forth great, organic, universal revolutions. It has not attacked the constitution as such but only a particular antiquated constitution; this is because the legislature acted as the representative of the people . . . In contrast to this, the executive has made all the petty revolutions, the retrograde revolutions, the reactions. Its revolutions were not fought against an old institution and on behalf of a new one; they were fought against the constitution itself, simply because the executive was the representative of the particular will, subjective caprice, the magical aspect of the will.[20]

As it currently existed, the legislature 'embodies the energy of the will [of the people] in its theoretical and not its practical form'. The point, Marx argued, learning his lesson from Hegel, was '*not to substitute the will for the law*' (i.e. not simply to discard law because it is formal or theoretical) but rather '*to discover and formulate the real law*' (my emphasis).[21]

In the functions of the legislature – ruling through law and on the basis of representation – Marx found the proper sphere of authority for the political state. Such was the nature of the radical republicanism – only just beginning to look outward to the democratization of civil society – that Marx counterposed to the Prussian constitutional monarchy as the embodiment of the rational state. His break from the idea of a 'rational state' itself was still far from complete.

## Civil society against the state

Marx's essay on the 'Jewish Question' took him one step further in his critique of the state. His immediate purpose was to defend the right of Jews to full political emancipation whether or not they retained their religious commitments; his immediate target was 'left-wing' currents represented by Bruno Bauer, who argued that Jews were not worthy of equal rights until they gave up their Judaism. Marx's political argument was twofold: first, while he was a critic of all religion, he affirmed the right of all to practise religion freely without state interference or discrimination and there was no reason to make an exception of the Jews; second, while the image of Judaism in particular was attached to 'the merchant' and 'the moneyman', in the modern world 'money has become a world power and the practical spirit of the Jews has become the practical spirit of the Christian peoples.'[22] In short, the idea that the Jew is fundamentally more rooted in money-making and commerce than the Christian was as erroneous as the idea that the Jew is fundamentally less eligible for human and political rights. Marx's defence of freedom of religion expressed the close association which he drew – in contrast to some other radical and socialist currents – between democracy and socialism. The theoretical significance of this essay goes well beyond its immediate subject matter. The question he posed concerned the meaning of political emancipation: what kind of emancipation, he asked, is involved in the emancipation of the Jews? In answering this, he incorporated for the first time a critique of bourgeois private property into his theory of the state.

Freedom of religion, Marx argued, does not mean freedom from religion but rather the freedom to be religious in whatever way one likes: no religion is to be suppressed by the state and none to be privileged. The liberal critique of religion was a critique of the power of the church over the state – either in the Catholic form of a competing authority or in the Protestant form of uniting its authority with that of the state – but it was not a critique of religion as such:

> The political emancipation of the Jew, the Christian, the religious man in general is the emancipation of *the state* from Judaism, from Christianity, from religion in general. The state emancipates itself from religion . . . by emancipating itself from state religion . . . A state can have emancipated itself from religion even if the overwhelming majority of the population is still religious . . . Political emancipation from religion is not complete and consistent emancipation from religion . . . political emancipation allows religion – but not privileged religion – to continue in existence . . . The right to be religious in whatever way one likes is expressly enumerated among the rights of man.[23]

Since Marx, following on from Feuerbach, saw that religion is a form of human alienation in which people worship as their gods what are in fact objects of their own creation, 'complete and consistent emancipation' required emancipation from religion in general. The conclusion he was faced with was that 'political emancipation' falls short of 'human emancipation'.

Marx then extended his analysis from religion to private property. Political emancipation signifies the abolition of privileges for private property but not the abolition of private property; the end of the state recognition of private property but not of its actual existence. Thus the abolition of property qualifications for the right to vote by no means abolishes private property but only its expression in law:

> The state as state annuls *private property*, man declares in a *political* way that private property is *abolished*, immediately the *property qualification* is abolished . . . And yet the political annulment of private property does not mean the abolition of private property; on the contrary it even presupposes it.[24]

Similarly the abolition of *legal* inequality does not abolish inequality in fact:

> The state in its own way abolishes distinctions based on birth, rank, education and occupation when it declares birth, rank,

education and occupation to be *non-political* distinctions . . . Nevertheless the state allows private property, education and occupation to *act* and assert their *particular* nature in *their* own way . . . Far from abolishing these *factual* distinctions, the state presupposes them in order to exist.[25]

The key to the limitations of political emancipation lies in the abstract character of the universality which it establishes. Individuals are equalized in the eyes of the law and the state by means of their abstraction as 'citizens' from all the real differences and distinctions which mark them off in reality from one another. To become a citizen of the state, the human being must be 'divested of his real individual life and filled with an unreal universality'.[26] The formalism of the state is the secular analogue to the spiritualism of the Christian god – and finds the ideal philosophical expression in Hegel's concept of 'mind' dissociated from all bodily and social attributes – inasmuch as all are abstractions from the real conditions of civil society. As citizens, people appear 'devoid of any recognizable character'; the form in which they exist is that of 'pure, unadorned individuality' whereby all their determinations in civil society – whether they are Jews, Christians, capitalists, labourers or tradespeople – are given no political status. The conclusion Marx reaches is that in modern society men and women lead a double life: on the one hand as citizens of the state, free and equal before the law, and on the other, as 'bourgeois' members of civil society:

Where the political state has attained its true development, man leads a double life, a heavenly and an earthly one, not only in thought and consciousness but in reality, in life: one life in the *political community* where he considers himself a communal being and one life in civil society where he functions as a private person, regards other people as a means, degrades himself to a means and becomes the plaything of alien powers. The political state is spiritually related to civil society in the same way as heaven is to earth.[27]

The image is drawn directly from Rousseau. But where Rousseau discovered a harmony between the general will and the particular, Marx saw nothing but an unresolved conflict between general interests and private interests, the political state and civil society, the communal citizen and the bourgeois egoist.

The lesson Marx drew was that in order to establish a truly rational state, the conditions of civil society had to be subjected to theoretical critique and practical transformation. There was no natural law of private property. The problem with political revolution alone is that instead of 'revolutionizing' civil society, it regards it as 'its *natural* basis'. It is only when civil society is transformed and society 'succeeds in abolishing ... the market and the conditions which gave rise to it,' it is only when political emancipation is accompanied by social emancipation that emancipation becomes complete. Political emancipation alone was a 'great step forward':

> We do not tell the Jews that they cannot be emancipated politically without emancipating themselves from Judaism, which is what Bauer tells them. We say instead: the fact that you can be emancipated politically without completely and absolutely renouncing Judaism shows that political emancipation is *by itself* not human emancipation.[28]

Marx was *not* saying here that the ideal of a democratic political state *in itself* is wrong, but only that *by itself* it is insufficient. He was not attacking the goal of a democratic republic, but arguing the need to ally a democratic republic with the social transformation of private property. A rational political state, in short, should not be treated as the totality of a rational society. *On the Jewish Question* was not a critique of the democratic republic as such, but only of the identification of the democratic republic with complete emancipation.

The achievement of political revolution was to end the separation between the life of the people and the state: it 'turned the affairs of the state into the affairs of the people ... it constituted the political state as a concern of the whole people ... '[29] Far from political democracy alienating the people from the state, Marx's position was that it overcame the old alienation of the people from the state. The limitations of political emancipation lay not in the state which it established but in its consequences for civil society:

> the perfection of the idealism of the state was at the same time the perfection of the materialism of civil society. The shaking off of the political yoke was at the same time the shaking off of

the bonds which had held in check the egoistic spirit of civil society. Political emancipation was at the same time the emancipation of civil society from politics, from even the *appearance* of a universal content.[30]

When Marx wrote of the 'emancipation' of civil society from politics, he was clearly being ironic. Far from being emancipatory, it gave free rein to egoism, competition, the treatment of one's fellow-human beings as means to one's own personal ends, to alien market forces over which people have no control; in short, to private property: 'he was not freed from private property, he received the freedom of property.' In this aspect of political emancipation – the release of private property from political constraints – Marx could see no advance. This came out sharply in his contrast between the 'rights of citizens' and the 'rights of man'. Whereas the former are political rights, exercised in common with others and involving participation in the community, the latter are private rights, exercised in isolation from others and involving withdrawal from the community.

> Not one of the so-called rights of man goes beyond egoistic man . . . an individual withdrawn into himself, his private interest and his private desires . . . The practical application of the right of man to freedom is the right of man to private property.[31]

Marx offered little more at this stage than a moral critique of egoism, picking up on the dark side of private property – as already outlined by classical jurisprudence – but not yet incorporating into his theory the positive significance which classical jurisprudence saw in private property, both for individual liberty and for the general development of society. Marx's contrast between the rights of the *citizen* and the rights of *man* was quite artificial; the constitution of 1793 from which he quotes is itself entitled 'Declarations of the rights of *Man* and of the *Citizen*', and made *no* distinction.

For Marx, the relation between the state and civil society was depicted as a contradiction between two opposing principles: universality and egoism. The state is predicated on civil society only in the sense that it 'asserts its universality in opposition to the elements [of civil society]'.[32] He addresses this contradiction in a

Hegelian fashion. The problem as he sees it is that the state is subordinated to civil society:

> the citizen is proclaimed the servant of egoistic man . . . the sphere in which man behaves as a communal being is degraded to a level below the sphere in which he behaves as a political being . . . political life declares itself to be a mere *means* whose goal is the life of civil society.[33]

In revolutionary times, when the political state is 'particularly self-confident', it may try to suppress civil society. But civil society is the 'presupposition' of the state; its suppression by the state can only mean violence and the guillotine; this 'political drama necessarily ends up with the restoration of religion, private property and all the elements of civil society.'[34] To bring about the dominance of the general interest over the particular, civil society has to be abolished – not by the state but by other means not yet specified.

The image of civil society on which this account was based was one of total unfreedom; the link between private property and individual liberty – vigorously defended by Smith and Hegel – appeared as a merely formal cover under which there actually lay generalized dependence.

The central problem lay in Marx and Engels's depiction of the capital–labour relation, the elements of which appeared in the *Economic and Philosophical Manuscripts* (1844). Workers were defined by their propertylessness, their relation to capital as one of propertylessness to property: 'workers sink to the level of a commodity, the most wretched commodity of all.' Workers themselves become a commodity since their labour, i.e. their life-activity, belongs not to themselves but to others: 'the external character of labour for the worker is demonstrated by the fact that it belongs not to him but to another, and that in it he belongs not to himself but to another.'[35] Who is this 'other' to whom workers and their labour belong? It is not God, nor nature, nor the instruments of production, but 'can be none other than man himself'. If the product of labour does not belong to the worker and if it confronts him as an alien power, this is possible only because it belongs to '*a man* other than the worker'.[36] Alienated labour, in short, is the *social* form taken by labour when it is organized in such a way that it belongs to the non-worker and is expropriated from the worker.

Marx showed that the capital–labour relation is not a natural fact of life but a transitory and historical relation between human beings based on the monopolization of property by a small class of non-workers, and alienation from property on the part of the mass of the workers. The great strength of Marx's approach was to reveal the social content behind the seemingly natural categories of capital and labour as a relation between expropriators and expropriated. But its weakness was to neglect the *form* in which the relation between capital and labour is expressed – that is, as a relation between free, equal and consenting partners. The 'free' wage-labourer, unlike the slave, is not owned by any particular capitalist, even though he or she is dependent on the capitalist class as a whole. The real difference between them emerges legally to the extent that – under the impetus of the requirements of capital as well as the struggles of workers – wage-labourers become free to move from one place to another and from one capitalist to another, to possess a sphere of 'free time', to withdraw their labour, to associate with each other, and so forth; even though the exercise of these freedoms is subjected to economic constraints. In the 1844 *Manuscripts* Marx was not yet able to connect form and content, freedom and exploitation, in his analysis of civil society. In *On the Jewish Question*, then, Marx portrayed the relation between civil society and the state as an antagonistic one, based on their mutual opposition. Civil society appeared as the sphere of pure egoism and slavery, while the rational state appeared as the sphere of pure universality and freedom. Marx, however, was soon to abandon this formulation of the problem.

# 3. The genesis of Marx's class theory of law and state

## Abandoning the rational state

Marx's early works gave a radical edge to classical jurisprudence, but they did not radically break from its principle. Marx rejected Hegel's conclusion about the form and content of the 'rational state' but retained this category as the basis of his theory, offering a critique of classical jurisprudence from the perspective of classical jurisprudence, but not yet transcending this perspective.

The new direction taken by Marx was to jettison a critique of existing authority relations based on how much or how little they corresponded with the idea of a 'rational state' and instead to see the actual state, as it was, as the historical and transitory product of definite social relations of production. Looking back in his Preface to the *Critique of Political Economy* (1858), Marx summarized the new position he and Engels had together constructed:

> I was led by my studies to the conclusion that legal relations as well as forms of state could neither be understood by themselves nor explained by the so-called general progress of the human mind, but that they are rooted in the material conditions of life, which are summed up by Hegel after the fashion of the English and French writers of the eighteenth century under the name *civil society* and that the anatomy of civil society is to be sought in political economy . . . The totality of these relations of production constitutes the economic structure on which legal and political superstructures arise . . .

It is the logic behind this conception which needs to be fleshed out.

The idea of the 'rational state' which Marx inherited from Hegel presupposed that there exists, as a timeless ideal, a form of state which genuinely represents the will of the people. When Marx discovered that not only the actual state but also Hegel's ideal state fell short of the rational state, his first reaction was not to abandon the concept of the rational state but rather to search deeper for its embodiment. The important thing, he said, is to grasp freedom 'in its essential character and not in its external relations'. Eventually, however, he discovered that the state is constituted by its corruptions and that the essence of the state is not something apart from its external relations but rather is its external relations. The apt image which Hal Draper[1] painted of Marx's development is that of his peeling away the layers of an onion in order to find its heart, only to discover that there is no heart, that the onion consists only of its layers. The task, as Marx put it, was no longer to find the essence of the state apart from social relations but in social relations. From the beginning, Marx was critical of the subordination of the state to private property: in his early works he regarded this as a corruption of the state's essence; in his later works he regarded it as the essence of the state's corruption.

The first partial expression of this new perspective was to be found in a brief note attached to Marx's critique of private property in the *Economic and Philosophical Manuscripts*, where *human* existence was equated with abolition of the state and law along with private property:

> Religion, family, state, law, morality, science, art, etc., are only *particular* ways of production and fall under its general law. The positive abolition of *private property*, as the appropriation of a *human* way of life, is therefore the positive abolition of all estrangement, hence the reversion of man from religion, family, state, etc., to his human, that is, social existence.[2]

This statement equated the realization of humanity not with the establishment of a rational state but with the abolition of the state *in toto*. The 'cause of social ills', as Marx put it in his article on the Silesian weavers' uprising (1844), lies 'in the *principle* of the state' and not in its corruption. The question, however, was what was the source of the principle of the state?

## *The German Ideology:* first steps in a new direction

In his earlier work Marx contrasted the freedom and universality of the state with the slavery and egoism of civil society, even when he sought to derive the state from civil society. Later he identified the character of the state with that of civil society. *The German Ideology* (1846), written in conjuction with Engels, provides a transitional (and often inadequate) version of this approach. It starts with a restatement of the 'old' theory that the state emerges out of the 'contradiction between particular and common interests',[3] but gives it a new twist. This was to analyse the contradiction between particular and common interests not as one between civil society and the state, but as one which enters into both civil society and the state. Marx and Engels now saw the state only as 'an *illusory* community' and in fact an '*alien* form . . . divorced from real individual and collective interests'; as something 'independent' of the real will of the people. The alienated character of Hegel's state no longer appeared as a deviation from the essence of the state, but rather as its essence. Their reasoning was that because individuals seek only their particular interests their common interest 'is asserted as an interest alien to them and independent to them'; the 'political spirit' was not so much emancipated as alienated by its formal separation from civil society. Capital and the state no longer appeared as contrasting but as like principles: each represented in its own way a 'social power . . . which arises through the co-operation of different individuals' and which appears to these individuals 'not as their own united power but as an alien force existing outside them, of the origin and goal of which they are ignorant'.[4]

Not only are capital and the state *analogous* in this sense, but once established the state becomes an instrument of capital:

> it is nothing more than the form of organization which the bourgeois are *compelled* to adopt . . . for the mutual guarantee of their property and interest . . . it is the form in which the individuals of a ruling class assert their common interests.[5]

While the form of the state arises independently of the will of the bourgeoisie, it soon becomes subjected to their socially determined will, since the state,

> purchased gradually by the owners of property by means of taxation, has fallen entirely into their hands through the national debt and its existence has become wholly dependent

on the commercial credit which owners of property, the bourgeois, extend to it, as reflected in the rise and fall of government securities on the stock exchange.[6]

The material conditions of life of individuals – 'their mode of production and form of intercourse', which by no means depend on the 'will' either of the rulers or the ruled, gives rise to the alien forms of law and the state and compel the individuals who rule 'to give their will, which is determined by these definite conditions, a universal expression as the will of the state, as law';[7] however, the *content* of law is 'always determined by the relations of the ruling class, as the civil and criminal law demonstrates in the clearest possible way.'[8]

The importance of these statements from *The German Ideology* is that they offer a materialist explanation of both the form and the content of law and the state, polemicizing against those who believe that either their form or their content is determined solely by the will or needs of men and women. On the other hand, these passages were Marx and Engels's first attempt to give a new direction to their critique of law and the state away from Hegel, and it is unfortunate that their sometimes incomplete and erroneous formulations, which they themselves later rejected, have become ossified as shorthand statements of their 'mature' theory.

Marx and Engels's first problem concerned their derivation of the *forms* of law and the state. They saw them as an 'alien forms' of authority estranged from individuals, but they attributed this not to private property but rather to the very fact of a division of labour:

the division of labour . . . implies the contradiction between the interests of the separate individual . . . and the common interest of all individuals . . . Out of this very contradiction between the particular and common interests, the common interest assumes an independent form as the state.[9]

Marx and Engels, however, had no answer as to why the division of labour as such should give rise to the alien form of the state. For example, their assertion that 'as soon as the division of labour comes into being, each man has an *exclusive* sphere of activity which is *forced* upon him and from which he *cannot escape*'[10] is clearly wrong. Marx and Engels projected characteristics belonging to the contemporary division of labour on to the division of labour in general. It depends on how the division of labour is organized as to whether, for example, individuals are forced into particular tasks or decide democratically among themselves on the allocation of labour; whether the allocation of labour takes place according to a conscious plan or according to market forces; whether individuals are attached rigidly to exclusive tasks or fluidly to multiple tasks; whether there is a rigid separation between mental and manual activity or a fusion of the two spheres; whether individuals are locked in one area of production or may move on to others; whether the relations of individuals with one another are personal and co-operative, or mediated by the exchange of commodities, and competitive. Only when the division of labour takes the form of the privatization of property do individuals appear as isolated and self-interested atoms, believing that social relations can be entered into at will, their relationships with each other based on mutual antagonism and their common interest taking the form of an alien power, since they are incapable themselves of constituting a common interest. The division of labour *per se* gives rise to the need for some social organ or organs to fulfil those public functions required if the various branches of the division of labour are to be integrated with one another – functions of internal policing, co-ordination, mutual defence, etc. – but it does not give rise necessarily to the alien form of the state as the means of performing these functions. Why the state should have emerged as the means of fulfilling communal tasks was a question which Marx and Engels did not, at this stage, satisfactorily resolve.

Since all societies, except perhaps the most primitive, are predicated on some division of labour, it would follow from this theory that the state and the law are eternal necessities. We are back again at a new version of natural law theory. Marx and Engels escaped this conclusion only by envisaging a utopia in which the division of labour is overcome in its entirety. This was the gist behind their famous depiction of communist society as one in which 'society makes it possible for me to do one thing today and another tomorrow, to hunt in the morning, fish in the afternoon, rear cattle in the evening, criticize after dinner . . .'[11] In communist society, the division of labour will be more mobile in order to allow for the many-sided development of the individual and the particular division between mental and manual labour will be abolished; but the division of labour as such will necessarily remain.

The implication of this theory with regard to the state was that the state, however alien a form it was, appeared omnipresent as long as there was a division of labour: what changed from one society to the next was only the nature of the class which lays hold of the state, but not the alien character of the state itself. Thus Marx and Engels had not yet overcome a tendency to naturalize law and the state, nor yet had they fully established their class theory of law and the state.

The second difficulty facing Marx and Engels concerned their derivation of the content of law and the state. It was determined, they argued, by the common economic interests of the ruling class: with the development of capital, so their argument ran, the apparent independence of the state from society becomes purely formal; real independence of the state

is only found nowadays in those countries where the estates have not yet completely developed into classes, where the estates, done away with in more advanced countries, still play a part and there exists a mixture, where consequently no section of the population can achieve dominance over the others.[12]

In other words, the separation of the political state from civil society idealized by Hegel turns out not to be the norm of bourgeois society but rather the peculiarity of Germany, where absolutism still ruled politically in the face of the rising economic power of the bourgeoisie. In fully developed bourgeois society, capital rules politically as well as economically. The view of 'the modern French, English and American writers . . . that the state exists only for the sake of private property'[13] was a truer representation than Hegel's of the developed bourgeois state. In other words, the formal independence of the state from society seemed to Marx only to have substance where, as in Germany, there is a balance of class forces and an absolutist state can set itself above them; in other situations the formal independence of the state appeared to Marx as a mere mirage beyond which lay class power, a reductionist view of the state which he was not to sustain.

Marx and Engels carried over from their own respective earlier works their conception of civil society as slavery and their moral critiques of egoism: only 'in imagination', Engels and Marx wrote in *The German Ideology*, 'do individuals seem freer under the dominance of the bourgeoisie than before . . . in reality of course they are to a greater extent governed by material forces.'[14] They argued correctly that freedom of property is formal, observing that

> the *jus utendi et abutendi* [the right to use and abuse] asserts . . . the illusion that private property is based solely on the private will, the arbitrary disposal of the thing. In practice, the *abutendi* has very definite economic limitations for the owner of private property, if he does not wish to see his property and hence his *jus abutendi* pass into other hands;[15]

but is is precisely this formal character that marks off the epoch of commodity production from other epochs. It is a 'juridical illusion' that social relations are based solely on will, but it is not an illusion that in a society based on private property social relations are mediated by acts of individual will.

Marx and Engel's tendency to treat the formal freedom and equality present in civil society as illusions was now reflected in their theory of the state; its formal character of communality was now also declared to be an illusion, behind which lay the unlimited power of private property. Their other comment of the *jus utendi et abutendi* – that it 'asserts *the fact* that private property has become entirely independent of the community [my emphasis]'[16] was not true. Rather, the idea that private property had become entirely independent of the community was also a juridic illusion. In reality the 'community' necessarily restricts the independence of private property – as Hegel appreciated – through the state. Historically it was untrue that the development of the state apparatus as an independent force separate from private property was an expression of the peculiar character of German absolutism; rather it became a general characteristic of all developed bourgeois societies, which required explanation rather than denial. The issue was not only to disclose that the form of the state has the power of private property as its content, but also to explain why the power of private property did – as a matter of historical fact – take the independent form of the state. Those democratic forms which Marx had previously identified with freedom and universality – the rule of law, representation, general suffrage – were now theorized as mere forms or illusions. There was a residue of the young Engels's anarchistic dismissal of democracy as 'nothing but hypocrisy'; of political liberty as 'sham liberty: the worst possible slavery, the appearance of liberty and therefore the reality of servitude', and his conclusion that 'we must have either a regular slavery – that is, an undisguised despotism, or real liberty and real equality, that is, Communism.'[17] It was only later that Marx and Engels, spurred on by their critiques of political economy, were able to theorize the contradictory rather than illusory character of the freedom, equality and independence manifested in the liberal state.

Directly linked to this problem was the static conception both of class and of the state which Marx and Engels offered. Drawing on Engels's critique in *The Condition of the Working Class inEngland* that the state is a class weapon with which 'the bourgeoisie defends its interests with all the power at its disposal', that the bourgeoisie is 'the chief, in fact, the only power in parliament', that the cabinet minister is 'the obedient servant of the bourgeoisie', etc., they presented the common interests of the bourgeoisie as the content of law and the state. But the bourgeoisie does not exist in a vacuum but rather in a definite relation to the other classes of civil society: workers, the old gentry, the petty bourgeoisie, the lumpenproletariat. The struggle between capital and labour is not static but depends on the level of development, organization and consciousness of each and on the alliances which each is able to forge with other classes. Capital is not just a 'thing' but rather the expression of a *relation* to labour; a relation that is not constant but shifts in accordance with the ebbs and flows of class struggle. The particular form taken by the state is similarly not static: from one period to the next it may become more or less alienated from the people, more or less subject to democratic control, more or less bureaucratic, more or less bound by rules of law, more or less permissive of working-class organization, etc. While the state in general is an alienated form of authority, the extent and form of this alienation are not fixed. Thus while it is true to say that the state serves the ruling class, it is nevertheless entirely insufficient, for the form taken by the state is determined not by the ruling class alone but by the relations between the ruling class and other classes. It is the capital–labour relations which determines the form of the state, and not capital alone. While parliamentary democracy and bureaucratic dictatorship are both forms of bourgeois domination, they are none the less *different* forms and reflect *different* relations between capital and labour.

The beginnings of such a view were already present in *The German Ideology* in Marx and Engels's comment that

> all struggles within the state, the struggle between democracy, aristocracy and monarchy, the struggle for the franchise, etc. are merely the illusory forms . . . in which the real struggles of the different classes are fought out among one another.[18]

Apart from the notion that the political form of class struggles is 'illusory' while class struggles themselves are 'real' – as if classes exist independently of their political forms – we see in this passage a more dynamic connection between forms of state and class relations than was allowed to appear in the main body of the theory of the state. Forms of state (fascism, democracy, liberalism, apartheid, bureaucratic dictatorship, etc.) and their content (whether its laws recognize a right to strike, a right to organize, a right to privacy, a right to jury trials, a right to freedom from arbitrary arrest and detentions, a right to demonstrate, a right to collective self-defence, etc.) are determined not by the will of the rulers alone but by the real relations between and within the classes which comprise bourgeois society.

# 4. Law, state and capital

## Political economy and jurisprudence: questions of method

*Capital* represents the maturation of Marx's critique of the economic forms of civil society and of his analysis of the social relations which lie concealed behind, and give rise to, these forms. His thesis was that economic categories can be understood only as the expression of a definite historical organization of labour. In the course of this critique the gulf which existed in his early writings between the surface economic forms of civil society (value, price, money, capital, wage-labour, etc.) was overcome, as he addressed the 'dialectical' question of why alienated labour should express itself in these forms. Marx offered a critique of political economy not only in the sense of replacing erroneous economic theories with better ones, but also in the sense of disclosing what kind of society provides the foundation for the emergence of an idependent economic sphere of life. In other words, he offered a social critique of economics in general, and not just an internal critique of one economic theory by another. The theoretical hypothesis which he defended was that the key to understanding economic categories lay in an exposition of the social relations according to which men and women organize the labour of society. It is thus misleading to call the economic sphere the 'base' of society on which legal, political and ideological superstructures rest; rather, the message which runs through *Capital* is that social relations of production constitute the base of society and that economic categories represent an expression of the base. The imagery which informs *Captial*, however, is not that of base and superstructure but rather that of 'form' and 'content': economics expressing the 'surface forms' of capitalist society, the 'inner content' or 'substance' of which comprises social relations of production.

The perspective from which Marx approached *Capital* was that of starting with economic forms, – e.g. value, price, money, capital, interest, profit, etc. – analysing the specific relations of production which lie hidden beneath these forms, and then explaining 'synthetically' why these relations of production necessarily express themselves in this economic way. This method has given rise to the impression that the economic expression of relations of production is their only expression, as if there is an exclusive association between economics and social relations of production which is not shared by other forms of social life. The result is that law, politics and ideology are in one way or another dissociated from relations of production: 'determined' by them perhaps, or 'relatively autonomous' of them, or only 'determined in the last instance', but not themselves a direct expression of relations of production in the same way as economics. Economics becomes a privileged sphere while law, politics and ideology appear as subordinate spheres. The basis of this privilege and subordination, however, is often quite arbitrary, appeals being made to supposedly self-evident truths that economics is more fundamental for the development of society than, say, the state. It seems to me that Marx at times identified 'economics' with relations of production and at times saw 'economics' as an expression of the surface forms assumed by certain definite relations of production. In the former case, he treats economics as a universal sphere in the sense that relations of production in all societies are said to determine the general organization of society; in the latter, he treats the emergence of the economic sphere as a historical event, in that it is only under particular conditions that relations of production assume the economic forms of value, money, capital, etc. The important point is not the verbal definition of 'economics' but the theoretical differentiation between the content of capitalist society – i.e. social relations of production – and its forms of appearance, i.e. value, money, capital, etc. In order to gain consistency, I believe that it would be most useful if the term 'economics' were reserved for the latter and thus clearly distinguished from its social content.

The theme which appears on the edges of *Capital* is that the social relations of capitalist production do not manifest themselves only in economic forms but also in juridic forms. In other words, it should be possible to do what Marx intended in his earlier years but then lost sight of as he delved deeper into his economic studies; that is, to complement his critique of political economy with a critique of jurisprudence: to start with juridic categories, analyse the social relations of production which lie hidden beneath them, and then explain 'synthetically' why these relations of production necessarily express themselves in juridic forms. Indeed, Marx outlined just such a programme of study in his preface to the *Economical Philosophical Manuscripts*:

> I shall therefore publish the critique of law, morals, politics, etc. in a series of separate independent pamphlets and finally attempt, in a special work, to present them once again as a connected whole, to show the relationship between the parts and to try to provide a critique of the speculative treatment of the material. That is why the present work only touches on the interconnection of political economy and the state, law, morals, civil life, etc. in so far as political economy itself particularly touches on these subjects.[1]

The traces of such an analysis in *Capital* point to a hypothesis that was not present in Marx's earlier writings – that the self-same relations of production which gave rise to the economic forms of capitalist society also gave rise to its juridic forms; that not only are economic and juridic categories both expressions of historical relations of production but that they are expressions of the same historical relations of production. But all this was only on the sidelines of Marx's critique of political economy: it appeared to many Marxists that social relations between people could only take the form of material relations between things (i.e. economics), ignoring the pressing fact that they also take the form of legal relations between persons, as owners of private property. *Capital* caught one side of the fetishism of capitalist society: that the economic forms assumed by the products of labour under definite relations of production – value, capital, wage-labour, etc. – appear as natural qualities of the products of labour themselves, as if it were the case that, as political economy thought, value is a natural property of anything produced by human hands, or that capital is a natural characteristic of the means of production as such, or that wage-labour is the natural form assumed by all labour. But it only touched on another side of the fetishism of capitalist society: that the legal forms assumed by producers under definite relations of production – ownership of private property, free will, equal right, law, state authority – appear as natural qualities of people, as if it were the case that, as jurisprudence assumed, they are attributes of human nature or human reason as such. The tangential influence of such a critique in Marx's work has led most interpreters to neglect this side of the question.

The practical result of this neglect has been most unfortunate: the idea that social relations between people have been reduced by capitalism to material relations between things will rightly be unconvincing to those who can see before their very eyes that capitalism also brings with it the idea of the integrity of the human personality, free will, equality before the law, rights of the individual and so forth. The critique of the materialist, i.e. economic, aspect of capitalist society will necessarily be one-sided and vulnerable, if it is not accompanied by a critique of its humanist (i.e. juridic) aspect. The critique of political economy has to be integrated with the critique of jurisprudence.

One consequence of this neglect among Marxists of juridic forms of capitalist relations of production has been to reduce them to the status of illusions or mirages. Such an approach is in complete contravention of the method Marx employed in his critique of political economy. When Marx used the term 'form' and contrasted it with 'content', he did not mean that the form is illusory and the content is real. When, for example, he discussed the value-form of commodities, his object was, first, to show the limitations of political economy which attempted to explain magnitudes of value (i.e. why products have one price rather than another) but ignored the form of value (i.e. why products bear prices at all); second, to show that the value-form is a social form, which presupposes the existence of definite social relations of production; third, to show that although the value-form is social, it appears either as a natural quality of material objects (vulgar political economy) or as a natural result of human labour (classical political economy); fourth, to show why social relations of commodity production must necessarily express themselves in the form of the value of things. The imagery of form and content is quite different from that of illusion and reality: the surface form of an object is not less real than its inner content, but it can be explained only by reference to its inner content. Similarly, the inner content of an object cannot be envisaged independently of its surface form, as if the one can be separated from the other. Once the value-form is established, it acts as a real constraint·on human behaviour and as a real mediation between human beings. The Russian Marxist economist Rubin, for instance, writing in the 1920s, has a useful discussion of the complementarity between the hidden process of 'reification', by means of which production relations between people give to products their specific economic form, and the overt process of 'personification', by means of which the value-form of product determines and mediates relations between people. Juridic forms of capitalist production relations are every bit as real as their economic forms. Just as Marx in no way meant that, because value, money, capital and wage-labour are forms of appearance of capitalist relations of production, they are not also real social forces that mediate relations between people and kick back at the people who create them; so too juridic forms of capitalist relations of production are also real social forces – there is nothing illusory about the law courts, the police and the prisons – which also mediate relations between people and constrain those who create them. The fact that Marx focused, in his theoretical writings, on the economic forms of capitalist productive relations and not on their juridic forms should not lead one to suppose that juridic forms are any less substantial than their economic counterparts.

The other major consequence of the neglect among Marxists of juridic forms has been not to discount them as fictions but to idealize them as eternal truths. The connections linking ideas of justice, law, rights and so forth to capitalist relations of production are lost from sight, with the result that these ideas, instead of appearing as what they are (that is, the ideas of real men and women in society), are abstracted from their human origins and acquire a life of their own. Such was the case with Proudhon, who saw 'justice' as an 'eternal idea' with which to attack aspects of capitalist society like usury or exploitation. Although this provided a critical standpoint from which to expose the hypocrisy associated with private property, Proudhon failed to see that his conception of justice reflected the self-same relations of production the economic forms of which he rejected. Thus, while the idea of 'free and equal exchange' which informs his concept of justice allowed him to be critical of capital and of usury, it also led him to be equally critical of the combination of workers into trade unions, on the grounds that:

> Each worker individually should dispose freely of his person and his hands, this can be tolerated; but that workers should undertake by combination to do violence to monopoly is something society cannot permit.[2]

It was precisely Proudhon's abstraction of juridic forms from capitalist relations of production which took Marx away from being an admirer of Proudhon into being his critic;

> Proudhon creates his ideal of justice, of *justice éternelle*, from the juridical relations that correspond to the production of commodities: he thereby proves, to the consolation of all good petty bourgeois, that the production of commodities is a form as eternal as justice . . . Do we really know any more about 'usury', when we say it contradicts *justice éternelle*, *équité éternelle*, *mutualité éternelle*, and other *vérités éternelles* . . . ?[3]

Proudhon serves here as an exemplar of an approach to law which has adherents within contemporary Marxism.

## On the idea of private property

Marx's critique of jurisprudence was – to the extent that he developed it – like his critique of political economy, not just an internal critique of one legal theory by another but an uncovering of the social foundation of legal thought in its entirety. It was a critique aimed at the fetishized character of law in which social relations between people appear in the form of private relations between people and things (rights of property) and thence in the form of personal subordination to an impersonal embodiment of those rights (government of laws rather than people). Just as it was necessary for Marx to complement his critique of religion with a critique of those social relations which gave rise to religion, so too his critique of law was complemented by a critique of relations that clothe themselves in legal mysteries.

The starting point for Marx's critique of law was private property, just as value was the starting point for his critique of political economy. Thus in his contribution to the *Critique of Political Economy*, he wrote that 'Hegel correctly takes ownership, the simplest legal relation of the subject, as the point of departure for the philosophy of law.' He regarded private property not as something separate from law – as if their connections were purely contingent – but rather as the elementary 'cell' of legal thought. The supercession of private property was therefore at once the supercession of law; the idealization of law, conversely, was the idealization of private property.

In the 1844 *Manuscripts* Marx contrasted the human way in which men and women relate to the natural world around them to the alienated appropriation of things in the form of private property. In the first case, people relate to the world through all their senses – seeing, hearing, tasting, smelling, etc. – and by so doing turn all objects into 'human objects, objectifications of themselves', which develop, realize and confirm their individuality. In the case of private property, sensual appropriation of objects is subordinated to possessing, having, owning things; appropriation of nature in the form of private property becomes a 'means of life' rather than a realization of one's individuality: 'private property has made us so stupid and one-sided that an object is only *ours* when we have it.'[5] The more people become what they own the less they are themselves, until even their personal qualities appear as possessions that can be bought and sold on the market place: 'the less you *are*, the less you give expression to your life, the more you *have*, the greater is your *alienated* life.'[6] From the perspective of jurisprudence, private property appears as the external embodiment of individual will in things; in fact it signifies the alienation of the individual, who is reduced to no more than an owner of things and whose identity is reduced to the things he or she owns. Thus private property was analysed by Marx in the *Manuscripts* as the alienation of 'human existence' and of a 'human way' of inhabiting nature.

The advance which Smith made over the mercantilists was that the latter treated private property 'as a purely objective being for man'[7] whereas Smith recognized that labour is the 'subjective essence' or 'principle' or private property. He translated Locke's natural law imperative that people have a right to the product of their own labour into the scientific doctrine that labour is the substance of private property. Smith never, however, once asked the question why this content has assumed this particular form, that is to say, why labour is expressed in private property. While all human labour produces material objects (i.e. use-values), the question which Marx posed was what specific kind of labour produces use-values in the alien form of private property. By ignoring the form of property Smith 'transfers private property into the very essence of man'; this illusion can be broken only by seeing private property as the product of a specific kind of labour, alienated labour, in which the objects of labour appear as something 'alien' to their producers: '*this* realization of labour appears as a *loss of reality* for the worker.'[8]

In the *Manuscripts* Marx based his critique of private property on a contrast between human and inhuman ways of appropriating nature: private property represents the dominance of the material world over 'the human element', while communism represents the triumph of the human element over the material world. Capitalist reality is condemned in the name of a communist ideal, the world of what *is* in the name of the world as it *should* be. The error of classical jurisprudence was to presuppose private property, while the strength of Proudhon was to expose it to critical examination. Marx's transition from utopian to scientific socialism, that is, from a radicalized natural law theory to historical materialism, led him to explore the juridic form of private property and the contradictory character of productive relations which express themselves in this form.

In his *Critique of Political Economy, Grundrisse* and *Capital*, the vast bulk of Marx's work was centred on a critique of the economic forms assumed by capitalist relations of production. No comparable critique of the fetish of private property, law and the state was written by Marx. We have, however, a basis for such a critique in Marx's own sporadic comments on jurisprudence, in his substantive analysis of capitalist relations of production and in the method he developed for his critique of political economy. In the section which follows, I shall just be skimming the surface of what is required for a critique of jurisprudence, in order to bring to light the dialectical view of bourgeois freedom and equality which informed Marx's later writings and the contradictory relation he saw between juridic forms and their substantive content.

Why, Marx asked, should private property, that is, a definite form of property, whose historical emergence classical jurisprudence had itself traced, none the less appear as a natural and rational institution valid for all times and places? Classical jurisprudence had squared this circle by treating all previous forms of property as distortions of private property by political and moral constraints: that is, private property appeared as a natural relation between people and things corrupted in all pre-capitalist societies by the imposition of external obligations. It seemed, in other words, as though private property was a starting point for analysis, even though its realization only came at the end of history with what was seen as the lifting of constraints upon it. The root of this mystique was that private property appeared as a relation between individuals and things constructed in private rather than as the expression of a definite social relation between people. In all societies, Marx argued, there must exist some form of property: 'production is always appropriation of nature by an individual within and with the help of a definite social organization. In this context, it is quite tautological to say that property (appropriation) is a condition of production' or that 'where no form of property exists there can be no production and no society either. Appropriation which appropriates nothing is a contradiction in terms.'[9] However, Marx adds, 'it is quite ridiculous to make a leap from this to a distinct form of property, e.g. private property.' Different forms of property express different relations of production; it is the nature of social relations between people that determines the form in which the natural world is appropriated by them.

In the *Grundrisse* Marx traces some of the characteristics of pre-capitalist forms of property which distinguished them from bourgeois forms of private property.

The key to these earlier forms was that appropriation of the objective conditions of labour (land, tools, etc.) took place not through labour but rather on the basis of the individual's existence as a member of the community. Ownership of land and of other instruments of labour was *presupposed* by productive activity and not the *result* of it. It was only as a member of a community that an individual could possess property, and the property that individuals possessed derived from their membership of a community. The notion that all individuals equally have a right to the product of their own labour was entirely alien to such societies.

For example, in 'clan communities' (of which oriental despotism was one example) the

communality of blood, languages, customs . . . is the first

presupposition for the appropriation of the objective condition of their life . . . They relate to the earth naively as the *property* of the community . . . Each individual conducts himself only as a link, as a member of this community, as . . . possessor. The *real appropriation* through the labour process happens under these *presuppositions*, which are not themselves the *product* of labour but appear as its natural or *divine* presuppositions.[10]

In the classical community of antiquity, communal property is separated from private property; on the one hand, individuals may become private proprietors of land; but on the other communal property is their bond and safeguard against internal and external foes.

Membership of the commune remains a presupposition for appropriation of land and soil, but as a member of the commune the individual is a private proprietor . . . The individual is placed in such conditions of earning his living as to make not the acquiring of wealth his object . . . but his own reproduction as a member of the community . . . The survival of the commune is the reproduction of all of its members as self-sustaining peasants, whose surplus time belongs precisely to the commune.[11]

Among German tribes, as a third example, the commune exists only 'as a periodic gathering-together of the commune members', settled not in cities but long distances apart in the country. The commune, in other words, comes into being only when the landed proprietors – whose economic existence is centred on the individual household – hold a meeting. Public land is merely a complement to individual property – land, that is, reserved for hunting, grazing, timber, etc., that cannot be divided if it is to serve these productive functions. Apart from this communal land, which is really no more than the common property of the individual proprietors, 'the commune exists only in the interrelation among these individual landed proprietors as such';[12] nevertheless membership of this commune remains a presupposition for the appropriation of land as property.

Since in all these societies it was only as a member of a community that an individual could possess property, it followed that 'an isolated individual could no more have property in land

and soil than he could speak . . . the individual can never appear here in the dot-like isolation in which he appears as mere free worker.'[13] Marx's purpose in these passages was not only to show – as classical jurisprudence has already perceived in its own way – that private property is a historical accomplishment, but also to demonstrate that all forms of property depend on social relations between people. If private property appears as a private relation between individuals and things, then this must be the mystified consequence of a particular organization of productive relations and not of a transubstantiation of the nature of property. Historically, what needs to be explained is not 'the *unity* of living and active humanity with the natural, inorganic conditions of their metabolic exchange with nature' – since originally human beings' relation to their natural conditions of production was presupposed, along with their own being as members of a community – but rather 'the *separation* between these inorganic conditions of human existence and his active existence.'[14] In other words, the idea that ownership of property could be an attribute of the abstract individual, taken in isolation from other people, is the juridic fetish of the modern age. The question is, where does this fetish derive from?

Before tracing Marx's answer to this, it should be noted that Marx no longer romanticized pre-bourgeois property relations as in any sense 'superior' to those of private property. If Marx's critique of the fetish of the abstract individual is taken as his sole yardstick for assessing different modes of production, it would be easy to conclude that bourgeois private property represents a regression from these older forms. Those commentaries which compare on the one side bourgeois private property, and on the other all other forms of property (primitive communist, ancient Greek, feudal, patriarchal, socialist, etc.) tend to obscure the particular restrictions associated with older forms of property which bourgeois private property broke asunder. Within traditional forms of property, although the individual was seen as a member of a community, relations within the community itself appeared to derive from divine or natural origins (as reflected in traditional natural law theory) and the origins of property in human labour were more or less completely obscured. Those who were not members of the community were deemed incapable of owning property (as was expressly articulated in Roman law); consequently slavery and serfdom – in which labour itself appeared among the objective conditions of production – emerged as necessary developments of these relations. Under slavery, as Marx put it, 'the worker is distinguishable only as *instrumentum vocale* from an animal which is *instrumentum semi-vocale* and from a lifeless implement, which is *instrumentum mutum*.'[15] Such forms of property founded on the labour of slaves, serfs, retainers, servant, etc., had as their natural basis the inequality of human beings and of their labour. Further, the classical view, according to which good citizens and human beings rather than wealth were the aim of production, '*seems* to be very lofty when contrasted to the modern world where production appears as the aim of mankind and wealth as the aim of production.'[16] But what is wealth, Marx asks, rejecting this classicist critique of modernity, 'other than the universality of individual needs, capacities, pleasures, productive forces . . . the full development of human mastery over the forces of nature, those of so-called nature as well as humanity's own nature?'[17] The mark of traditional property relations was *restricted* development of the forces of production, of society and of the individual. The fault of private property was not that it broke through these restrictions, nor that it aimed at the unlimited production of wealth, nor that it was premissed on 'the equality and equivalence of all kinds of labour in so far as they are human labour in general',[18] nor that it posited property as a human institution predicated on human labour – these were, as Marx learnt from Smith and Hegel, its great strengths. Rather, its defect lay in the alienated form in which these achievements were secured. The separation of property from its presuppositions in the community represented a twofold process: on the one hand the cutting of the real ties which bind individuals to the community of which they are part, the rise of the mythology of property as a private attribute, the pursuit of private interest without regard for the interests of others, the treatment of others as means to one's own private ends; on the other the breaking of the real chains which subordinated the development of the individual and the forces of production to reproducing the limited, one-sided aims of the natural community. Marx thus abandoned his earlier conception of civil society as the worst possible slavery in favour of a dialectical view of its historical progressiveness. This new position was reflected politically in his attacks on 'Feudal Socialism', whose protagonists were anti-capitalist from the perspective of the old order without being pro-socialist.

## Freedom, equality and commodity production

From where then does private property, as a determinate form of property, actually emerge? The society which gives rise to it is one that is based on private production by isolated producers whose contact with each other is mediated entirely through the exchange of their products on the market. In such a society, producers are free to produce what and how much they wish; they are equal in that no one producer can force any other to produce against his or her will, nor expropriate the means of production or the products of other producers against their will. They are independent in that they are all entitled to pursue their own private interests regardless of what others think or do. Their contact with other producers is a matter left to their own desires and needs, and contact with each other takes the form of a free and equal exchange in which one individual alienates his or her own private property in return for the private property that belongs to another. In so doing they give up unneeded things in return for useful things for the mutual benefit of each party. In short, a society based on petty commodity production provided the historical foundation for private property.

Under these circumstances, the exchange relation appears as a self-sufficient relation, divorced from any particular mode of production, between free and equal property owners who enter a voluntary contract in pursuit of their own self-interest. The exchange relation itself makes no reference to the circumstances in which individuals seek to exchange, nor to the characteristics of the commodities offered for exchange. In exchange, Marx argues,

> all inherent contradictions of bourgeois society appear extinguished . . . and *bourgeois democracy even more than the bourgeois economists* [i.e. jurisprudence more than political economy] takes refuge in this aspect. In so far as the commodity is conceived of only as exchange value [or in juridic terms as private property] and the relation . . . as the exchange of these exchange values [i.e. of private property] . . . then the individuals, the subjects between whom this process goes on are simply and only conceived of as exchangers [i.e. as

of owners of private property]. As far as their formal character is concerned, there is no distinction between them . . . As subjects of exchange, their relation is therefore that of *equality*. It is impossible to find any trace of distinction, not to speak of contradiction between them, not even a difference. Furthermore, the commodities which they exchange are as exchange values [i.e. as private property] equivalent . . . The content of the exchange, which lies altogether outside its economic [and juridic] character, far from endangering the equality of individuals, rather makes their natural difference into the basis of their social equality . . . Only the difference between their needs and between their products gives rise to exchange and to their social equation in exchange; these natural differences are therefore the preconditions of their social equality in the act of exchange.[19]

Exchange appears not only as a relation of equality between property owners but also as one of freedom and mutual respect for the freedom of others:

each confronts the other as owner of the object of the other's need, this proves that each of them reaches beyond his own particular need . . . as a *human being* and that they relate to each other as human beings . . . [Thus] there enters in addition to the quality of equality, that of *freedom*. Although individual A feels a need for the commodity of individual B, he does not appropriate it by force, nor vice versa, but rather they recognize one another reciprocally as proprietors, as persons whose will penetrates their commodities. Accordingly, the juridical moment of the Person enters here.[20]

Out of this relation there appears to emerge, behind the backs of the parties to the exchange, a common interest, one that is not counterposed to the particular interests of individuals but rather based precisely on the reciprocal development of self-interest. In other words, it is not an alien 'common interest' which arises but one that cannot be separated from the autonomous development of each individual. The only compulsion which enters the relation is one that stems not from an alien force but only from my own needs, drives and nature. The exchange relation appears as natural and rational because it respects and embodies these human qualities of equality, freedom, mutual respect and mutual need. To the extent that exchange relations comprise the means of association between owners of private property, it would therefore seem that they represent a truly human form of social contact based on the integrity, as well as the needs, of the private individual. In exchange relations, owners of private property

> must place themselves in relation to one another as persons whose will resides in those objects and must behave in such a way that each does not appropriate the commodity of the other and alienate his own except through an act to which both parties consent . . . This juridical relation, whose form is the contract, whether as part of a developed legal system or not, is a relation between two wills which mirrors the economic relation.[21]

While it appears that the eternal human qualities of freedom and equality are respected in exchange relations, in fact exchange relations are their material basis:

> as pure ideas they are merely the idealized expression of this basis, as developed in juridical, political, social relations, they are merely this basis to a higher power . . . Equality and freedom developed to this extent are exactly the opposite of the freedom and equality in the world of antiquity, where developed exchange value (and thus private property) was not their basis but where, rather, the development of that basis destroyed them. Equality and freedom presuppose relations of production as yet unrealized in the ancient world and in the middle ages.[22]

Marx saw the development of juridic freedom and equality as a great advance. No longer did they appear to him as an ideal, when applied to the state, or as an empty form or illusion when applied to civil society. Rather than rest his analysis on the forced abstraction of the state from civil society and of civil society from the state, he now viewed juridic relations between free and equal owners of private property – alongside economic relations between commodities bearing value – as antithetical social forms, the secret to whose riddles lay in the unravelling of the social relations of commodity production. He was now in a position to explore the contradictory character of the formal freedoms and equalities traversing state and civil society alike.

The myth of private property as a private relation between individuals and things is dissolved once the abstraction of exchange from production is abandoned. The presupposition of exchange is a definite organization of production: one which forces producers to exchange their products – for they cannot survive nor reproduce except by exchanging their products – and which determines socially the form and content of their private interests: 'the private interest is itself a socially determined interest, which can be achieved only within the conditions laid down by society and with the means provided by society.'[23] The real point of departure is not the private individual as he or she appears at the moment of exchange but rather 'individuals producing in society – hence socially determined individuals'.[24]

The presuppositions of commodity production are, first, an extended division of labour (though Marx now clearly saw what he and Engels had confused in their earlier writings, namely that although

> the division of labour is a necessary condition for commodity production . . . the converse does not hold; commodity production is not a necessary condition for the social division of labour . . . Only the products of mutually independent acts of labour, performed in isolation, can confront each other as commodities.[25]

Second, the dissolution of all relations of personal dependence, such as those that characterized feudal relations between serfs and lords, vassals and suzerains, laypersons and clerics, and of all community restraints on the ownership and use of property; third, 'the all-sided dependence of the producers on one another',[26] since the individual act of private production presupposes that individuals will find available in the market the things necessary to satisfy their needs. In short, commodity exchange is premissed on the reciprocal and all-sided dependence of commodity producers which compels them to exchange. The positive aspect of this development was that for the first time objective social connections were made not only between all producers within a community but, as the world market inexorably grows, between all producers in the world: 'this objective social connection is certainly preferable to the lack of any connection or to a merely local connection . . .

Individuals cannot gain mastery over their own social connections before they have created them.'[27] The alien character of the bond between commodity producers consists, therefore, not in the fact of their mutual interdependence but in its mode. Both the form of their interconnections – a contract between two private parties based on the exchange of their property – and their content – the terms on which such contracts for the exchange of goods are made – are entirely out of the control of the producers and thus become an alien force above them:

> Ties of personal dependence are exploded . . . Individuals seem independent but they appear thus only for someone who abstracts from these conditions [of production] . . . The definedness of individuals, which in the former case appears as the personal restriction of the individual by another, appears in the latter case as developed into an objective restriction of the individual by relations independent of him . . . These external relations are very far from being an abolition of 'relations of dependence'; they are rather the dissolution of these relations in a general form . . . Individuals are now ruled by abstractions, whereas earlier they depended upon one another. The abstraction is nothing more than the theoretical expression of those material relations which are their lord and master.[28]

Since commodity producers labour privately, in isolation from one another,

> the social character of [their] activity appears as something alien and objective, confronting the individuals not as their relation to one another but as their subordination to relations which subsist independently of them and which arise out of collisions between mutually indifferent individuals.[29]

Equality before the law is a formal property of exchange relations between private property owners. In general, this appearance of equality is dissolved once one explores the content of exchange. In a famous passage in his *Critique of the Gotha Programme*, Marx wrote that the equal rights of parties to an exchange necessarily entail as their consequences substantive inequality:

> Equal right . . . is a right of inequality in its content like every right. Right by its nature can only consist in the application of an equal standard in so far as they are brought under an equal point of view, are taken from one definite side only . . . To avoid all these defects, right instead of being equal would have to be unequal.[30]

In other words, equal treatment of unequal individuals – and individuals would not be individuals if they were not unequal – leads to inequality. In Anatole France's famous example, a law forbidding the rich and the poor equally from sleeping under the bridges of Paris would be most unequal in its effects. While, however, a tension between equal rights and substantive inequality is a tension in all exchange relations and reveals the folly of those who would idealize the mediation of social relations by law, the nature and degree of that inequality are determined by productive relations. It is an entirely abstract critique of law that leaves the matter at that and fails to investigate how 'the form and content [of equal right] are changed'[31] as productive relations themselves change. While equality before the law always means inequality in fact, it is compatible with entirely different levels and forms of inequality. In *Capital*, Marx analysed how the content of equal right changed with the development of capitalist relations of production, changes which reveal a dynamic relation between juridic forms of equality and their social content. It should be noted here that Marx did not analyse how forms of equal right changed with the development of capitalist relations of production – this was beyond his scope in a critique of political economy – and it is a question to which I return later.

## Freedom, equality and capitalist relations of production

Where commodity production is sporadic or peripheral, exchange takes the form of occasional barter between isolated individuals or groups (in the first instance, usually one tribe exchanging surplus goods with another). The terms of the exchange are determined by the producers themselves and each producer has to defend his or her rights of private property by force of arms: even club law, as Marx put it, is law.[32] With the generalization of commodity production, one commodity becomes the embodiment of human labour in the abstract and assumes the economic form of money. Competition between producers will ensure that commodities exchange at their values, that is, according to the socially necessary labour time that enters their production. There is no guarantee that the actual labour-time of the individual will correspond with the labour-time that is socially necessary. For instance, a peasant farmer on good land will, other things being equal, be more productive than a peasant on bad land. Equal right in these circumstances entails that some producers exchange their commodities for more than their actual labour-time and some for less; that is, a particular mode of inequality which will lead to the impoverishment of some and enrichment of others (as illustrated, for example, in the differentiation of the peasantry in pre-capitalist societies): 'if one grows impoverished and the other grows wealthier then this is of their own free will . . . even inheritance does not prejudice this natural freedom and equality.'[33] Under these circumstances producers may have to be forced to be free, since a good deal of coercion will be required to ensure that proprietors' rights to free exchange are guaranteed against those who are impoverished as a consequence. For free and and equal exchange to be sustained under the pressure of these substantive inequalities, a force is required – over and beyond that exercised by the producers themselves – to protect property rights. From where is this force to arise? We shall see that the problem and its solution arose simultaneously with the emergence of law as the independent and objective form assumed by property right. I shall reserve exploration of this formal aspect of the question, which Marx did not pursue, till later.

With the means of production becoming the property of some and the non-property of the vast majority, the economic forms of capital and wage-labour emerge. The relation between them still takes the form of free and equal exchange between commodity producers, but the particular form and content of this exchange have changed:

> The sphere of circulation of commodity exchange, within whose boundaries the sale and purchase of labour power goes on, is in fact a very Eden of the innate rights of man. It is the exclusive realm of Freedom, Equality, Property and Bentham. Freedom because both buyer and seller of a commodity, let us

say labour-power, are determined only by their own free will. They contract as free persons, who are equal before the law ... Equality because each enters into relations with the other as with a simple owner of commodities and they exchange equivalent with equivalent. Property because each disposes only what is his own. And Bentham because each looks only to his own advantage. The only force bringing them together is the selfishness, the gain and the private interest of each.[34]

On the surface of capitalist society the relation between capitalist and worker is a simple exchange, each obtaining an equivalent from the other: the one obtaining money (in the form of a wage) and the other a use-value, labour-power. In the movement which proceeds on the surface of the bourgeois world,

a worker who buys a loaf of bread and a millionaire who does the same appear in this act as simple buyers . . . all other aspects are extinguished . . . the content of these purchases appears as completely irrelevant compared with the formal aspect.[35]

So too the exchange between capitalist and worker appears just like any other exchange and each appears as an equal; in fact the exchange between capitalist and worker expresses a completely different social relation from that between two petty commodity producers. Nobody enters exchange as an abstract individual but rather as an individual rooted in definite social relations: 'not relations between individual and individual, but between worker and capitalist, between farmer and landlord, etc. Wipe out these relations and you annihilate all society.'[36]

The distinctive feature of the exchange between capitalist and worker, which differentiates it from exchange between buyers and sellers in general, lies in its content. A new commodity has entered the market which did not previously exist as a commodity: namely labour-power. Its historical presupposition lay in the double freedom of the worker: freedom, on the one hand, from relations of personal dependence, bondage, servitude, etc., and on the other from ownership of the means of production and subsistence. Similarly, the buyer of this new commodity, labour-power, is no longer a simple buyer who seeks to use it as an object of personal consumption (as in the case of a householder employing a servant), but rather one who uses it specifically for the production of surplus value.

The wage-form obscures this relation. It appears that workers exchange not their labour-power, but rather their labour in return for a wage. Since workers are employed by the day, the week, the year, the piece, etc., it appears as though they are paid for the entire labour. The only question then becomes whether workers receive a fair day's wage for a fair day's work, i.e. whether the exchange of equivalents is in fact being upheld. In fact the wage-form constitutes only the surface of a relation inherently based on exploitation, but it is this form which above all generates bourgeois ideas of justice, freedom and equality:

> The wage-form thus extinguishes every trace of the division of the working day into necessary labour and surplus labour, into paid labour and unpaid labour. All labour appears as paid labour . . . We may therefore understand the decisive importance of the transformation of the value and price of labour-power into the form of wages or into the value and price of labour itself. *All the notions of justice* held by both the worker and the capitalist, all the mystifications of the capitalist mode of production, *all capitalism's illusions about freedom*, all the apologetic tricks of vulgar economics, have as their basis the form of appearance discussed above, which makes the actual relations invisible and indeed presents to the eye the precise opposite to that relation.[37]

Marx's recognition that workers sell their labour-power and not their labour was of crucial significance for his analysis of the substantive inequality which lies behind equal exchange between capitalist and labourer. The hidden secret behind the exchange between capital and labour is that workers receive in the form of wages a value equivalent to the value of their labour-power and not of their 'labour', and the value of their labour-power is less than the value which their labour – put to use by the capitalist – is able to generate. Part of the value so created is expropriated without return by the capitalist as surplus value. In this case, unlike that of petty commodity production, unpaid surplus labour and dependence on capital provide the content of equal right. The inequalities characteristic of petty commodity production do not disappear. They persist in the wage-form. Unequal individuals receiving the same wage will derive unequal benefits from it. But over and above these persisting inequalities, there are further inequalities of a new order.

When we turn to the reproduction of capitalist society, we see that the real content of the exchange between capital and labour has changed once more. Previously the exchange between capital and labour consisted of the expropriation of part of the workers' labour. But Marx then asked, what is the nature of the capital which the capitalist exchanges with labour-power? The capitalist says that he worked hard for it, or that it is the product of his own labour. Even if this view of primitive accumulation were true (it ignores primitive accumulation based on robbery and international pillage), after several periods of production the entire capital owned by the capitalist will consist of capitalized surplus value, that is, the product of the labour of workers expropriated by the capitalist and turned into capital. It is now revealed that the exchange between capital and labour is in content no exchange at all, since the capital which exchanges for labour is but the expropriated labour of workers from a previous period in transmuted form:

> The capitalist, it is true, pays him the value of the commodity [labour-power] in money, but this money is merely the transmuted form of the product of his labour . . . The capitalist class is constantly giving to the working class drafts in the form of money on a portion of the product produced by the latter and appropriated by the former.[38]

Under these circumstances the content of the exchange relation, that Eden of innate rights, is utterly transformed. Beneath the surface of equal exchange we now find, when we view the matter from the perspective of capital as a whole and labour as a whole, an inversion of the exchange of equivalents; the appropriation of the product of one 'owner' by another without equivalent:

> Each individual transaction continues to conform to the laws of commodity exchange with the capitalist always buying labour-power and the workers always selling it at what we shall assume is its real value. It is quite evident from this that the laws of appropriation of private property laws, based on the production and circulation of commodities, become

changed *into their direct opposite* through their own internal and inexorable dialectic. The exchange of equivalents, the original operation with which we started, is now turned round in such a way that there is only an *apparent exchange*, since firstly the capital which is exchanged for labour power is itself merely a portion of the product of others which has been appropriated without equivalent; and secondly this capitial must not only be replaced by its producer, the worker, but replaced with an added surplus. *The relation of exchange between capitalist and worker becomes a mere semblance belonging only to the process of circulation, it becomes a mere form which is alien to the content of the transaction itself and merely mystifies it.* The constant sale and purchase of labour-power is the form; the content is the constant appropriation by the capitalist without equivalent of a portion of the labour of others . . . Originally, the rights of property seemed to us to be grounded in man's own labour. Some such assumption was at least necessary since only commodity owners with equal rights confronted each other and the sole means of appropriating the commodities of others was the alienation of a man's own commodities, commodities which however could only be produced by labour. Now, however, property turns out to be the right on the part of the capitalist to appropriate the unpaid labour of others or its product and the impossibility of the worker of appropriating his own product. The separation of property from labour thus becomes the necessary consequence of a law that apparently originated in their identity.[39]

Under these new relations of production, in which the content of equal right has undergone such enormous change, so too does its form. Just as capital represents means of production alienated from their producers, so the function of enforcing equal rights between capital and wage-labour gives rise to a new form of legal authority, the state, that is, a public power alienated from the people, an independent force distinct from society which acquires its own institutions and its own personnel. But this aspect of capitalist relations of production is not pursued in *Capital*. These passages show how the content of inequality is transformed with the reproduction of capitalist relations of production: while on the surface a free and equal exchange of equivalents proceeds apace, beneath the surface the law which presupposed ownership of the products of one's own labour 'turns into . . . through a necessary dialectic an absolute divorce of property and appropriation of alien labour without exchange.'[40] Thus, while equal right always means inequality, it does not always mean the same inequality: differences between one form of inequality and another are a matter of great significance for the individuals involved.

The story of the connection between capitalist relations of production and equal rights does not, of course, end here; rather this is its beginning. The socialization of labour under capital leads to the organization of the working class, who assert their rights as free labourers against the rights of capitalists as free owners of private property. Right is set against right, as Marx put it, and the outcome in law is the result of a struggle of class forces. Marx portrays this process vividly in his account of struggles over the ten-hour day:

> The capitalist maintains his rights as a purchaser when he tries to make the working day as long as possible, and where possible, to make two working days out of one. On the other hand, the peculiar nature of the commodity sold implies a limit to its consumption by the purchaser, and the worker maintains his right as a seller when he wishes to reduce the working day to a particular normal length. There is here therefore an antinomy, of right against right, both equally bearing the seal of the law of exchange. Between equal rights, force decides.[41]

Relations of production between capital and labour are not static: they are not once given, forever fixed. Nothing is more stultifying in my view, and less in the spirit of *Capital*, than to freeze its analysis of the capital–labour relation into a motionless frame. The content of inequality is not static, even though no amount of tinkering with the wages and conditions of work will abolish the exploitative nature of the capital–labour relation itself.

However, Marx's argument that with the reproduction of the capital-labour relation exchange becomes a 'mere semblance', a 'mere form . . . alien to the content of the transaction', a mere 'mystification', may give rise to the idea that, however real and important formal equality was in petty commodity production, it loses all substance with the development of capitalism. This theme is present in the *Grundrisse* and in *Capital*. It mirrors the view of civil society as 'the worst possible slavery' put forward in *The German Ideology*. Marx was also, however, developing another, quite different view of the significance of formal freedom and equality, which grasped far more adequately their contradictory character.

The *juridic* significance of Marx's discovery that workers sell their labour-power and not themselves or their labour was this: it enabled him to see that workers do not, as he previously thought, 'sink to the level of a commodity, the most wretched commodity of all', but remain at all times owners of a commodity that is, labour-power. They are guardians of a commodity rather than being themselves commodities; they are in this sense free workers rather than slaves. Capitalist production, in other words, based on relations of exploitation and domination, was revealed as compatible with – not at odds with – juridic freedom and equality. Thus capitalist reproduction does not imply an 'absolute divorce' between workers and property, since possession of one's own labour-power as private property is the presupposition of wage-labour. At the end of one cycle of production and beginning of the next, the workers themselves are reproduced as workers, still – if we exclude consideration of the state – in need of selling their labour-power in order to survive, but still also free and equal possessors of one vital piece of property which remains theirs, their own capacity to labour. Workers are not 'free of *all* belongings and possessions . . . of all property', as Marx continued to state in some passages of the *Grundrisse*.[42] Their labour-power remained their own, and this differentiation from slavery was a matter of juridic as well as economic importance. Marx was beginning to see, in the *Grundrisse*, that:

As a slave, the worker has exchange value; as a free wage-worker, he has no value, it is rather his power of disposing of his labour which has value . . . The worker is thereby formally posited as a person who is something for himself *apart from* his labour and who alienates his life-expressions only *as a means towards his own life* . . . [for example], the sphere of his consumption is not qualitatively restricted, only quantitatively. This distinguishes him from the slave.[43]

The fact that workers are owners of their labour-power and only grant temporary disposal of it to capital, is, as Rosdolsky has clearly argued, 'of decisive importance, since it counts as one of those features of the relation of wage-labour which raises it historically above earlier modes of exploitation'. In slavery, direct producers themselves belong to individual particular owners; in serfdom, direct producers appear 'as a moment of property land itself . . . an appendage of the soil exactly like draught-cattle'. The wage-labourer, by contrast, 'belongs to himself' and sells his or her property 'to a particular capitalist whom he confronts as an independent individual'. This grants to workers, as Rosdolsky put it, 'a wide field of choice, of arbitrary will, hence of formal freedom, which the producers of other class societies lacked and without which the workers' struggle for liberation would be simply inconceivable.'[44] By exchanging labour-power for money, the worker even becomes 'a co-participant in general wealth up to the limit of his equivalent'.

Marx never overcame his ambivalence between his conception of bourgeois equality and freedom as 'only a semblance and a deceptive semblance' and his realization that 'this semblance exists nevertheless as an illusion on his [the worker's] part and to a certain degree on the other side, and thus essentially modifies his relation by comparison to that of workers in other modes of production.' If this 'semblance' has such a palpable reality, then it should no longer be called a semblance. At the end of the day, what is important is not how Marx resolved – or failed to resolve – his own ambivalence, but how we resolve the problem which he expressed.

The main point is this. Workers under capitalism are not propertyless. They remain at all times owners of private property, at best in the form of personal possessions (means of subsistence) and at worst in the form of labour-capacity alone. It is this fact which turns ideologies centred around the sanctity of private property into viable means of persuasion rather than alien means of mere oppression. Marxists should relate to this rather than simply denounce private property as something entirely oppressive and bad, from which workers are entirely expropriated and in which they have no interest. Juridic freedom and equality, far from losing their social base with the extended reproduction of capital, are granted a new foundation with the socialization of labour and its collective organization. This is a story beyond the scope of *Capital* itself, but is one whose interpretation may be greatly informed by reading *Capital*.

# 5. Bourgeois and socialist democracy

## Bourgeois democracy

The crucial phenomenon with which Marx and Engels tried to come to grips in their political writings on Britain, France and Germany was the growth in the power and autonomy of the state bureaucracy and the subordination to it of the elective assembly and the judiciary. They witnessed the decline of the liberal form of the 'legal state' – which in some countries had only a shortlived and precarious existence – and the rise of bureaucratic statism. Their critique was directed against the autonomy of the executive within the state – its interference in elections, its suppression of civil liberties, its corruption of democratic forms for thoroughly undemocratic ends, etc. – and against the autonomy of the state from society. They saw the state bureaucracy as an 'appalling parasitic body', which in a country like France had come to 'choke all the pores' of society:[1] either it ruled behind a thin veneer of democratic and legal forms which it turned increasingly into a 'democratic swindle', a 'democracy of unfreedom' (for example, by granting civil liberties like freedom of speech with 'escape clauses' like 'except when it contravenes the public interest' which effectively withdraw the original freedom); or it ruled directly without even this democratic veneer, putting itself forward as the universal class, above politics and class differences and representative of the nation as a whole. In opposition to the power of the bureaucracy, Marx and Engels fought for the dominance of the legislature and the judiciary over the executive. 'Escape clauses' must be removed from civil liberties: if rights to a free press, free assembly, free speech come into conflict with the needs of state, then too bad for the state. Parliament must assert its command over ministerial posts and break the grip of the executive over the cabinet. Judicial independence from the executive must be upheld;

Marx attacked constitutional provisions which 'deprived the courts of law of their ancient right of cancelling administrative decrees'.[2] Hal Draper recounts Marx's praise – written in 1859 – for the Hessian Constitution (of 1831), based on the grounds that 'there is no other constitution which restrains the power of the executive within limits so narrow, makes the administration more dependent on the legislature and confides such a supreme control [of the executive] to the judicial benches.'[3] Marx paid tribute to the fact that 'the courts of law, empowered to decide definitively upon all acts of the Executive, were rendered omnipotent.' Real judicial independence meant, for Marx, independence from the bureaucracy; the sham judicial independence that was developing meant, in fact, subordination to the executive and domination over the popular legislature. The courts, instead of being empowered to cancel administrative decrees on behalf of the assembly, cancelled the assembly's decisions on behalf of the administration. Instead of the judiciary being elected by the people or the legislature in order to serve as a counterweight to the executive, they were appointed by the executive to serve as a counterweight to the people and its legislature. Marx attacked the doctrine of 'the separation of powers', which he saw as a shoddy compromise between the legislature and the bureaucracy, the effect of which was to free the executive from popular control. He called for 'unity of power' in the representative assembly and for the assembly to take the necessary steps to implement it: simplify the state administration, augment its accountability to representative bodies, reduce the army of officials as far as possible, upend its hierarchical structures of internal authority. He called for civil society to create organs of its own, independent of governmental power, and for the assembly to support the initiatives of civil society: in order to integrate struggles to democratize the state with struggles over self-organization and self-activity outside the state.

Representative democracy backed by the rule of law and bureaucratic government backed by administrative decree appeared to Marx as the two poles of bourgeois authority. He recognized both as bourgeois forms of domination: his initial tendency to see the bureaucracy as a hangover from the absolutist state of the old order[4] (a view derived from the French experience but entirely inapplicable to Britain) gave way to the realization that the development of bureaucracy is a thoroughly modern, bourgeois phenomenon taking place in all bourgeois states. Either the old bureaucracy was 'bourgeoisified' (as in France) or a bourgeois bureaucracy was built anew – (as in Britain). But, although representative democracy and bureaucratic government (the latter illustrated by Bonapartism) were both bourgeois forms of state, they were different forms of bourgeois state. Marx reserved particularly biting criticism for those 'true socialists' who either ignored the differences or, in reaction against the repressive policies carried out by the Republic of 1848, put their support, either actively or passively, behind Bonaparte's coup. The conclusion to be drawn from the sham liberties of the 1848 Republic was not that all political liberties are a sham but that sham liberties must be turned into real liberties. The lesson to be drawn from the true socialists was that it is possible to be 'anti-capitalist' without being 'pro-proletarian'. The proletariat needs political liberty both as means for their own social ends and as an end in itself. Political democracy 'puts entirely new weapons in the hands of the proletariat for the struggle against the bourgeoisie' (like freedom of the press and of association) and 'obtains an entirely different status for the proletariat, a status as a recognized party.'[5]

## Socialist democracy

Marx's commitment to political liberty as an integral part of socialism was apparent not only in his criticisms of authoritarian and bureaucratic forms of bourgeois state but also in his conception of the form of authority appropriate to socialist societies led by the working class. His views on socialist democracy have often been misinterpreted by Marxists, who have either obscured the formal distinctions between bourgeois and socialist democracy (as if they expressed the same form of government) or overstated the gulf between them (as if socialist democracy were an entirely different breed of animal from its bourgeois counterpart). In fact, in Marx's writings there was a strong thread of continuity between them, even though he did not identify the one with the other.

'Equal right', Marx wrote in the passage from his *Critique of the Gotha Programme* which we have already cited, 'is in principle bourgeois right . . . it is a right of inequality in its content like any right.'[6] These words are a useful reminder of the limits of law to those who would idealize it as an unqualified good; they have, however, been used by other Marxists to dismiss law entirely as a bourgeois form of regulation, to write off its claims to equality and to look elsewhere for socialist forms of authority.

How far this was from Marx's view should be evident from the immediate context within which these words were written. Even in a very advanced stage of socialism, when all labour is considered equal to any other labour and when workers receive in wages an equivalent to the amount of labour they have contributed to the total social labour according to the principle 'to each according to his or her labour', even then it would be necessary for regulation to take the legal form of protection of equal right. It is true that equal right would still entail inequality, since some people are more equipped to labour than others, and some have greater needs than others. It is true that

> unequal individuals (and they would not be different individuals if they were not unequal) are measurable by an equal standard in so far as they are brought under an equal point of view, are taken from one *definite* side only, for instance, in the present case, are regarded *only as workers* and nothing more is seen of them, everything else being ignored.[7]

It is further true that only when 'the narrow horizon of bourgeois right is crossed in its entirety' and when 'society inscribes on its banners: From each according to his ability, to each according to his needs!'[8] that the limits of human equality and individuality can be reached. In regarding the limits of bourgeois right, however, it should not be overlooked that Marx believed 'equal right' to be a necessity in so advanced a stage of socialism as one in which class inequalities had been abolished in their entirety. For Marx, 'bourgeois right', was not a temporary hangover from capitalist society, to be eradicated as soon as practicable, but a principle which was to govern socialist society until the point of its transformation into complete communism. In the period of transition, however, both the form and content of law would be changed: labour and the means of consumption are the only commodities that can be exchanged, and the means of production have ceased to be commodities in private hands:

> Here obviously the same principle prevails as that which regulates the exchange of equal values. *Content and form are*

*changed*, because under the altered circumstances no one can give anything except his labour and because on the other hand nothing can pass to the ownership of individuals except individual means of consumption.[9]

This passage poses a question: what forms will law take in socialist society and what will be the content of its regulations? Marx provides no clear answer, but he has said enough to show that in his view law in some form or other is a vital part of the transition to communism.

The more general question, of which this is part, was that of analysing the forms of authority appropriate for the emancipation of labour, just as classical jurisprudence had in its time analysed the forms of authority appropriate to the emancipation of private property. But their methods were different: what was crucial for Marx was to start with a historical analysis of capitalist society and to uncover the social dynamics latent within it; not to start with natural law and deduce forms of authority from it. Analysis of existing forms of law and state revealed to Marx that it was not sufficient for the proletariat merely to take over this apparatus and use it for its own ends. Why not? Because capitalist relations of production determine the form itself of the capitalist state: they impose limits on the democracy of even the most democratic bourgeois states, and they generate in actuality forms of state that are not democratic at all. The *real* state against which the Paris Commune revolted, for instance, was not a bourgeois democracy but the Second Empire of Louis Bonaparte, born out of the destruction of the 'social republic' of 1848 and dominated by a massive state bureaucracy, entirely alienated from the people and allied with the speculating and corrupt giants of the bourgeoisie. This certainly was not a form of authority appropriate for any kind of emancipation. Any democrat could see that this apparatus had to be 'smashed' and replaced by a new form of power. The originality of Marx's work lay in his analysis of what this new form would be: a form of state more democratic than any that had existed, or could exist, under bourgeois rule. What made this possible was that the social base of this state was to be no longer the exploitation of the majority by the minority but rather the dominance of the mass of the people over the exploiting minority. It was crucial to discover the '*political form* under which the economic emancipation of labour could be accomplished'. This meant not dreaming up an ideal form, in the manner of utopians; nor dismissing the whole question of form, in the manner of anti-authoritarians; nor posing republican forms as a limit which should not be overstepped; rather it called for an analysis of the dynamics of capitalist societies and of socialist revolutions. Although Marx and Engels only initiated this process in their theoretical and political writings they were able, on the basis of their limited experience, to draw tentative conclusions about what particular forms of authority were appropriate.

The rise and fall of the Paris Commune, which Marx saw as a prologue – a 'glorious harbinger' – of a socialist form of authority, provided him with one occasion for giving empirical substance to his theoretical ideas. He tried to draw lessons, first from what it did, and second from what it would have done if it had survived. The principle which he saw embodied in the Commune was that of a transition from a 'special power' alienated from the people to a power under their control; from a power which sought to monopolize political life to one which opened it up to the people. The 'haughteous masters' of the people were to be replaced by its 'removable servants'; 'mock responsibility' was to give way to 'real responsibility'. The Commune represented, in Marx's eyes, 'the re-absorption of the state power by society as its own living force instead of as forces controlling and subduing it'.[10] Radical democracy was its keynote: the extension of representation from parliament to the bureaucracy, the judiciary, and the army; universalization of suffrage (though Marx was silent on the age of majority); strict accountability of delegates to their electors and revocability at short notice; abolition of the division of powers between legislature and executive in favour of legislative dominance; abolition of internal hierarchies within the state officialdom; popular organization independent of the state; replacement of the army by the 'people armed'.

Marx conceived of the Commune as itself a transitory form of power: through the gradual extension of democratic controls over the state and of popular organization outside the state (Marx was very vague about what form this would take), the independence of the state from society would be gradually dissolved. The endpoint of the process was the withering away of the state: the final realization of the general will could be achieved not through the state, but through its abolition. The extreme pole of democracy lay not in a particular form of state power, but in a form of power which transcended the state.

What was the place of law in this scenario? It is clear from our discussion above that Marx saw a place for law right up to the final dissolution of the state. Even in the most advanced stages of the transition law would still be needed to enforce relations of equivalence, but both its form and its content would be radically transformed. Marx, however, offered only hints concerning how they would be transformed. The judiciary, whose complete independence from the executive he supported in the 1850s, 'were to be divested of that *sham* independence which has but served to mask their abject subserviency to all succeeding governments' and were to be made *truly* independent by being made 'elective, responsible and revocable'. The Commune, he foresaw, 'would have transformed the peasant's present bloodsuckers, the notary, advocate, executor and other judicial vampires, into salaried communal agents'. Hal Draper points out that Marx's view seemed to be that judicial functions were not to be subordinated to the Commune, and that in this respect Marx recognized the validity of a separation of powers.

Marx saw in the law a means of inhibiting the power of government and of protecting the rights of the people; but it was not just as an instrument that Marx valued the law. The principle of the rational state, which he inherited from Hegel, was that of a synthesis between the universal will of the whole and the particular will of the individual. In the *Manuscripts*, for example, he had rejected the crude communism which

> negates the *personality* of man in every sphere . . . extends the category of *worker* to all men . . . and returns to the *unnatural* simplicity of the *poor*, unrefined man who has no needs and who has not even reached the state of private property, let alone gone beyond it.[11]

In *The German Ideology* Marx's objection to capitalist productive relations is that 'never in any earlier period have they taken on a form so indifferent to the intercourse of individuals *as individuals*'[12] and his idea of communism 'corresponds to the development of individuals into *complete individuals*'.[13] The Commune, Marx wrote, 'wanted to make *individual property a truth* by transforming the means of production, land and capital, now chiefly the means of enslaving and exploiting labour, into mere instruments of free and associated labour'. Communism meant not the subordination of the individual to the collective, but rather the realization of the individual through the collective and the realization of the collective through the individual. A genuine synthesis between the universal and the particular was to be achieved: not a fake synthesis, which really meant either the subordination of the individual to the state or the subordination of the state to private interest. Marx was for the development, expression, and realization of the individual as an individual, not for the suppression of individuality by the state. His objection to capitalism lay not in its 'individualism' but in the *limits* of its individualism. On the one hand the bourgeoisie raises 'the rights of the individual' as its slogan; on the other it suppresses individuality under the weight of the police, of bureaucracy, of hierarchy and, most especially, of the homogeneous and soul-destroying labour to which it subjects most of the people. The individualism proclaimed by the bourgeoisie was not its fault but its strength; the suppression of individuality, however, was the dark side of the capitalist coin.

It was not, therefore, a question of subordinating individual right to the general good but rather the extension of individual right beyond the narrow horizons of bourgeois right. Form and content must be changed. The right of the capitalist to exploit and of the bureaucracy to oppress the mass of the population was to be abolished; but this signified not the abolition but the enlargement of individual rights. Law was not just an instrument but a principle of socialist transition. The reader may remember that Hobbes demolished the idea of natural right by taking it to its limit: by extending it to mean the right of all to everything, natural right perished by its own abundance. With private property serving as his premiss Hobbes saw, in the limitless extension of natural right, a spectre to be suppressed by the state. Marx, with human emancipation as his premiss, saw in the limitless extension of right a path to genuine communism. It was through the combined extension of democracy and law that a real synthesis of the universal and the particular could be achieved.

Was this a utopia? Are the state and the rule of law necessary properties of any complex, democratic society? To answer this it is necessary to see what the doctrine of the withering away of the state did *not* mean. First, it was not the same as the anarchist dream of the abolition of all authority in the name of the limitless freedom of the individual. Expressed here, in Marx's view, was the mythology of petty bourgeois commodity production in the form of unbounded egoism. The abolition of state authority and the abolition of authority in general are not the same; the final goal of Marx and that of the anarchists were *not* identical. Second, the withering away of the state did not mean the end of public functions; in any society there are communal tasks to be done – adjudication of disputes, internal regulation, general planning, external defence (if the society has foes beyond its borders), the organization of production and distribution, and so forth. In the Commune, some public functions immediately diminished: 'the Commune made that catchword of bourgeois revolutions, cheap government, a reality by destroying the two greatest sources of expenditure – the standing army and state functionaries',[14] though it could perhaps have made government cheaper still if it had expropriated the National Bank. The function of policing was also diminished; in the Commune 'no more corpses at the morgue, no nocturnal burglaries, scarcely any robberies; in fact for the first time since the days of February, 1848, the streets of Paris were safe and that without any police of any kind.'[15] The function of policing, to the extent that it was still necessary, was performed by the popular militia. Third, the withering away of the state did not mean the dissolution of a division of labour for the performance of communal functions: the allocation of communal tasks to particular individuals was still necessary, though now it took the form not of hierarchical investiture but of universal suffrage:

> Universal suffrage was to serve the people, constituted in Communes, as individual suffrage serves every other employer in the search for workmen and managers in his business. And it is well known that companies, like individuals, in matters of real business generally know how to put the right man in the right job.[16]

What the withering away of the state did mean was the dissolution of an alien force, separated from the people, constituting an independent branch of the division of labour. It was the social form of the state that Marx saw as surpassable, not its technical functions.

'Right', Marx argued in another much-cited passage from *Critique of the Gotha Programme*, 'can never be higher than the economic structure of society and its cultural development conditioned thereby'.[17] The narrow horizons of bourgeois right and democracy derive from the material conditions of capitalist production: the exploitation of the majority by the minority is compatible only with limited democracy and limited right. Similarly the surpassing of these limits cannot be achieved by an act of will alone, but itself depends on definite material conditions. On the edges of Marx's analysis of the Commune, a separate problem was emerging: the relation between democratic forms of government and the practical needs of the revolution. The Commune was on the one hand 'the political form at last discovered under which to work out the economic emancipation of labour', and on the other 'a working-class government, the produce of the struggle of the producing against the appropriating class'. The form of the Commune was radical democracy, its content was the rule of labour over capital. No automatic synthesis between form and content could be presupposed. The Commune was, after all, rapidly defeated, the communards of Paris horribly massacred at the vengeful hands of Thiers's mercenaries, supported by the bourgeoisie under the flag of 'order and justice'. Was the democratic form of the Commune incompatible with its success? Marx argued – on the periphery of his celebration of it – that the Commune was insufficiently resolute in 'smashing' the old bureaucratic-military machine. They should have marched at once on Versailles but missed their opportunity 'because of moral scruples'; the Central Committee surrendered its power too soon to the Commune, 'again from a too "honourable" scrupulosity.'[18] Would the Commune, Marx asked, 'not have shamefully betrayed its trust by affecting to keep up all the decencies and appearances of liberalism as in a time of profound peace?'[19] There was a real tension, emerging from the material conditions of the Commune's existence, between its success as an organ of class rule and its success as a prefigurative form of socialist government. For instance, the failure of the communards to take decisive military action against Thiers's regrouping forces at Versailles was linked to the fact that they organized elections in Paris instead. In theory, perhaps, they could do both; in practice they could either send their best forces out to fight or use these forces at home to organize elections. They could not do both. This failure was linked to the fact that their commitment to liberal principles of free speech, free assembly, free criticism of government allowed the Commune's enemies to regroup in Paris and would have made it very difficult to send the flower of the Commune's youth out of the city to fight. It was linked to the fact that the precipitate transfer of power from the Central Committee to the Commune left the latter without the kind of audacious leadership capable of taking the initiative against Thiers. It was linked to the fact that, although the introduction of elections into the army allowed for the successful expulsion of officers committed to the bourgeoisie, this was not an adequate means of rapidly reconstructing an effective fighting force. This real tension between form and content, democracy and class struggle, was to impress itself on later Marxists looking back on the Commune and attempting to draw from it lessons for their own struggles. Kautsky came down in favour of its democratic form – which he used to contrast with the Bolshevik's dictatorship of the proletariat – and pretended that there was no conflict with its class content. Trotsky came down in favour of its class content and argued that the Commune, like the Bolsheviks, had to forgo temporarily their democratic principles in order to win and to survive. He had the merit of looking the issue square in the face, which Kautsky certainly did not. The immediate dilemmas confronting the Commune were symptomatic of a larger tension between a 'fuller democracy' (Lenin's phrase) as the political form of socialist government and 'dictatorship of the proletariat' (described by Lenin as 'unrestricted power, beyond law, resting on force in the strictest sense of the word') as its class content. It seems to me that Marx posed the problem but by no means resolved it.

Marx's vision of socialist forms of power was based on his knowledge of bourgeois revolutions, of bourgeois theories of power, of bourgeois forms of power and finally on the first faltering attempts at socialist revolution. Marx did not provide a blueprint for the future; but he did draw a sketch of the principles of socialist power, as he saw them. They are not complete nor static; they need to be filled out, expanded and revised in the light of our experience. Forms of socialist power borne out of developed monopoly capital in the 'West' and out of the state bureaucracy that passes for 'socialism' in the 'East' cannot simply mirror the forms established by the Commune. Perhaps there still lingered in Marx a touch of his old master. Was the Paris Commune to Marx what the Prussian monarchy was to Hegel: the embodiment of the idea of the rational state?

# 6. The contradictory foundation of law and the state

## The law-form, the money-form and the generalization of commodity production

Marx warned that in his economic writings he tended to deal with 'the state, law, morality ... only *in so far* as political economy itself professes to deal with these subjects', and Engels in turn commented that he and Marx 'neglected the formal side of political, juridical and other ideological notions – the way in which these notions come about – for the sake of their inner content'.[1] This was not entirely true; as we have seen, Marx and Engels did have many things to say about juridic forms. However, they never traced the logic and history of the development of law and the state in anything like the detail in which they traced the development of money and capital. The connections between private property and value, law and money, and finally state and capital, provide a crucial starting point for analysis of juridic forms. Just as value, money and capital are not things but economic expressions of definite productive relations, so too private property, law and the state are not impersonal abstract entities but juridic expressions of the same relations. Just as Marx sought to unravel the contradictory character of money and capital, so too subsequent Marxists need to unravel the contradictory character of law and the state. This parallel was noted in a fine comparison between state and money found in Trotsky's *The Revolution Betrayed* and approvingly cited by Rosdolsky in *The Making of Marx's Capital*:

> These two problems, state and money, have a number of traits in common, for they both reduce themselves in the last analysis to the problem: productivity of labour. State compulsion like money compulsion is an inheritance from the class society, which is incapable of defining the relations of

man to man except in the form of fetishes, churchly or secular, after appointing to defend them the most alarming of all fetishes, the state, with a great knife between its teeth. In a communist society the state and money will disappear. Their gradual dying away ought consequently to begin under socialism. We shall be able to speak of the actual triumph of socialism only at that historical moment when the state turns into a semi-state, and money begins to lose its magic power. This will mean that socialism, having freed itself from capitalist fetishes, is beginning to create a more lucid, free and worthy relation among men. Such characteristically anarchist demands as the 'abolition of money', 'abolition of wages', or 'liquidation' of the state and family, possess interest merely as models of mechanical thinking. Money cannot be arbitrarily 'abolished', nor the state and the old family 'liquidated'. They have to exhaust their historic mission, evaporate and fall away.[2]

What I have to offer here are some tentative suggestions as to how a Marxist critique of the juridic forms of law and state might be developed on the basis of Marx's critique of the economic forms of money and capital.

Marx analysed in depth the economic expression of the rule of people by 'abstractions': far from exchange co-ordinating the needs of one producer directly with those of another through the direct exchange of use values, their needs are related only through the equation of their products as 'values', and thus through the mediation of money. The fact of this mediation introduces into the classical parable of symmetrical and harmonious exchange, 'antithesis and contradiction':

The simple fact that the commodity exists doubly, its one aspect as a specific product whose natural form of existence ideally contains its exchange value, and in the other aspect as manifest exchange value (money) in which all connection with the natural form of the product is stripped away . . . this double *differentiated* existence must develop into a difference . . . this contradiction between the commodity's particular natural qualities and its general social qualities contains from the beginning the possibility that these two separated forms in which the commodity exists are not convertible into one another . . . As soon as money has become an external thing alongside the commodity, the exchangeability of the commodity becomes bound up with external conditions which may or may not be present.[3]

Money, the embodiment of exchange value in its independent form, is the real abstraction which gains mastery over the people who create it. What Marx only touched upon was the juridic expression of this abstraction. The abstraction of labour is manifest in the form of the value of commodities, in which all trace of the material substance of products disappears and in which they appear simply as a materialization of a certain amount of abstract labour-time. It also manifests itself in the form of the ownership of private property, in which all trace of the material substance of producers disappears and in which they appear simply as free and equal juridic subjects regardless of their real needs or of what they actually own. Like their products, commodity producers also appear in a double form, their natural form and their juridic form. To paraphrase Marx, not an atom of matter enters into the objectivity of commodity producers as owners of private property in contrast to their coarsely sensuous existence as physical human beings. We may twist and turn individuals as we wish; it remains impossible to grasp them as owners of property, as juridic subjects.

Commodity producers are abstracted in this way only because they work independently of each other in private:

since the producers do not come into social contact until they exchange the products of their labour, the specific social characteristics of their private labours appear only within this exchange . . . To the producers, therefore, the social relations between their labours appear as what they are, i.e. they do not appear as *direct* social relations between persons in their work, but rather as *material relations between persons* and *social relations between things*.[4]

The economic expression of this organization of labour, i.e. social relations between things, has been analysed by Marxists at length. Its juridic expression, 'material relations between persons' – persons being treated solely as owners of private property, from this viewpoint only, to the exclusion of all other qualities, needs, desires, etc. – has received comparatively little attention. The simple fact that commodity producers exist doubly as specific individuals with specific needs and as abstracted owners of rights must develop into 'antithesis and contradiction'. This double existence contains from the beginning the possibility that individuals will not be able to translate their needs into rights and their rights back into the fulfilment of their needs. As soon as rights become an external thing alongside the commodity producer, the exchangeability of the property of producers into rights to the property of others – a condition of their survival – becomes bound up with external conditions which may or may not be present. The mediation of relations between people in the form of a contract between free and equal subjects is a strange and mysterious phenomenon, as 'abounding in metaphysical subtleties and theological niceties'[5] as the parallel and simultaneous mediation of relations between two commodities by money. Just as value expresses itself independently, first in the form of money and then in the form of capital, so too ownership of private property expresses itself independently, first in the form of law and then in the form of the state.

With the generalization of commodity exchange, rights of ownership assume the independent form of a 'third party' who represents, in his or her person, rights of ownership in general. Just as a specific commodity – e.g. gold – takes on the social form of money, so too a specific individual or group of individuals takes on the social form of law. In bourgeois countries which emerged out of feudalism this function was played in part, for example, by feudal lords who discovered in their juridic role a lucrative supplement to their private revenues. But just as there is nothing in the nature of gold itself that makes it money, so too there was nothing in the nature of feudal lords to make them 'the law'. While Marx analysed in detail why the development of commodity production necessarily generates money as the objective and independent form taken by exchange value, he only hinted at the parallel process by which it generates law as the objective and independent form taken by private property. I shall tentatively follow his clues.

We have seen that, as owners of private property, individuals differ from themselves as natural, sensuous human beings. In simple exchanges, rights of ownership were immediately identified with producers; it was their immediate quality from which they were soon to split, so that on one side there arose individual producers, and on the other side rights. Law presents rights of ownership to individuals as something different from themselves: in the form of law, producers relate to their rights as something outside themselves. It arises from the essence of private property that a specific person or group will obtain the privilege of representing the rights of all producers. The individuals who don the mantle of law serve as the personification of abstract right – of rights abstracted from particular commodity producers. They acquire this property not by virtue of their natural capacities, nor by virtue of their being themselves commodity producers with their own private interests like everyone else, but by their role in the system of exchange as a kind of 'universal equivalent' in whom all owners of private property seek to represent their rights. Specific individuals are socially selected because of their natural capacities, just as gold was selected as the money commodity because of its natural qualities of divisibility, durability, etc., to serve as the universal equivalent of private rights (but just as the natural qualities of gold do not make it money, so too the natural capacities of these people do not make them the personification of right). Henceforth, commodity producers can bring themselves into relation with one another as owners of private property, indirectly, only by bringing themselves into an opposing relation with some other individuals who serve as the universal equivalent of their rights. The natural form of these persons thereby becomes the socially recognized equivalent form: their word, as it is said, is law; they are the law. The generalization of exchange develops the opposition between the natural individual and the owner of private property which is latent in the nature of the commodity producer and generates the drive towards an independent form of right which 'finds neither rest nor peace' until an independent form has been achieved by the differentiation of commodity producers into owners of private property and the law. Law, then, is a *social* power, the result of the development of social relations of commodity production. The discovery that law is product of human activity was made in the last quarter of the seventeenth century (by Hobbes), but this was merely a first step in discovering how, why and by what means human activity becomes law.

'A negro is a negro and only becomes a slave in certain relations.' Marx used this analogy to show that gold is a mineral that becomes a commodity only in certain relations, and money with the development of these relations. So too a particular individual becomes an owner of private property only under certain relations, and the embodiment of law with the development of these relations. Torn from these relations, an individual is no more law than gold, in itself, is money. Looked at from the other side, just as the abstraction of money is a social form taken by a particular commodity, so the abstraction of law is a social form taken by a particular commodity producer or set of commodity producers. All authority is a relation between people; it is a mystification to contrast a government of laws to a government of people, since a government of laws is but the fetishized form taken by the government of people under certain definite circumstances. Further, the person or persons who embody legal authority are themselves private property owners, albeit ones socially selected to perform a particular function in commodity production; thus it is also a mystification to contrast the rule of law with the rule of private interests, since the rule of law is the fetishized form taken by the rule of private interests under determinate social relations. The law is itself, as Marx commented, a private interest.

## The contradictory functions of law

Marx differentiated the emergence of the form of money from the functions which it is called upon to perform once established. In this manner, rather than assuming the functionality of money, – that is, that money performs its functions rationally and successfully – he explored the necessarily contradictory ways in which it performs its multiple functions and the tensions between its forms and functions. So too he laid the basis for, but did not himself offer, an analogous exploration of the contradictory functions of law. Drawing on Marx's analysis of the functions of money, I offer here some tentative suggestions concerning the functions of law.

The first function of law is to serve as '*a measure of right*' (this is my terminology): commodity producers, as it were, hang a ticket on their products declaring their right to own and exchange them. Since the juridic form of commodities is quite distinct from their real bodily form, 'the guardian of the commodities must lend them his tongue'[6] to communicate to the outside world that they are his or hers. Since the expression of their rights in law is a purely ideal act involving no actual transaction, we may use purely imaginary law to perform this operation. The law does not have to be present in any palpable shape. All commodity producers know that they are nowhere near turning the products of their labour into rights to the property of others, nowhere near realizing their claims to property simply by this statement of ownership. But although the law which performs the function of measure of right is imaginary, the form in which individuals express their property rights depends on the substance of the legal system. For example in a primitive legal system, where one individual simply *is* the law, producers will assert their rights by appealing to the imaginary approval of this individual (like Adam Smith's 'impartial observer'). In a developed legal system, where law is a codified product of many individuals and many generations, the form in which individuals must assert their property rights is by reference to this or that statutory clause or common-law decision. In other words law assumes a second function which depends entirely on its content, that of a *'normative standard'*. The forms in which property owners express their claims depends on the substance of law and will vary from one legal system to the next. As measure of right and as normative standard, the law performs quite different functions. It is the measure of right as the social incarnation of free and equal human labour; it is a normative standard as a self-sufficient body of rules. As a measure of right, the law refers outside itself to convert the labour of commodity producers into legal entitlements; as a normative standard, it refers internally to its own codification, derivation and systematization of norms. This latter function has given rise to the wildest theories, like those of 'legal formalism', according to which the study of law must be limited to that of its own formal arrangements, regardless of its relation to the external world. Confusion arises since any legal term, say, criminal damage, refers both to the rights of property owners and to a conventional body of legal norms. By giving privilege to one or other function of law, a very one-sided view of what law 'essentially' is will emerge: either a 'formalism' (exemplified by Hans Kelsen) which abstracts law altogether from its social content, or an 'abstract materialism' which sees law as no more than an ideological expression of social relations (see Reisner).

These dual functions of law appear sharply in those cases where substantive social issues cohabit with purely formal legal issues. For example during debates on women's suffrage, supporters of votes for women asserted the right of women to vote on the basis of the Reform Act of 1867 which established the right to vote of every '*man*' householder. The argument shifted from the rights of women to the meaning of the legal category of 'man': whether, like the Latin *homo*, it meant human being, male and female alike, or whether it was gender-specific.[7] The democratic argument for women's rights was lost, 'man' was legally defined in its narrow masculine sense. The case reveals, however, that whether women had a right to vote was a question which hung, on the one side, on the recognition of women's labour as equal human labour carrying with it the same juridic entitlements as men's labour; on the other side, it was a question of law which could be determined only by reference to the particular norms of a particular legal order. The assertion of a right of ownership is, similarly, a tricky business, since the owner must look over one shoulder to his or her place in the social relations of production, and at the same time over the other shoulder to a conventional legal system. The normative form of law is compatible with – indeed it will necessarily engender – an incongruity between rights of private property and normative standards, between 'natural rights' and 'positive law'. This possibility is inherent in the normative form itself and, far from being a defect, it makes the normative form an adequate one for a mode of production in which the regulation of labour by society asserts itself only indirectly, after the event, as 'the precarious result of constant irregularities' (Marx). It is only after the event, in the course of exchange, that private producers have their rights to own the products of their labour socially validated in the form of law. If private property rights in one area of production are not reflected in the normative standards of law, then producers will move out of that area of production into another. If, conversely, the normative standard of law upholds rights in one area of production which are not reflected in private property, then producers will move into that area. The normative form of law is not only compatible with an incongruity between rights of private property (as determined by a definite form of labour) and normative standards; it may cease altogether to express private property rights, despite the fact that law is nothing but the objectification of these rights. Things which in and of themselves are not private property, things in which no abstract labour is embodied, like conscience, honour, reputation, etc., can acquire the form of private property through the law; one can be sued or punished for violating rights to them, just as one can alienate them in order to acquire rights to another commodity.

A third function of law is that of *'mediation'* or *'medium of association'* between commodity producers: commodity producers can relate to one another only as owners of private property whose mutual bond takes the legal form of a contract. This, of course, is a *particular* form of human association, entirely different either from one based on personal dependence (a master-servant relation) or from one based on mutual co-operation, concern for each other's needs, etc. The specific character of law as a mediation between individuals is that individuals relate to each other exclusively in terms of the property they own and the rights which they thereby possess, and are indifferent to all other aspects of people. As far as a legal relation is concerned, it matters only that the rights of each party are secured, regardless of all other consequences for the individuals in question. Whether one individual is impoverished and another enriched by relations based on their rights of private property is a question outside the ambit of legal relations themselves. The law serves as a means of inhibition over what one individual may do to another; it states that they must treat each other as free and equal subjects – but only from one point of view, that of property ownership. In legal relations individuals relate to each other solely as means to their private ends; this does not mean that they can act towards others in any way they like, but it does mean that their concern for others is limited to concern for the rights of others as property owners, while everything else about the needs, capacities and desires of others becomes a matter of complete indifference. Subjects of a legal relation relate to each other as autonomous entities, mutually competitive, self-involved, for whom (in Hobbes's image) the law provides the *only* form in which they take into consideration the interests of others.

The last function of law that I shall consider is that of being a *'means of regulating relations'* between people. As such, the law must have a real material existence, a palpable bodily form; it must possess the physical means of adjudicating in disputes between contending parties, of apprehending individuals and of enforcing its decisions. In more developed legal systems, a division of labour grows up between the various functions of apprehension (the police), of adjudication (the courts) and of punishment (the penal system). Law is a specific means of regulating disputes, with its own peculiar characteristics. This is the function of law in which its objectivity and independence stand out most firmly. The law not only arbitrates between conflicting private interests, but also becomes itself a particular interest which enters into disputes with other particular interests and then arbitrates between itself and these other interests. Thus the law may come into conflict with certain kinds of activities which are objected to in the main by the law itself but not by the vast majority of individuals in the community. This seems to have been the case, for example, in eighteenth-century laws against smuggling and poaching. This separation of law as an autonomous force alongside other private interests is inherent in this function of law. The police, to take a modern instance, as a corporate body representative of the law, become a powerful private interest in their own right. From its servile role in which the law appeared as a mere medium of association, a mere mediation between property owners, it suddenly changes into the Lord and God of the world of property owners. With its bodily independence, law now represents not simply the rights of one commodity owner against another, but rather the rights of one particular commodity owner (the law itself) against all others.

Although law possesses a substance of its own, it appears at the same time as the embodiment of the universal rights of all property owners. It is a *general* power, as opposed to its diffusion and fragmentation in a world of private property owners; with the development of law the idea of power in general becomes real. The substance of law is power itself, abstracted from its particular mode of existence: not power through ownership of this or that property, but power as such irrespective of what or whom it is power over. In the form of law, power becomes in itself an object of greed and ambition. There are, however, limits to the independence of law. For law derives from transactions between private property owners and disappears with their termination; its autonomous existence is transitory. When law becomes fully independent of circulation between property owners, then it is no longer merely law but takes on the new social form of the state, as we shall see. In its independence from exchange, law latently contains its potential as the state but is not to be identified with the state.

From the perspective of law, the individual's essence is that of being a property owner, while the real needs, desires, capacities, etc., of the individual appear as mere abstractions, the phenomenal form in which the individual's essence is manifested. From this perspective, rationality consists in acting as the ideal property owner: respect for the rights of others, indifference to others except in regard to their rights, pursuit of self-interest within the bounds of the law, observance of the law. It is this perspective which Hegel and the other representatives of classical jurisprudence reflected and idealized. This is the juridic illusion under which one's formal existence appears as one's real existence, while one's real existence appears as a formality. In its function as regulator of social relations the law needs to exercise real force over individuals, but force appears in a wholly mystified shape. Relations of domination and subordination between people appear in the fetishized form of a relation between reason and unreason. The individuals who function as law serve as mirrors to other individuals of their own rational, human existence; in the activities of those who represent the law, others discover the reflection of their 'true' selves. So it appears that law is on the side of reason, that reason is on the side of law, and that subordination to the law is subordinate to one's own rational being.

This is the basis on which an ideal synthesis of coercion and consent is founded. The law coerces those who oppose it and designates them criminals, but it does so in the name of the criminals themselves. Since criminals appear as violators of a law which embodies the universal rights of all, including themselves, power appears accordingly not as an alien force inflicted by another but as self-punishment, the force of reason over unreason, humanity over inhumanity, conscience over guilt. The real punisher appears as no more than a mirror of, and means of enforcing, the criminal's own rational will and interests. There seems to be no opposition between the criminal and the law, since the law is the personification of the criminal's own sense of right. Power no longer appears as what it is, the subjection of one individual to another, but rather as the realization of reason and humanity. Criminals, as it is said, are punished for their own good and for the good of society as a whole, whether or not they are reformed as individuals and whether or not the punishment succeeds in protecting society. In law, power is exercised in the name of the community; but simultaneously the law becomes the community while the real community appears as an abstraction. In this context violation of the law can appear only as guilt, that is, as a violation of one's own true self. The language of law is indifferent to everything about people and their acts except the categories of 'guilt' and 'innocence', 'liability' and 'non-liability', into which they are forced to fit. The law presupposes that all, as individuals, possess a will, are free and equal human beings – and this is a great advance over the old order – but it recognizes only our will, freedom and equality as property owners. So it sees no contradiction in suppressing with the utmost vigour the real will of individuals in order that their rational will may prevail, in treating people most unfreely so that they may be forced to be free. Law and coercion are by no means counterposed; rather, that coercion should take the form of law is the expression of the fact that private property rules humankind, that the individual's formal existence as a property owner rules his or her real existence as a sensuous human being.

All the contradictions of law emerge most sharply in its functions as means of regulation. The law seems to engender community and common humanity, but at the same time, it produces mutual isolation, indifference and antagonism. The law is predicated on equality, but establishes the sharpest differentiation between the judges and the judged, the police and the policed, the gaolers and the gaoled. The law presupposes universal freedom, but justifies universal coercion precisely in freedom's name. The law posits will and rationality as the universal attributes of humankind, but negates manifestations of will and reason which contravene the dictates of the law. These contradictions lie at the heart of law: between abstract collectivity and mutual antagonism; between abstract equality and the splitting of society into two parts; between abstract freedom and general coercion; between abstract reason and the suppression of reasoning that does not accord with private property; in short, between the juridic form of the individual as property owner and the natural form of the individual as producer, consumer and social being with real individual needs. Various forms of law may correspond better to social production relations at various stages; one form may remedy evils against which another is powerless: but, to paraphrase Marx's discussion of money,[8] as long as they remain forms of law and as long as law remains an essential relation of production, none of them is capable of overcoming the contradictions inherent in juridic relations.

## The state-form, the capital form and capitalist relations of production

Just as money is a developed form of value and capital is a developed form of money, so too law is a developed form of juridic right and the state is a developed form of law. This relation between law and the state has given rise to two opposing kinds of misconception. On the one hand, it may appear that all juridic categories – including 'law' and 'state' – are so many names for the same relation, and this crude inability to grasp real distinctions is represented as a discovery of the inner nature of juridic relations. It seems that there is only one single juridic relation which takes on different names, or that the differences that do occur are not 'fundamental'.

Thus some critiques of 'the legal form' treat the turning of law into the state not as a real transformation of the legal form, but merely as its extension or consolidation. They see that the state emerges out of law but then treat the state merely as a consolidation or quantitative extension of law, rather than as its real transformation. The state appears to embody no principles that are not to be found in the simple legal form itself. The move from law to state should be regarded, like the move from money to capital, as a transition from a lower, simpler form of social life to one that is higher and more complex; in the course of this transition the state acquires properties that go beyond the properties of law as such: 'it can be regarded as a higher realization, as it can be said that man is a developed ape.'[9] Just as, with the transition from money to capital, money does not disappear but rather reappears in a new form and with new functions as money capital, so too, with the transition from law to state, the law reappears in a new form and with new functions as state law. Law as state law possesses properties which transcend its properties simply as law, just as money-capital has properties not possessed by money as such.

Confusion arises when properties belonging to law as state law are attributed to law as such, since the form of appearance is identical in each case. With the emergence of the state, law persists as *one* of the forms taken by the state but not as its *only* form; the state also takes the form of a bureaucracy, an army, an assembly, etc., and law, which pre-existed the state and makes up one of its presuppositions, now becomes only one of the forms assumed by state power. There is, of course, no inevitability that law will grow into the state, in the same way as money does not always grow into capital. None the less, just as 'the concept of value precedes that of capital but requires for its full development a mode of production founded on capital' (i.e the generalization of commodity exchange takes place only with the transformation of commodity into capitalist production), so too the concept of law precedes that of the state but requires for its full development the establishment of the state. It comes as no surprise, then, that bourgeois jurists and their socialist critics sometimes consider the state as the creator of laws (without seeing that it is but a development of law) and sometimes portray it as no more than a sum of laws (without seeing that it expresses a qualitative transformation of law and not just a quantitative aggregate).

The alternative misconception about the relation between law and state is one that divorces the state from law, as if two entirely distinct principles were at stake. It appears that there exist no essential connections between them, or, to put the matter the other way round, that whatever connections do exist are purely contingent. It is imagined by some bourgeois and socialist critics that the 'rule of law' is essentially or originally a system of universal freedom and equality, but that it is perverted by the development of the state. To such a view, the correct response should be that the state represents precisely the development of the system of freedom and equality found in law, and takes to a higher level the contradictions already latent within this system. Just as, to pursue Marx's analogy, the distinctions between ape and human being, money and capital, do not mean that they are unrelated, so too appreciation of the real distinctions between law and state should not lead us to draw a watertight divide between the two, as if one were not the direct progeny of the other.

The state, like capital, is the expression of definite social relations of production. Capital, Marx demonstrated, 'is not a thing but rather a definite social production relation, belonging to a definite historical formation of society, which is manifested in a thing and lends this thing a specific social character.'[10] Thus the definition of capital as, say, accumulated means of production ignores the specific social form of capital: namely, that accumulated means of production become capital only when they are 'mono-polised by a certain section of society . . . and confront living labour-power as products and working conditions rendered independent of this very labour-power'.[11] If the specific form of capital is abstracted away and only its material content is emphasized, then nothing is easier than to demonstrate that capital is a necessary condition of all developed human production. The same argument applies equally to the state. If the state is defined as a means for regulating society, it does not follow that all such means are state means. If the state is defined as an agency of social control, it does not follow that all social control is state control. If the state is defined as something which functions for the reproduction of capitalist relations of production, it does not follow that everything which performs this function is the state. The state necessarily comprises a body of armed men, but not every body of armed men constitutes part of a state. The state administers justice and the police, but not all administration of justice and not all policing are state justice and state policing. The form of the state is what marks its specific social character; if exclusive attention is paid to its material content at the expense of its form, then the state will appear as the necessary condition of any and every complex social order. The first question, then, is to explore the presuppositions of the state form with regard both to its affinity to and distinction from the legal form.

The state realizes the quality which was only latent in law, that of its independent existence outside the process of circulation. In law as such we have seen that juridic rights have already acquired an objective form, but only as a transitory expression of circulation. In the state, the independence and objectivity of law are confirmed with the establishment of a state apparatus which perpetuates and increases itself in the course of circulation. In the simple circulation of commodities, where producers exchange their products for money and then money for products which will be consumed as use-values (the process Marx refers to through the formula C-M-C), law exists independently only as a regulator of the process of circulation; it loses this character as soon as the circulation process is completed and the commodity which has exchanged itself for another commodity through the medium of on the one hand money, and on the other a juridic contract between commodity producers, steps out of circulation in order to be consumed or destroyed. Looked at juridically, the process of circulation requires a move from private owner, to legally enforcible contract, to private owner. In this circuit the independence of law is transitory while private consumption of use-values, the meeting of private needs, or in many cases the failure to meet private needs, is the outcome. The repetition of the process is not presupposed within the conditions of the exchange as such. Simple circulation of this sort does not, as Marx put it, 'carry within itself the principle of self-renewal . . . Commodities constantly have to be thrown into it from the outside, like fuel into a fire. Otherwise it flickers out in indifference.'[12] If one property owner forms a contract with another, then the legal moment disappears as soon as the contract is fulfilled and the parties to it step outside this relation and turn to the direct satisfaction of their respective needs.

As soon, however, as law not only becomes independent of property owners themselves but maintains and develops itself through the process of circulation, then it no longer remains law but becomes the state. The fact that law may, under some historical circumstances, be the first form taken by the state by no means contradicts this development, but does obscure the real transition that is taking place. The circuit of capital which Marx analyses is that of money turning itself into commodities (means of production and labour-power), which turns itself through a productive process into new commodities and then back again into more money; he designates it by the formula M-C-C-M.[13] Viewed juridically, both the beginning and the end of this process require the existence of law; for money – unlike objects of direct need – retains its function as money only in the context of a definite legal order which guarantees the functioning of a particular commodity as money, i.e. legal tender. Self-preservation and self-expansion of law provide the first formal criteria which mark the turning of law into state, that is, the emergence of a state machinery which obtains a real and lasting independence of its own.

With the extension of simple commodity exchange, the various parties to the exchange necessarily establish a legal authority to regulate the circulation process – as was ideally envisaged in the social contract theories of classical jurisprudence – but the objective existence of this legal authority is precarious, dependent on a voluntary transfer of surplus product from the producers to the legal authority. The precondition for the emergence of a permanent state apparatus – and the state, as Marx said, is nothing without its apparatus – is, first, the production of a surplus over and above the immediate needs of the parties to the exchange; and, second, the development of means whereby part of this surplus is channelled into a state machinery. These conditions for turning law into state are met only with the transformation of commodity into capitalist production (though the real history of the state, like the real history of capital, does not follow in any simple way this formal exposition).

With the self-perpetuation of the law as state law, there also develops the differentiation of the state itself. Law becomes now only one of the forms assumed by the state, though historically it often arose as the first form taken by the state. The state constantly changes its particular forms in accord with the new functions it is called upon to perform. It moves perpetually from law, to bureaucracy, to legislation, to armed force, to education to welfare, to police, etc., and it exists at once in all these forms. It is the relation of the state's particular forms to the whole that determines the significance of each of its particular forms. Thus the significance of law in the context of a representative legislature is quite different from the significance of law outside this context. The attachment of law to a developed apparatus of policing and punishment alters the properties of law in comparison with a situation in which law is not so attached. The subsuming of law to a state bureaucracy, with, for example, the bureaucratic appointment of a judiciary, gives to law a social character it would not otherwise possess. Just as money-capital is not the only form of capital, so too state law is not the only form of state. However, this relation between state and law gives rise to great confusion when properties are attributed to law as such which are in fact properties of a particular kind of state law. Thus, some bourgeois and socialist writers ascribe to the law as such democratic properties which it possesses only as one form of a democratic state. Conversely, others ascribe to law as such negative properties – e.g.

being an instrument of class oppression – which it acquires by virtue of its placement within the capitalist state as a whole.

The substantive character of the state lies in its expropriation of power from the mass of the people and its monopolization by a small minority. It is this aspect of the state form which Lenin caught so well in *State and Revolution*: the state is a special force alienated from society, a public power which arises out of society but places itself above it. As an armed force, the state is not the people armed but the separation of armed force from the people and its monopolization by the state. As a police, the state is not the self-regulation of society by its own members but rather the alien regulation of society by a police hierarchy. As law, the state is not merely the administration of justice but, rather, the expropriation of the means of administering justice by the state. As economic regulator, the state is not just planner of production and distribution but represents the loss of these functions for the people themselves. In short, the form of the state presupposes the development of an alien power, separated from the mass of the people.

For such a power to come into being, a definite historical process was required which possessed a twofold character: on the one hand, the separation of the means of exercising legal authority from feudal lords, princes, private capitals and other personal potentates of pre-capitalist society; and on the other, the accumulation of the means of exercising legal authority by a special body of people. This general historical process left its mark on the state in quite different ways in different societies. In previous forms of class society, political power was fused with economic exploitation, as Marx frequently emphasized, and class rule tended accordingly to be the direct rule of one class over another. It was only with the development of capital that class rule began to take the indirect form of state rule. Marx thus dates the beginnings of the state in the declining years of feudalism and in the emergence of merchant capital. Witness, for example, his comments in *The Civil War in France* that 'centralized state power . . . *originating from the Middle Ages . . . developed in the nineteenth century* and with the development of class antagonism *between capital and labour* . . . assumed more and more the character of a machine of class rule.'[14] With this in mind, Engels' brief comments deriving the state from class antagonism in general and characterizing the state as the means of suppression owned by 'the most powerful, economically dominant class', whichever that class may be – comments which have had enormous influence on twentieth-century Marxist theory of the state, both 'revolutionary' (Lenin) and 'reformist' (Kautsky) – did not coincide with Marx's stated views and, more importantly, did not take into account the formal aspects of state power. This 'class-theory' of the state laid itself open to the criticism (which we find in Colletti and Pashukanis) that while it explained the class content of the state, it did not explain why class rule should assume the particular form of state power. Feudalism, for instance, was manifestly a class society but the state-form was largely undeveloped.

Although the state is in general an alien force above society, the form, content and extent of this alienation is, of course, not fixed. The democratic republic is premissed on a degree of alienation quite distinct from, and far preferable to, say, absolutist monarchy, apartheid or a fascist dictatorship. Accountability of the police to democratically representative bodies; access of citizens to state secrets; subordination of bureaucracy to parliament and courts; openness of courts to the public; participation of the public in the administration of justice (albeit in the highly limited role of jury service, in which the sole function of ordinary citizens is to decide on the guilt or non-guilt of an individual under certain restrictive conditions); subjection of what goes on inside police stations and prisons to public scrutiny; rights of citizens not to be subjected by the police to arbitrary search, stop, arrest, detention and interrogation; rights of citizens to organize themselves independently of the state (in free trade unions uninhibited legally from taking collective action, in political movements uninhibited legally from demonstrating political commitments, in self-defence groups against racist attacks or against police harassment), etc., etc. – all such matters inhibit the alienation of the state from society. The erosion of such rights and freedoms marks a change for the worse in the relation of the state to society. At the same time the police, the courts, the bureaucracy, etc., remain from the point of view of society alien powers over which society may exercise more or less influence but which belong to that which is opposed to society, the state. In general, it is as absurd to turn an appreciation of the alien character of the state into a reason for abstaining from democratic struggles as it is to abstract democracy from its alien basis as state democracy.

The opposition between state and labour is the juridic expression of capitalist relations of production, whose economic expression is the opposition between capital and labour. In both cases, living labour constructs forces which stand against it as the alienated form of its own powers. Capital represents the appropriation without equivalent of the products of labour, while the state represents the appropriation without equivalent of the powers of the labourer. Just as the right to the products of one's own labour turns 'through its own necessary dialectic' into the expropriation of the products of one's own labour, at the same time the private right of individuals to dispose of their property as they will turns into the expropriation of this right by the state as the monopolizer of legal authority. The owner of private property, who started life as an autonomous and self-directing atom, becomes the mere bearer of only those rights granted by state laws whose interpretation, application and enforcement are prerogatives of the state itself. Just as capital presupposes the divorce of labour from all commodities except labour-power, so the state presupposes the divorce of labour from all rights except ownership of one's own labour-power. This exception is not insignificant: the juridic freedom and equality of labour distinguish capitalism from other forms of class society and serve as a necessary counterpoint to the power of capital and the state.

The state is the juridic aspect of capital; created by labour, it turns into the antithesis of labour. Thus the state, like capital in general, should be seen not as a thing but as a class relation. The class character of the state lies not merely in who controls it, nor in what functions it performs, but in the form of the state itself; just as the class character of capital in general lies not in the fact that it is controlled by capitalists, nor in the functions it performs, but in capital itself as a social relation. The state is not something alien to capital, it is rather an aspect of capital, a definite form which capital takes in the course of its internal differentiation. The state may thus be transferred from one set of individuals to another and may be put to new uses, but it remains the state, the independent, juridic form taken by the capital-labour relation. As an independent form of capital, the relation between the state and other forms of capital is contradictory. The state is at once a guarantee for the production and circulation of surplus value and itself a drain on surplus value, with its own corporate interests, its own social base, its own needs and pressures. The state derives from private property, but it also becomes an alien form in opposition to private property, since it assumes unto itself the rights associated with private property. The state becomes the real abstraction of the power of capital: an object of greed and ambition in its own right. Private property and the state are complementary poles: dependent on each other for their mutual survival, but antithetical to each other not merely as competitors for the lion's share of surplus value but as embodiments of private right and socialized power respectively. The state represents the socialization of power in an alien, capitalist form; consequently its relation both to capital and to labour is inherently contradictory. Workers need the social power of the state against the private rights of capital, but they do not need the state's alienated form. Capitalists need the state's alienated form as its guarantee against labour, but live in apprehension of its social power. If the contradictory character of the relation between state and capital is missed, then all is missed. The state does not transcend the contradictions inherent in capital; rather, in its own particular way, it necessarily embodies them.

# 7. Twentieth-century theories

## The withering away of law and the state: Evgeni Pashukanis

One of the most serious attempts to collate and to develop Marx's theory of law was made by the Russian legal theorist Evgeni Pashukanis. His most important text, *Law and Marxism*, was written in 1924 as one contribution to the extremely rich theoretical discussions on law and the state which were held in the early years of the Bolshevik revolution. The particular strength of Pashukanis's work was that he sought to derive a Marxist theory of law not merely from this or that occasion on which Marx happened to comment about the law, but from the method which Marx developed in his critique of political economy. He developed both the analogy between and the common derivation of commodity fetishism and legal fetishism, of the theory of value and the theory of right. Thus he analysed law as a historical form of regulation expressing the emergence of definite social relations between individuals, just as Marx analysed value and capital as the expression of definite social relations. Pashukanis demonstrated that the category of 'law' is not a generic category that can be applied to the authority relations of any and every society, but rather a specific category valid only as a representation of a particular kind of authority relation. This constituted a great advance over theories of law which either ignored the form of law and equated law with authority in general, or idealized the form of law, dissociated it from social relations and presented it as the natural and eternal condition of any and every social order. Pashukanis's brief critiques of 'vulgar materialism', i.e. theories of law which subordinate the form of law to its content, and of 'formalism', i.e. theories of law which subordinate the content of law to its form, still stand today as a valid and important starting point for Marxist theories of law.

The political significance of Pashukanis's theory lay in his rejection of economism, in the sense that he saw the transition to communism as signifying not only a transformation of economic relations but, alongside that, also a transformation of authority relations between individuals. His great strength lay in the clarity with which he saw that legal forms of authority have characteristics which make them unsuitable as a basis on which communist society should be regulated, however necessary they may be in the course of the transition to communism.

Pashukanis brought out the fetishism of legal relations, that is, the abstraction of legal subjects from their real qualities as natural and social individuals; the formal character of legal equality and freedom which abstract from rather than overcome the real inequalities and dependencies which mark relations between individuals in society; the manner in which legal relations express and reproduce social relations based on the conflict of private interests, mutual indifference and all-round competitiveness rather than relations based on mutual co-operation, love, comradeship, the collective pursuit of a common goal. Imagine, he said, what a marriage would look like if it were based purely on the defence of private rights and the putting forward of legal claims; such a 'marriage' might be necessary in bourgeois society but could not possibly be the goal of how individuals should relate to one another under communism. A legal relation is a definite kind of relation, which first of all has to be distinguished from other kinds and then has to be criticized from the perspective of the co-operative, communal ways in which individuals should relate to each other under communism, where the atomistic pursuit by individuals of their private interests gives way to the collective pursuit by individuals of their common interests. In private law, Pashukanis writes,

> The a priori assumptions of legal thought are clothed in the flesh and blood of two disputing parties defending their own rights . . . the dogma of private law is nothing more than an endless chain of arguments pro and contra imaginary claims . . . The basic assumption of legal regulation is thus the opposition of private interests. At the same time, the latter is the logical premise of the legal form.[1]

Pashukanis showed how, in the course of their development, legal relations take on the objective form of a third party representing the law, who acts as a mediator between the conflicting claims of rival parties. The fetishism of law is thereby increased, as a social relation of domination between one individual and another appears in the mystified form of mutual subordination to an impersonal authority; authority, in other words, is abstracted from the relations between people of which it is in fact an expression. The 'law' appears as a subject in its own right divorced from individuals; at the same time, it appears as neutral arbitrator between rival claimants, whereas it in fact puts its social weight behind one claimant or another and so 'resolves' disputes by virtue of its power rather than its impartiality. In this role the law represents itself as the public interest, whereas in reality it is one private interest among others. The emergence of the state takes this fetishism to its highest point, since class relations take the form not of direct domination of one class by another but of indirect domination, mediated by the state. This mediation, Pashukanis argued, on the one hand mystifies power, since class domination no longer appears as what it is, and on the other creates a mighty apparatus that crushes society beneath its weight. This was not, Pashukanis concluded, the form of power suitable for communist society. Pashukanis's abstract language may easily obscure the nub of a fine argument, which has its roots deep within Marxism.

At the same time, however, Pashukanis did not simply reflect Marx, he also gave his theory of law his own mark and character, which diverged significantly from that of Marx and in my view signified a regression from Marx and not an advance over him. This divergence was both theoretical and political.

Whereas Marx derived law from relations of commodity production, Pashukanis derived it from commodity exchange. This was the essence of their difference. Marx wrote that 'the relationship of rulers and ruled' is determined by the specific economic form in which unpaid surplus labour is pumped out of direct producers', that is:

> It is always the direct relationship of the owners of the conditions of production to the direct producers – a relation always naturally corresponding to a definite stage in the development of the methods of labour and thereby its social

productivity – which reveals the innermost secret, the hidden basis of the entire social structure.[2]

Pashukanis, by contrast, argued that the elementary legal category from which all other legal categories arise, that of 'juridic subject', emerges out of relations of exchange between what he alternatively calls 'guardians of commodities' or 'owners of private property'. Theoretically, Pashukanis's confusion stemmed from the fact that Marx first wrote about the emergence of juridic forms in *Capital* at the beginning of his chapter on 'The Process of Exchange' and this led Pashukanis – and many others since – to believe that Marx derived juridic forms from exchange, which was not the case and which belied the method he created for analysing economic forms. Pashukanis argued that in exchange, just as the product takes on the form of value, so too the owner takes on the form of juridic subject. But the analogue should not be between produce and owner, but rather between product and producer. It is the producers of commodities who appear in exchange relations as no more than owners of private property, regardless of how they acquired that property, or of what that property comprises, or of what they need to reproduce that property. If one looks only at the surface of society, then – as we have traced in our review of Marx – exchange appears not as what it is, a moment in the cycle of production, but in abstraction from productive relations.

This was the view taken by bourgeois jurisprudence when it idealized the freedom, equality, security and independence of exchangers, but it was also the perspective of Pashukanis when he revealed the dark side – competitiveness, mutual indifference, egoism – of the exchange relation. Marx's analysis – and this is particularly clear in the *Grundrisse* – focused on both these aspects of exchange: it is as erroneous to give privilege to the freedom and equality of exchange relations as their only truth as it is to give privilege to private interest and disregard for others, which they also express. For Marx, the point was to grasp that the form of exchange possesses both these characteristics (i.e. of equality, freedom, etc., and of egoism, mutual indifference, etc.); it was as one-sided of Pashukanis to subordinate equality and freedom to egoism and mutual indifference as it was of bourgeois jurisprudence to do the reverse. Pashukanis offered a 'negative' critique of forms of law which ignored its egalitarian and democratic aspects, in contrast to bourgeois jurisprudence, which offered a 'positive' idealization of forms of law which ignored what have been called its 'effects of isolation and individuation'. Both Pashukanis and bourgeois jurisprudence thereby miss the contradictory nature of legal forms; Pashukanis offered an abstract negation of bourgeois jurisprudence, simply reversing its portrayal of law, highlighting its dark side over its light side, without yet seeing law in, as Marx called it, its 'multi-facetedness'.

On the other hand, Marx revealed that the content of exchange is determined by relations of production and that quite different relations of production (e.g. simple commodity production, capitalist production, state capitalist production, socialist production, etc.) will be expressed and mediated in exchange. Pashukanis and bourgeois jurisprudence have in common their abstraction of exchange from relations of production. The consequence of Pashukanis's abstraction of exchange from production was to give his approach to law an entirely different coloration from that of Marx's (one which lost sight of the dialectic). Instead of seeing both the content and forms of law as determined by and changing with the development of productive relations, Pashukanis isolated law from its content and reduced quite different forms of law, expressing qualitatively different social relations, to a single, static and illusory 'legal form'. Marx expressed the contradictory aspects of the form of law when he wrote that 'the real point' about exchange

> is not that each individual's pursuit of his private interest promotes the totality of private interests, the general interest. One could just as well deduce from this abstract phrase that each individual reciprocally blocks the assertion of others' interests, so that, instead of a general affirmation, this war of all against all produces a general negation.

The real point, he immediately added, is to break from this abstract way of posing the issue and instead relate form to content:

> The point is rather that the private interest is already a socially determined interest . . . its content as well as the form and means of its realization, is given by social conditions independent of all.[3]

Thus, as Marx adds in the *Critique of the Gotha Programme*, both the form and the content of exchange are changed with the transition from capitalist to socialist relations of production, even though exchange itself persists until the communist principle of 'to each according to their needs, from each according to their abilities' finally breaks exchange relations down in their entirety. This whole process, going on beneath the surface of exchange, was made invisible by Pashukanis's theory of law.

Pashukanis derived the legal category of 'juridic subject' from the 'owner of private property' or 'guardian of commodities'. In so doing, he thought he was moving from the juridic form to its social content; in fact, however, the idea of owning private property is itself a juridic form. Instead of moving from a juridic form to its social content, he was in reality moving from one juridic form to another. In other words, Pashukanis never escaped the realm of juridic forms; in spite of his awareness of the pitfalls of formalism, this was precisely what he ended up offering. The problem stemmed from his often-stated conviction that the category of 'abstract juridic subject' is the elementary category of law, whereas it is in fact a developed legal category which depends on the generalization of legal relations. Pashukanis recognized this at one point in his discussion when he observed that in the early stages of legal relations, reflected in feudal custom,

> every right is thought of merely as an attribute of a specific concrete subject . . . Each right was a privilege . . . Each city, each estate, each guild lived according to its law which followed a man wherever he was. The idea of a formal legal status, common to all citizens, general for all people, was absent in this period . . . To the extent that in the Middle Ages the *abstract concept of legal subject was absent*, so also the idea of an objective norm was mixed and merged in the establishment of concrete privileges and liberties.[4]

The elementary legal category is that of 'owner of private property', one in which the individual is still attached to particular possessions and not yet abstracted as a juridic subject in general. While Pashukanis thought that in moving from 'the juridic subject' to the 'owner of commodity' he was moving from the juridic form to its social content, in fact he was moving from a developed legal form to the elementary legal form.

Pashukanis's abstraction of exchange from production led him to offer an entirely abstract critique of law. While he learnt from Marx that equality before the law necessarily entails inequality in fact, he did not appear to learn either that equality before the law provides a measure – albeit limited and formal, but not illusory – of equality, or that the inequalities which it entails are of an entirely different order depending on whether they derive from commodity, capitalist or socialist relations of production. Opposition to inequality in general should not blind us to the distinctions between one kind of inequality and another. At the same time, while he learnt from Marx that exchange gives rise to the legal form, he did not learn that, depending on the nature of productive relations in which it is inserted, exchange gives rise to different legal forms. Opposition to the legal form in general should not blind us to the distinctions between one legal form and another. Pashukanis explained the development of legal forms – from subjective rights to objective law to the state – entirely in terms of the extension, deepening and generalization of exchange relations. Thus, as far as its effects on juridic forms was concerned, Pashukanis saw the transition from petty commodity production to capitalist production and then from capitalist production to socialist production purely in terms of the generalization and restriction of exchange respectively, and not in terms of the transformation of productive relations. Different legal forms seemed to Pashukanis to represent merely the quantitative extent to which exchange was present in society, rather than any qualitative difference in productive relations. Thus all legal forms appeared to him to express the same basic relation of exchange. While Pashukanis's strength was to see the common origins of right, law and state as the three fundamental juridic forms, he failed to perceive the distinctions between them. It was as if an economist were to equate money and capital simply because they both derived from value. This is why class relations appeared to Pashukanis as external and unrelated to the form of the state; in his eyes, the state derived from the generalization of exchange relations and not from the development of capitalist relations of production. Class domination in Pashukanis's theory was therefore reflected in external intrusions into the state – in the buying up of the state by the banks, in the corruption of the state or in the abandonment of the state in favour of direct, naked force; it was concealed by the state-form, but it was not expressed in the state-form. Such were the theoretical limitations of Pashukanis's formalism.

Pashukanis's *Law and Marxism* was not merely an abstract theoretical critique of law but was intended and served as a political intervention into the politics of the transition period. The strength of his intervention lay in his attempt to grasp the transitory function of law in the transition to socialism against those who, on the one hand, wished to abolish law immediately on the grounds that it was a bourgeois form of regulation which had no place in socialist society, and against those who, on the other, uncritically accepted legal forms of regulation as appropriate for communist society and who thus wished merely to substitute proletarian for bourgeois law. To Pashukanis law appeared unequivocally as a bourgeois form of regulation, but also as one which was temporarily necessary under socialism until conditions were such that 'the narrow horizon of bourgeois right' could be transcended in its entirety.

The timeliness of Pashukanis's intervention – *Law and Marxism* appeared in 1924 – was this. In the first period of Bolshevik rule, that known as 'war communism', the erosion of legal forms under the exigencies of civil war gave rise to utopian dreams of moving immediately (as Lenin put it, 'by direct assault') to a society in which law and state would no longer exist, just as the financial breakdown characteristic of this period also gave rise to utopian illusions about the immediate withering away of money. In the second period of Bolshevik rule, that known as 'The New Economic Policy', the restoration of legality, along with that of exchange relations, the market, currency stability, etc., gave rise to conservative ideas of 'proletarian law' and 'proletarian state' which subordinated the Marxist critique of the bourgeois character of law and the state. Against the first tendency Pashukanis argued that 'law could never be higher than the economic conditions of society' and that the Soviet Union was not yet ripe for its abolition; against the second he argued that the concept of 'proletarian law' is a contradiction in terms, given the bourgeois nature of the form of law itself. The long-term goal should remain the withering away of law in its entirety; the immediate prospect, on the other hand, was the gradual withering away of the legal form. It was the strength of this dual critique of legal theory which undoubtedly won for Pashukanis his enormous reputation in the Soviet Union.

Pashukanis traced the logic of the connection between commodity exchange and legal regulation, and on this basis argued for the twofold nature of the transition to communism: it was to be both an economic process involving the replacement of market relations by planned production and distribution, and a juridic process involving the replacement of legal regulation by what Pashukanis called 'technical' forms of regulation. In this respect, the charge that Pashukanis was 'economistic' is not strong, since he conceived of the transition as comprising not only a transformation of economic relations but also a self-conscious and planned transformation of authority relations.

The real problem, however, in Pashukanis's intervention lay in its abstractness. The principal issues which divided left, centre and right in the Soviet Union (personified respectively by Trotsky, Stalin and Bukharin) was not over whether or not there was a connection between exchange and law, but rather over the extent to which and forms in which exchange and legal relations should be reinstituted. The New Economic Policy, and with it the new legal policy, both reflected and brought about a massive proliferation of exchange relations. The key questions concerned, first, the *content* of exchange: to what extent private property rights should be upheld, what were to be the limits of inheritance, to what degree was private employment of labour to be permitted, on what terms was the 'city' to exchange with the 'country', were state companies to have the right to dismiss workers, were workers to have the right to criticize and dismiss their managers, what rights of appeal against the decision of the bureaucracy were to be granted to citizens, what level of wages were workers to receive, were private entrepreneurs to have the right to foreign exchange with external capitalists? etc. But Pashukanis's formalism led him to ignore, or at least relegate, questions of juridic content. This saved him from taking political sides, but it also divorced his analysis from many of the concrete issues of the day. The other key question concerned the *forms* of exchange: how, for instance, were the courts to be organized, were judges to be elected and revocable and if so on what basis, how far would the independence of the judiciary from the bureaucracy be upheld, what rights of working-class organization independently of the state would be upheld, to what extent would the bureaucracy be subordinated to popular representative assemblies, would inner party democracy be restored, what forms would punishment of criminals take? etc. Pashukanis subordinated analysis of the forms of law and state appropriate to socialist transition to the single question of the quantitative reduction of legal regulations. It seemed to him that the transition was marked merely by the gradual restriction of commodity exchange rather than by a transformation of relations of production, and by the gradual restriction of legal relations rather than by their transformation. The struggle for qualitatively new forms of law and state – forms that would be more democratic than any that were possible in bourgeois society – was subordinated by Pashukanis to a struggle simply for *less* law. This abstract perspective was directly associated with a theory of law which derived its development solely from the generalization of exchange and its withering away solely from the restriction of exchange.

The most unfortunate aspect of Pashukanis's approach lay in his conception of the relation between law and state. His emphasis on the 'withering away' of law in anticipation of the 'withering away' of the state meant in effect the subordination of legal forms of the state to the state's other forms, and especially to the bureaucracy. Thus Pashukanis reversed Marx's doctrine of the independence of the judiciary from the executive. In the context of Pashukanis's silence on the question of political democracy, his intervention could only lend support for precisely what Marx saw as the very mark of the alienation of the state from society, namely the uninhibited power of the bureaucracy. This dimension of his work was reinforced by his entirely uncritical embrace of 'technical' forms of regulation as the 'socialist' alternative to law.

He argued that while the opposition of private interests is the premiss of law, 'unity of purpose' is the premiss of 'technical regulation'. In bourgeois society, he believed, both forms coexist, with technical regulation being embodied in the organization of postal and railroad services, military affairs, doctor-patient relationships, the education of criminals, and most important of all – though Pashukanis was not consistent on this one – in the internal organization of the capitalist enterprise. He believed that under socialism, as the state sector gradually won predominance over the private sector, so technical forms of authority would predominate over legal forms. What gave rise to Pashukanis's naively uncritical view of authority relations within the state bureaucracy and enterprises was his blindness to productive relations and his conviction that bourgeois society left its mark only in the form of exchange. For Marx, by contrast, capitalist relations of production determined not only legal forms but also the bureaucratic forms of authority which are instituted within the workplace and within the state. Pashukanis's inability to follow this side of Marx's critique of capitalism led to an uncritical view of the internal relations which characterized the state sector in the Soviet Union. Law is not the only form of regulation assumed by capitalist productive relations, and thus the elimination of law does not entail the elimination of bourgeois forms of regulation *in toto*.

The theoretical source of Pashukanis's concept of 'technical regulation' derived, I believe, from his misunderstanding of Marx's category of the 'technical division of labour'. Marx differentiated in *Capital* between the division of labour in society among independent units of production based on the exchange of commodities, which he called 'social', and the division of labour within the workplace among related units of production based on planned allocation of labour and distribution of products, which he called 'technical'. But by the concept of 'technical division of labour' he did not mean that the division of labour did not take a socially determinate, capitalist form. Every form of co-operative labour, Marx argued, requires that there be instituted some form of regulation in order to accomplish the purely technical task of co-ordinating the various elements within the co-operative labour process. But what form of regulation depends on the social character of co-operation? Marx distinguished between the technical characteristics of co-operation in general (those of increasing the productivity of labour, of socializing individuals, etc.) and the social characteristics of capitalist co-operation (the prime purpose of which is the production and expropriation of surplus value). The problem of imposing discipline under these circumstances is that of imposing capitalist discipline, i.e the regulation by capital of alienated labour.

Since it is only the capitalist who can bring together labourers so as to allow them to co-operate in the labour process, it is the capitalist who appears as the personification of the conditions of social production:

Through the co-operation of numerous wage labourers, the

command of capital develops into a requirement for carrying on the labour process itself, into a real condition of production. That a capitalist should command in the field of production is now as indispensable as that a general should command in the field of battle.[5]

In manufacture, co-operation on the basis of handicraft leaves the independence of the producer partially intact; the task of grinding down this independence gives rise to a special supervisory force. The capitalist

hands over the work of direct and constant supervision of the individual workers and groups of workers to a special kind of wage-labourer. An industrial army under the command of a capitalist requires, like a real army, officers (managers) and NCOs (foreman, overseers) who command during the labour process in the name of capital.[6]

Since handicraft skill is still the basis of manufacture and 'since the mechanism of manufacture as a whole possesses no objective framework which would be independent of the workers themselves, capital is constantly compelled to wrestle with the insubordination of the workers.'

The battles that were fought out between labour and capital moved to a new terrain, however, as capital turned to the introduction of machinery as the basis for meeting the contradictions unleashed between the narrow technical basis of manufacture and the productive forces which it generated. It is always the case formally, in capitalist production, that it is the conditions of production which employ the worker rather than the worker employing the conditions of production. However, 'it is only with the coming of machinery that the inversion first acquires a technical and palpable reality.' The authority of the capitalist was now technically integrated with the very machinery of production, a fusion premissed no longer on the appendage of the tool to the craftsperson but rather on the appendage of the worker to the machine. Thus were born all the illusions about 'technical' control which Pashukanis inherited. Technical forms of regulation were accompanied by the establishment of authoritarian hierarchies of control within the workplace, but these hierarchies appeared as the technical conditions of production:

On the basis of capitalist production, the mass of direct producers is confronted by the social character of production in the form of strictly regulating authority and a social mechanism of the labour-process organized on a complete hierarchy – this authority reaching its bearers, however, only as the personification of the conditions of labour in contrast to labour and not as political or theocratic rulers as under earlier modes of production.[7]

Pashukanis cited this passage but failed to integrate it into his analysis.

Marx's analysis revealed the dual nature of the authority of the capitalist: he is in charge of the technical tasks of co-ordination which belong to any form of large-scale productive enterprise, and at the same time he is in charge of the process of extracting surplus value out of the labour of workers, a task which exists only under certain definite conditions of production. Thus the technical and capitalist functions of the capitalist's control of the workplace coexist, but they assume the appearance of representing the conditions of production alone. The class nature of authority appears as if it were a purely technical authority, even when this authority is imposed in the most arbitrary of ways. What we in fact see here is not technical control but a definite class form of control emerging out of capitalist production relations.

Pashukanis transposed his technicist conception of capitalist productive relations on to productive relations within the state sector of the Soviet economy; he could then pass off bureaucratic forms of control within this sector as merely technical. The theoretical ground was thus cleared for an uncritical view of social relations of production within the arena of state-planned production. Pashukanis – like many other Marxists of the time – conceived of the transition from capitalism to socialism simply in terms of the replacement of commodity exchange by planned production, which he equated with the replacement of bourgeois (i.e. legal) forms of regulation by socialist (i.e technical) forms:

Until the task of the construction of a single, planned economy is realized, so long as the market bond between individuals and groups of enterprises remains, the form of law will also remain in force this long . . . The form of private property remains almost unchanged in the transitional period in small scale peasantry and crafts economy... To the extent that state enterprises are subordinated to the conditions of circulation, so the bond between them is shaped not in the form of technical subordination but in the form of exchange ... Thus a purely legal procedure for regulating relations becomes possible and necessary; however, along with this there has been preserved and with the passage of time undoubtedly will be strengthened direct, that is, technical management... in the form of programmes, production and distribution plans etc ... Its gradual victory will mean the gradual withering away of the legal form in general.[8]

Every co-operative labour process assumes some social form in which technical tasks are fulfilled. There is no way by which the 'technical' can somehow replace the social; no higher form of society is possible in which social forms of control can metamorphose themselves into purely technical forms. What always has to be considered is the interaction of technical and social factors. This is true of capitalist production, but is also true of planned production under socialism. Failure to see this led Pashukanis to accompany his negative critique of legal fetishism with an uncritical adoption of technical fetishism.

Such was Pashukanis's logic in *Law and Marxism*. As the years went by, so the logic was played out. For example, in 1929 Pashukanis accepted Stalin's view that communism was being achieved with the introduction of the First Five-Year Plan, and he drew the conclusion that 'the role of the pure juridical super-structure, the role of law, is now diminishing and from this one can infer the general rule that technical regulation becomes more effective as the role of law becomes weaker and less significant.' This was written at the time when bureaucratic terror and the suppression of independent organization of workers and peasants were reaching a crescendo. Trotsky offered the wry observation, in *Revolution Betrayed*, that when in 1931 Stalin declared that 'the last relics of capitalist elements in our economy have been liquidated', certain 'incautious Moscow theoreticians' took this on faith and inferred the withering way of law and state. Pashukanis, more cautiously, hedged his bets and saved his skin for a few years (until 1937) by positing the abolition of law without the abolition of state. Thus the bureaucratic form of the state was to survive as the embodiment of technical regulation, while the legal form was to wither away as the embodiment of bourgeois fetishism. Not only did Pashukanis invert the relationship between law and bureaucracy envisaged by Marx, he lost all sight of the democratic nature of Marx's critique of the state, according to which its withering away was to be the result of its ever more radical democratization. Pashukanis's over-critical view of law, combined with his uncritical view of bureaucracy, formed an unfortunate mixture, especially in the context of a regime which increasingly identified the bureaucracy with the state and the state with the people.

### Rule of law and class struggle: Edward Thompson

*Appreciation*
One of the great strengths of Edward Thompson's recent contributions to Marxist theory of law and the state lies in the close ties he draws between theory and politics. In a period in which theories of law and the state have often been confined to academe and dissociated from class struggle, Thompson's passionately polemical concerns come as a welcome antidote to the dangers of academicism and sterility facing contemporary Marxism.

Thompson's polemic was directed against threats to civil liberties and democratic rights emanating from the modern state. In the terms of his own preferred imagery, the branches of the 'liberty tree' are being lopped off one by one by the state, and the 'free-born Englishman' is in danger of becoming a chattel to state power. Thompson's list of attacks on liberty is a long one. It includes

> the management of news, the blackmailing of politicians, the political vetting of civil servants, the clipping of the coinage of civil liberties, the enlargement of police powers, the dissemination of calumny against dissenters, the corruption of the jury system, the surveillance and intimidation of radicals, the management of state trials, the orchestration through the media of a 'law and order' *grande peur* and the cry of 'national interest',[1]

not to speak of the rapid erosion of trade union rights to strike in sympathy with fellow-workers, to picket or even, under some cicumstances, to belong to a union. The principal 'muggers of the constitution', to employ Thompson's vivid phrase, are not the 'criminals, terrorists and subversives' upon whom blame is heaped by the right; they come rather from the state itself – not from below but from above.

In the context of this drift toward an authoritarian state it is essential, Thompson argued, that modern Marxism put its own house in order: its ambivalence about civil liberties and its tendency to dismiss all law as merely an instrument of or camouflage for class rule must be abandoned. If civil liberties are merely an illusion obscuring the harsh realities of class rule, then the only significance of their loss is that it clarifies the class struggle. If law is merely an instrument of capital, then attacks on democratic rights initiated by the state present no danger to the working class. If all states are 'inherently profoundly authoritarian' and if all inhibitions on their power are 'masks or disguises or tricks to provide it with ideological legitimation', then the move from one form of state to another will appear to make no essential difference, and the erosion of inhibitions on state power will merely clarify its repressive nature. Such a rhetoric, Thompson argued, reduces Marx's democratic critique of the state to no more than a cynicism; it has nothing in common with genuine Marxism and is bankrupt historically, theoretically and politically.

Politically, cynicism leads to a dulling of 'the nerve of outrage' when liberties are removed. If rights are just an illusion covering up exploitation and oppression, then they are not worth fighting for. Historically, cynicism leads Marxists to devalue popular struggles against wealth and power for the achievement of political liberty. On the basis of twentieth-century experience, 'even the most exalted thinker' ought to be able to note the difference between a state based on the rule of law and one based on 'the exercise of arbitrary, extra-legal authority'. If the only significant distinction observed is that between different 'modes of production' – feudal, capitalist and socialist – then distinctions which are equally important, between one form of bourgeois rule and another, are lost from sight. Political liberty under bourgeois rule is not just a device of capital but represents the tangible achievement of struggles from below, and can be secured only through the continued pursuit of such struggles.

Theoretically, Thompson polemicized against an 'essentialism' according to which 'a platonic notion of the true, ideal capitalist state' is substituted for analysis and critique of actual capitalist states in all their diversity. He attacked the base-superstructure model which presents law as merely 'part of the superstructure of productive forces and relations'. He rejected the 'reductionism' in which the law appears to define 'what shall be property and what shall be crime' in ways necessarily 'confirming and consolidating class power'. Law, Thompson argues, should be seen not just as an instrument of class domination, nor just as a force that functions for the reproduction of class relations, but also as a 'form of mediation' between and within the classes. Its function is not just to serve power and wealth but also to impose 'effective inhibitions upon power' and to subject 'the ruling class to its own rules'. It acts not just as a means of repression but also as 'a defence of the citizen from power's all-inclusive claims'. It not only throws a veil over the class struggle, it also shapes it. If law is to be effective as a form of legitimation for the rulers, then the rulers must to some degree live up to its own universal and egalitarian standards.

Thompson rejects the major theoretical premiss which under-writes these tendencies within Marxism: that is, the isolation of the law as a distinctive part of the 'superstructure' separate from its 'base'; or, in structuralist language, the conception of law as a determinate 'level' separate from that of 'economics' (the determining level), politics and ideology. These abstractions, he argues, afford a Marxist legitimation for 'carrying on with age-old academic procedures of isolation which are abjectly disintegrative of the enterprise of historical materialism, the understanding of the full historical process'.[2] It is not possible to understand law in isolation from productive relations, just as it is not possible to understand productive relations in isolation from law. They intermingle so intimately that the isolation of one from the other can be done only by means of a forced abstraction. Thus he writes of his studies of the eighteenth century:

> I found that law did not keep politely to a 'level' but was at *every* bloody level; it was imbricated within the mode of production and productive relations themselves (as property rights, definitions of agrarian practice) and was simultaneously present in the philosophy of Locke; it intruded brusquely

within alien categories, reappearing bewigged and gowned in the guise of ideology; it danced a cotillion with religion, moralizing over the theatre of Tyburn; it was an arm of politics and politics was one of its arms; it was an academic discipline, subjected to the rigour of its own autonomous logic; it contributed to the self-identity both of rulers and of ruled; above all, it afforded an arena for class struggle, within which alternative notions of law were fought out.[3]

In other words, productive relations are meaningful only in terms of their definition at law: 'men enjoyed petty property rights or agrarian use rights whose definition was inconceivable without the forms of law.' What unites these different 'levels' or 'instances' – or rather what makes problematic their initial separation – is the fact that they reflect the unitary experience of real historical actors:

We are talking about men and women, in their material life, in their determinate relationships, in their experience of these and in their self-consciousness of this experience . . . class experience will find simultaneous expression in all these 'instances', 'levels', institutions and activities. It is the 'same unitary experience' which gives rise to fear of the crowd in 'politics' reappearing as contempt for manual labour among the genteel reappearing as Black Acts in the 'law' reappearing as doctrines of subordination in 'religion'.[4]

Productive relations, in other words, are themselves legal, political and cultural as well as economic; the relation between capital and labour is one whose class character appears only via its multiple forms of expression. Law is not a servant of economics, even in the last instance; they both reflect, rather, the same 'unitary' class experience. Indeed,

the very category of economics – the notion that it is possible to isolate economic phenomena from non-economic social relations, that all human obligations can be dissolved except the cash-nexus – was the product of a particular phase of capitalist development.

Capitalist society is founded upon 'forms of exploitation which are simultaneously economic, moral and cultural'; social and cultural phenomena, like the law, do not 'trail after the economic at some remote remove' but are, rather, 'immersed in the same nexus of relationship'. If we accept the metaphor of base-superstructure, the base should be seen as 'not just economic but human – a characteristic human relationship entered into involuntarily in the productive process'. Law is as immediate an aspect of this human relationship as is economics. Just as Marx submitted economic categories to 'the test of history', so too, Thompson argues, legal categories must be submitted to the same test: not reified as a self-sufficient and eternal sphere of social life but grasped as the historical expression of definite productive relations.

The reverse side of the coin of cynicism towards law and the state, Thompson argues, is an equally dangerous doctrine which identifies Marxism with the 'bureaucratic statism' both of the official labour and social-democratic parties in the West and of Stalinism and its heirs in the East. This doctrine portrays the state 'in *all* its aspects' as a 'public good, a defence of working people or of the little man against private vested interests'. A distinction must be made, Thompson maintains, between the different elements of the state. While the legal and representative institution of the state constitutes its democratic element, the bureaucracy constitutes the omnipresent danger to democracy. Despotism, Thompson concludes, means the subordination of the state as a whole to bureaucracy; liberty means the subordination of the bureaucracy to control by parliament and the law. The consequence of the bureaucratic statism of the official left is that 'the dividing line between the welfare state and the police state became obscure and bureaucracy in every form waxed fat in this obscurity.' The welfare state is not the same as the police state, but the elevation of the state executive in the former paves the way for the emergence of the latter.

The key concept Thompson invokes in his critique is that of 'the rule of law': its presence or lack of presence marks, in his view, the difference between liberty and despotism. The importance of Thompson's approach is that it restores the classic liberal usage of the concept of 'the rule of law' against its corruption in contemporary conservative thought. According to the latter, whatever the state dictates is law and the doctrine of the 'rule of law' means an unconditional obligation to obey the state's laws, regardless of their form or content. From this point of view, according to which law is defined only in terms of its origin, any measure enacted by the state – even the most draconian police measure – is law. The state cannot, by this account, violate the rule of law, because it appears as its embodiment. The classical liberal conception of the rule of law, by contrast, was based on what Thompson called a 'bloody-minded' distrust of the state. The state's commands were legitimate only if they accorded with definite formal standards of conduct. The state could not do anything it wished and declare it to be law; rather the state remained a bona fide state – and not a mere private force – only if it followed dictates associated with the rule of law. Thus a doctrine which started off as offering an ideal against which existing states should be measured, as an inhibition on state power and as a precaution against despotism, has been turned by modern conservatism – in the name of liberalism, Adam Smith, etc. – into a travesty of its former self. It has become little more than an apology for state power. Thompson has performed a great service in returning to the liberal ideal of the rule of law in order to expose the poverty of present-day conservatism. This usage of the concept of 'rule of law' also reveals the shortcomings of a Marxism which either reduces law to class dictatorship or elevates the state as a whole as a human good.

Thompson's depiction both of 'statist' and 'nihilistic' currents within contemporary Marxism is somewhat caricatured; there are few Marxists or Marxist movements which fit neatly and four-square into either of these images. His target is often broad and he tends to conflate diverse currents; for example, a dismissive attitude to law affects some kinds of 'libertarian' Marxism which reject all forms of authority equally, including law, and some kinds of 'authoritarian' Marxism which reject all forms of inhibition on working-class power, including legal inhibitions. Their common position on law should not obscure their distinct starting points, even though it may facilitate a movement from one to the other. Sometimes Thompson's target is misplaced, as when his offhand dismissal of 'Leninism' cuts a swathe through the historical record of Lenin's firm commitment to struggles for political liberty. However, the general thrust of Thompson's critique of statist and nihilistic currents within Marxist theory of law and the state is in my view pertinent, correct and in accord with Marx's own writings.

The problem lies not in Thompson's critique as such, but in the alternative he puts forward. In rejecting 'economism' and the 'vulgar Marxist' conceptions of law and the state with which it is associated, Thompson comes close to abandoning Marxist criticism of the rule of law in its entirety in favour of a resuscitated liberalism. In itself this is, of course, no fault; we should not adhere to Marxism dogmatically. I wish to show, however, the contradictions inherent in Thompson's alternative, not in order to return to economism but rather to deepen and extend a Marxist critique of it.

## Critique

Thompson's repeated comment that the rule of law is 'an unqualified human good' is not only a case of his bending the stick too far away from legal nihilism and from bureaucratic statism. After all, the rule of law does not have to be an unqualified human good for its superiority over authoritarianism to be recognized and acted upon. There is no doubt but that liberal forms of bourgeois rule are preferable, from the point of view of democracy and the working class, to authoritarian forms, even though both remain forms of bourgeois state based on class exploitation. The liberal state does not have to be abstracted from its class content for its value to be recognized and its institutions to be defended against forces of reaction. That Thompson's defence of the rule of law was unqualified reveals the shortcomings of his general method.

Thompson's initial rejection of reductionism turns into its opposite when he too reduces the multiple functions of law to one essential function: that of inhibiting power. From an initial position which held that law is not only a means of domination and obfuscation but also a restraint upon the state and a defence against repression, Thompson concludes that the defining characteristic of the rule of law lies in the one function of inhibition. His objections to monolithic views of the function of law do not prevent him from replacing one monolith by another. He recognizes other functions but sees inhibition as essential. A critical understanding of the rule of law requires that we comprehend the many functions of law and the conflicts between them; not that we give privilege to one function of law as law's essence.

So, too, Thompson's original argument that the law should be seen not just as an instrument of one class or another, nor simply in terms of its functions or for reproducing class relations, but also in terms of its form of mediation gives way to Thompson himself reducing the form of law to its function. In his view, the form of law is defined by its function of inhibition, with the result that the specific characteristics of legal inhibitions on state sovereignty are lost from sight. Law is not the only form of inhibition on state power; there are also the political institutions of representative democracy, not to speak of the independent organization of the working class on one side and the interests of capital and of other states on the other. The law possesses definite social characteristics as a means of inhibition on the power of the executive – and definite limits. It tends to work through individual cases, thus bringing with it the danger that it might 'individuate' the collective struggles of the working class. It imposes formal standards of comparability which might neglect the unequal class consequences of executive policy and practice. It imposes sanctions only after the event, that is, after a specific abuse of power by the executive has taken place. It functions through the mediation of courts, the judiciary, and the legal profession, who have their own specific class characteristics. For instance, the law serves as a vital inhibition on the power of the police: it requires the police to bring detainees to court; it allows for civil suits and criminal prosecutions against the police; it permits the judiciary, under certain (ever more restricted) circumstances, to exclude evidence improperly obtained by the police; it provides a public forum in which the police may be interrogated. But it is not the only form of inhibition on the police; there are also political restraints in the shape of local authority police committees and parliament, and unofficial restraints in the shape of trade-union picket lines, self-defence groups and, on the other side, those arising from the organized pressure of capital. In this context legal inhibitions on police power, while remaining a vital means of defending individual liberty and working-class democracy, possess limitations that derive from the form of law itself and which therefore naturally lead working-class organizations to weigh up, in any given situation, the strengths and weaknesses of the various means, including, but not restricted to, legal means by which police powers may be inhibited. Such considerations are ruled out theoretically when the form of law and its function of inhibiting state power are fused together as one.

The definition of law as an inhibition of power presupposes the existence of a power alienated from the people, which needs to be inhibited. In the early stages of liberal thought the idea of the rule of law was invoked to inhibit the authority of the absolute sovereign, but not to transform the nature of the state itself. In later stages the idea of the rule of law was tied to the transformation of the state itself from absolutism to liberalism and thence to democracy. By picking up on the 'inhibitory' rather than the 'transformative' side of this liberal concept, Thompson presupposes the presence of the alien power of the state. To see the rule of law as an unqualified good, then, means accepting the presence of the bourgeois state as given and immutable. This 'pessimistic determinism', to use Thompson's own term, appears in his projections of the socialist future, where Thompson surmises that even the rise of working-class power, based on egalitarian productive relations, will require 'the negative restriction of bourgeois legalism', and concludes that any belief to the contrary is a 'utopian projection' without historical warrant. While this position reflects a well-justified rejection of the claims of various socialist states to have overcome their alienation from the people – the very idea of the state, according to Marx, socialist or otherwise, implies an alienation from the people – it explicitly surrenders the vista offered by Marx of the democratization of the state to the point of its dissolution. While Marx saw a place for legal inhibitions on state power as long as the state existed, he also saw, as the final goal of communism, the dissolution of the state, and with it the need for inhibitions on its power. The more immediate significance, however, of this theory of 'inhibition' can be again seen in the example of the police: far from challenging the institution of the police itself, Thompson justifies its existence by reference to its legitimate functions of internal regulation without asking in what ways these functions could be performed other than through the hierarchical bureaucracy of the police, and seeks only to inhibit its powers through legal controls. The perspective of transforming the police from a corporate entity above society to a function democratically controlled by society gives way to the more limited perspective of inhibiting police power.

Thompson's defence of the rule of law as an unqualified good does not mean that he is blind to the class nature of the actual deployment of law, but he conceived of class domination as an intrusion of 'class-bound procedures' into law and not as an essential characteristic of law itself. Thus he has himself demonstrated how, when considered as an institution ('the courts with their class rhetoric and class procedures') or as personnel ('the judges, the lawyers, the justices of the peace'), the law may be assimilated to the needs and interests of the ruling class:

> But all that is entailed in 'the law' is not subsumed in these institutions. The law may be seen as ideology or as particular rules and sanctions which stand in a definite and active relationship (often in a field of conflict) to social norms; and finally it may be seen simply in terms of its own logic, rules and procedures, that is, simply *as law*.[5]

In other words, although Thompson is well aware of the class forces which affect the actual administration of law, he argues that the rule of law contains at its core a 'logic of equity' that is above class determination, and held that his own historical studies support his case. This is at first sight surprising, since they relate for the most part to the ways in which the ruling class and the state have turned the law into little more than an instrument of their own private interests and how economic forces

> actually grabbed hold of the law, throttled it and forced it to change its language and to will into existence forms appropriate to the mode of production, such as enclosure acts and new case-law excluding customary common rights.[6]

But for Thompson the determination of law by its economic base reflects not the essence of law but its distortion. Concerning his study of the bloody Black Acts of the eighteenth century, Thompson comments that it was 'centred upon a bad law, drawn by bad legislators and enlarged by the interpretation of bad judges'. Far from being an indictment of the rule of law itself, it was rather an indictment of the 'corruption' of law: 'We feel contempt not because we are contemptuous of the notion of a just and equitable law but because this notion has been betrayed by its own professors.'[7] It is the idea of law which stands, for Thompson, as the standard against which to measure the actual corruption of law:

> If I judge the Black Act to be atrocious, this is not only from

> some standpoint in natural justice and not only from the standpoint of those whom the Act oppressed, but also according to some ideal notion of the standards to which the 'law', as a regulator of human conflicts of interest, must always seek to transcend the inequalities of class power which, instrumentally, it is harnessed to serve.[8]

In other words there exists, according to Thompson, a core component in the idea of law, which is not locatable in a base-superstructure model and which is not reducible to the logic of a class-based functionalism or instrumentalism.

In these passages Thompson comes close to reproducing the 'essentialism' which in his theoretical programme he sought to exorcize. The 'idea' of law is abstracted from its actual deployment in bourgeois society, so that its external manifestations appear as a corruption of its essence. The key question, then, is to identify the rational kernel of law apart from its mystical and class-ridden shell. If we transfer vegetable metaphors, as Thompson peels away the corrupted outer layers of the onion he may find that it is an arbitrary decision where its rational heart begins. Thompson himself is not very helpful in identifying what he means by the idea of law. At times he refers to the principle of equality embodied in law, which provides a minimum guarantee of liberty in spite of the limitations of its formal character. At times he refers to the principle of 'equity', which in legal terms refers to the use of discretionary powers by the courts to compensate for unfair decisions emanating from the rigid application of formal rules. In one passage he defines the rule of law as 'the regulation of conflicts according to rules of law which are exactly defined and have palpable and material evidence – which rules attain towards consensual consent and are subject to interrogation and reform'. At other times he seems to include in his idea of the rule of law more substantive notions about parliamentary democracy, individual liberty and labour movement rights of organization. In his essays on the state of the nation, he presents the libertarians of the left as the protectors of the 'institutions of this country': 'not the law-and-order brigade but the defenders of civil liberties are attempting to uphold the constitution and the rule of law.' In this version, the rule of law would appear to refer to the judicial wing of the bourgeois state that existed up to the recent wave of attacks on traditional liberties. The fact that 'the rule of law' is for Thompson an elastic concept does not mean that it is purely rhetorical. But it does allow him to slip from a position that correctly asserts the significance of formal equality and freedom before the law as a minimum guarantee of liberty to one that depicts twentieth-century British justice as the incarnation of the rule of law. Thompson rightly rejects the dangerous conclusion that, because equality before the law is merely formal or negative, it should be discarded in favour of substantive justice. This is a view which has historically been adopted by the right (see, for example, Franz Neumann's account of Nazi 'legal theory' in *Behemoth*) even though the grounds for it have sometimes been laid by the left. But he draws the equally untenable conclusion that the principal institutions of the liberal bourgeois state – parliament, jury trial, 'independent judiciary', 'impartial' police, etc. – are not only preferable to authoritarianism but are the last word in a free society.

## The historical record

Thompson claims to draw his theoretical conclusions about the rule of law from his historical studies; however, the main theme which runs through his historical writings on the eighteenth century is a different one: that of a struggle between laws representing absolute and exclusive rights of bourgeois private property and popular movements – falsely defined as criminal by the upper classes and by subsequent orthodox historians – holding on to the use-rights of the traditional moral economy. Thus in *The Making of the English Working Class* (1963) he writes that the food riots were 'a last desperate effort of the people to reimpose the older moral economy as against the economy of the free market . . . a last desperate attempt to enforce the old paternalist consumer-protection'. In *Peculiarities of the English* (1965) he argues that until the late eighteenth century

> the common people adhered to a deeply felt 'moral economy'
> in which the very notion of an 'economic price' for corn (that
> is, a dissociation between economic values on the one hand
> and social and moral obligation on the other) was an outrage
> to their culture . . . The very category of economics – the
> notion that it is possible to isolate economic from non-

economic social relations, that all human obligations can be dissolved except the cash-nexus – was the product of a particular phase of capitalist evolution.

Plebeian movements in the eighteenth century and working class movements during the industrial revolution should by this account be read as 'a movement of resistance to the annunciation of economic man' and to the laws which heralded it. The 'Marxist humanism' which Thompson represents thus looks back to these struggles with particular favour, since they were valiant attempts, analogous to modern struggles to attain humane welfare services, to hold on to human values in the context of economic dehumanization.

In *Whigs and Hunters* (1975) Thompson pursues this theme in his account of the Black Act, which 'signalled the onset of the flood-tide of eighteenth century retributive justice'. He argues that the Act represented the culmination of a social and economic struggle through which a 'customary' economy of forest-dwellers was destroyed and replaced by a market-oriented regime based on 'capitalist property rights'. In Thompson's view, 'the forest conflict was in origin a conflict between users and exploiters.' During the eighteenth century 'one legal decision after another signalled that the lawyers had become converted to notions of absolute property ownership and that . . . the law abhorred the messy complexities of coincident use-right.' The traditional rights of the poor either received 'perfunctory compensation' or were simply redefined as crimes. Thus the Blacks (the poachers and forest-dwellers against whom the Black Act was directed) shared something of the character of Hobsbawm's social bandits: they enforced the definition of rights to which the country people were habituated and resisted the development of laws protecting the rights of absolute and exclusive private property. The dominant motif of *Eighteenth Century British Society* is that 'plebeian culture is rebellious in defence of custom':

> capitalist logic and 'non-economic' customary behaviour are in active and conscious conflict as in resistance to new patterns of consumption . . . of time-discipline and to technical innovation or work rationalization which threaten to disrupt customary usage . . . Hence we can read eighteenth

century social history as a succession of confrontations between an innovative market economy and the customary moral economy of the plebs.[9]

Thompson does at times modify this version of events. In '*The Making* . . .' he shows how this appeal to the past was sometimes no more than a cloth in which thoroughly new rights were dressed. 'All reformers before Paine', he commented, 'commenced with the "the corruption of the constitution" ', the constitution in question being imaginary versions of the Revolution of 1688 or even of old Saxon law. Such antiquarian arguments were even used to justify the modern demand for manhood suffrage. So too in '*Eighteenth Century* . . .' Thompson distinguished between the form and content of popular rebellious culture: 'this is a conservative culture in its forms; these appeal to custom and seek to reinforce traditional usage . . . But the content of this culture cannot so easily be described as conservative.' However, the general picture he painted about food-rioters, poachers, Blacks, smugglers, wreckers, writers of anonymous threatening letters and the like was one of plebeian rebellion in defence of traditional use-rights against laws representing unequivocally the requirements of the newly emergent capitalist economy.

Two questions arise: first, how well does this account fit the facts, and second, how much support does it offer to Thompson's defence of the rule of law? On both counts, there are problems.

It is an oversimplification – and ultimately wrong – to reduce all these eighteenth-century struggles to a conflict between traditional use-rights and legally enforced private property rights. 'Plebeian' rebellion crossed class lines and many of its participants were advocates of, and not rebels against, absolute property rights. Although I am not qualified as a historian of the eighteen century, on the basis of Thompson's own historical evidence the picture seems to be more mixed than he allows and less easily fitted into the mould of 'primitive rebellion'.

For example, the popular struggles of poachers and foresters against the Black Act were supported by a cross-class alliance of some small gentry, peasants, capitalist farmers who rented land, labourers, merchants and craftspeople. This broad support arose from the particular class character of poaching laws which declared that, to be eligible to hunt game, one had to be a freeholder earning a minimum of £100 a year. This included the large gentry landowners and excluded all others. Thus capitalist farmers were opposed to these laws because they were excluded from a privilege reserved for the large gentry, because they were deprived of valuable rights to the use of land reserved for the pleasures of the hunt, and because the hunt caused damage to their farms.

It is not surprising, therefore, to find 'middling men' among the foremost in protest against these laws as an 'unconstitutional oppression'. Further, as the commercial exploitation of game by innkeepers, poulterers and victuallers became more viable, so too their resentment against game laws, which prohibited the selling of game, joined up with the resentment of the farmers. Game was important, as Doug Hay put it, because it symbolized 'land' against commerce:

> Game laws were the only enforceable remnant of the mass of statutes that once fixed status among Englishmen . . . Game could not be legally bought and sold because it was meant to symbolize prerogatives, to show that its owner held power and prestige in landed society.[10]

It was, in short, a traditional form of property right that the game laws expressed. The large gentry were – if we are to believe Christopher Hill's account – less concerned with the setting in motion of productive forces characteristic of productive capital than with the appropriation of a finished product:

> Landlords sought prestige through conspicuous investment rather than conspicuous consumption – buildings, parks, paintings. But such investment, though it created some employment, stimulated the economy far less than a planned programme of investment in the capital goods sector and in improving communications would have done. [11]

The form of the game laws was itself archaic. They set up the right to hunt game as an exclusive privilege of the landed gentry, and achieved this through property qualifications. Such laws were first established in 1389, when the qualification for hunting 'gentlemen's game' was set at owning a freehold worth at least £40 a year and lasting 99 years. Wealth itself, unconnected with the land, was excluded from such privileges. In other words, the law recognized privileges based on property qualification; it embodied differential rights and duties based on rank and status. The bourgeois conception of the rule of law that accompanied the development of bourgeois private property, by contrast, was based on the abolition of legal privileges.

The administration and implementation of the law was equally imbued with traditional elements. The basis of law enforcement was the 'manor'. The lord of the manor had the power to appoint a gamekeeper who served public and private functions at once: his public function was to enforce the law, his private function was to serve as servant of the landowner. The sharp division between public and private functions established within liberal legal thought was not yet present.

The same interpenetration of the public and the private was present in the judicial system. Thompson demonstrated the direct links between landowners and the judiciary, with little evidence of that separation of powers advocated by liberalism and established only in the nineteenth century. Doug Hay has demonstrated how the extensive use of discretionary 'crown pardons' by the judiciary was given on the basis of personal pleas of mercy by the local gentry. It held the victim in a position of personal debt to the landlord and expressed the explicit employment of mechanisms of social control based on personal dependence. Terror and obligation were the two sides of this relation of direct domination. Even the execution of the penalty displayed this traditional class character. The public hanging was a military ceremony which manifested the coercive power of the monarch over his people. Punishment was not applied in the name of the 'people', as became the case in the bourgeois epoch, but was imposed over the people as a show of superior might. It was a ceremony which was intended to manifest the direct domination of the rulers over the ruled or, as Hay put the matter, an exercise in 'terror'. The execution was done in public and the penalty was painful (the victim was choked to death by the hangman's noose rather than having his neck 'painlessly' broken) so that the people might witness the power of the ruling class at work and even see the personal prerogative of the king or the landowner in the case of a last-minute pardon. If offenders were not hanged, they might be transported to the colonies in privately-owned boats, and on arrival would be subjected to forced labour on behalf of private property. If, by chance, offenders went to prison, they would find the prisons run for profit by their keepers, and explicit divisions based on rank and wealth practised within them.

The game laws, in short, cannot be seen simply as the embodiment of bourgeois private property, nor can opposition to them be simply fitted into the category of defence of a traditional moral economy. The rebels were as much concerned with the emancipation of private property from traditional fetters as with the defence of use-rights. This side of the question slipped into Thompson's own account in *Whigs and Hunters*, when he commented on the 'archaic' character of the crown's claims and of the laws which declared that land, whether or not privately owned, 'might not be fenced so high that the deer could not pass through them to their customary feeding grounds'; that 'no timber could be felled without licence from the forest officers'; and that deer 'might not be killed on any pretence whatsoever'. In these instances the forest struggles might equally be real as a popular defence of absolute private property over traditional use-rights claimed by the crown.

The case of excise laws raises similar problems. Widespread popular opposition to them arose from the narrow class interests which these laws expressed. They articulated an alliance between monopoly trading companies – like the East India Company – and the state. For the former, a royal charter meant monopoly rights as well as the protection of the British navy over their trading routes. For the latter it meant a lucrative source of income. It represented the supremacy of merchant capital and a mercantile state.

Opposition to the excise laws came from merchants and 'middling men' desirous of gaining some share in the lucrative international trade in tea and other reserved commodities; from the middle classes eager to see lower prices for tea – both for their own sakes and to lower the value of labour-power – and from the 'poor', for whom smuggling meant, for some, work on ships or the opportunity to get a foot in the door of commodity exchange, or at least access to what had been luxury commodities on the popular market.

It would appear inadequate to present smuggling as a 'plebeian' activity based on the defence of an 'older moral economy'. In the earlier years of the eighteenth century smuggling was predominantly the business of small entrepreneurs who acquired the capital necessary for the pursuit of this trade through one-off ventures like theft; however, as the scale of trade widened, the initial capital necessary to enter the market became increasingly substantial. Smuggling was not only a 'plebeian' but also a bourgeois movement which drew behind it popular support from sections of the population who opposed the vestiges of class privilege and the restrictions on trade represented by the excise laws. This is why bourgeois thinkers like Adam Smith were at the forefront of criticism of the excise laws (just as he was of the game laws). There was no way by which the right to free international trade could legitimately be translated into a traditional custom. Indeed, Smith pointed out that the very term 'customs' – as in 'customs duty' – derived from the fact that they were 'customary payments which had been in use for time immemorial': 'They appear to have been originally considered as taxes upon the profits of merchants . . . originating in the barbarous times of feudal anarchy.'[12] Tradition was in favour of the 'customs'; it was in the name of 'natural law', i.e. modernity, that opposition to it was waged. Smith developed an elaborate critique of the excise laws and campaigned for their repeal, for the lowering of excise duties and for the end of royal prerogatives to trade. This was not the stuff of primitive rebellion.

It is remarkable how the idea of primitive rebellion against laws expressing the development of private property and capitalist economic relations has taken root in Thompson's work, in spite of the contradictory elements which also ran through his accounts. It is as if the particular moral he drew from his study of struggles around the price of grain is unproblematically extendable to all other areas of eighteenth-century struggle. The reason behind this, I believe, is that there lay an untested prejudice running through his historical work, resistant to empirical refutation: a romanticism which sees in pre-bourgeois property relations a 'human' state of affairs which the mass of the people wished to hold on to, and which sees in the development of capitalist property an unmitigated evil which the mass of the people more or less consciously resist. Both in form and content, however, the laws concerning excise and game were becoming, in the eighteenth century, increasingly archaic. In Marx's language, the legal and political superstructure was becoming a block on the development of productive forces. Popular forms of rebellion were as much attempts to break through these blocks as attempts to hold on to a past idyll.

Thompson's conclusions reflected precisely the instrumentalist view of law as a protector of bourgeois private property which he now rightly rejects, for it would appear that this view fails to fit the historical facts as he presents them. The final chapter on the 'rule of law', in *Whigs and Hunters*, which presents the rule of law as 'an unqualified human good' seems to me, therefore, to be in part a self-criticism: Thompson's attempt to break from his own past perspective. His alternative, however, does not solve the problem either.

Thompson's history reveals not so much the 'corruption' of the rule of law in the eighteenth century but the fact that this rule of law was in large measure still an image in the eye of classical jurisprudence and not yet a fully accomplished reality. It was still in possession of all kinds of traditional characteristics – unequal privileges, the fusion of public and private functions, a scarcely existent base in 'consensual assent' – which were later to be superseded. Thompson can turn this period into one of the 'corruption' of law only by turning the law itself into a timeless ideal rather than a specific social form of regulation coming into being in this period.

At one moment Thompson presents the conflict between traditional use-rights and private property rights as one between two 'alternative' notions of the rule of law. In this view Thompson recognizes that the form of law changes from one period to the next (e.g. from natural law to positive law); that its content changes (e.g. from the defence of use-rights to that of absolute property rights); that its institution changes (e.g. from forest to magistrates' courts). But the rule of law itself appears in Thompson's eyes to transcend these historical transformations; 'it is not possible to conceive of any complex society without law.' However, traditional natural law conceptions of property did not possess the egalitarian, universal and humanistic properties Thompson associates with the 'rule of law'. It is not possible to marry traditional natural law theory – rooted in privilege, inequality, dependence, obligation and immutable laws – with any of Thompson's definitions of 'the rule of law'.

At other times, he treats the rule of law as an ideal which emerged out of 'the work of sixteenth and seventeenth century jurists, supported by the practical struggles of such men as Hampden and Lilburne'; which was passed down 'as a legacy' to the eighteenth century but violated systematically in practice; to which the bourgeoisie finally succumbed in the nineteenth century after a period of direct repression, as exemplified by the Peterloo massacre; and which is now being threatened by an increasingly authoritarian state. As an expression of bourgeois ascendancy, however, the rule of law was directly connected with the emergence of absolute private property right. Private property and the rule of law cannot be dissociated from one another. Thompson's over-critical view of private property makes a poor partner for his under-critical view of the rule of law. The same Adam Smith who is the arch-villain in the saga of private property is at once the hero in the saga of the rule of law. Just as private property is not an unqualified human bad, so too the rule of law is not an unqualified human good; they both reflect the limited character of bourgeois emancipation. The final contradiction in Thompson's theorizing about law is that his idealization of the rule of law violates his own humanistic belief in the 'unitary' character of law, economics, politics and culture. Under the rule of law, as Trotsky put it, 'the landlord, the labourer, the capitalist, the proletarian, the minister, the bootblack are equal as "citizens" and as "legislators" '; the abstraction of juridic subjects from their experience as producers is completed. The rule of law expresses the very fetish of law as a force remote from productive relations that Thompson so powerfully criticizes.

## Conclusion

That Marxism must ally with liberalism in defence of civil liberties and democratic rights against their erosion by the state is beyond question. One way of reading Thompson is to see him as offering a critique of a sterile, sectarian Marxism that abstains from this joint struggle. The important question, however, is not whether an alliance between Marxism and liberalism is necessary, but rather on what terms it should be forged. By presenting the liberal idea of the 'rule of law' as an unqualified human good, and by excluding a Marxist critique of its limitations, Thompson advocates an alliance based in effect on the subordination of Marxism to liberalism. With the nightmare of Stalinist and authoritarian right-wing states before his eyes, Thompson perceives that workers prefer the 'rule of law' to both and are right to do so; but he thereby surrenders the vista of a far more radical democracy than that envisaged in liberal constitutions, put forward by Marx. In a context in which the right wing is successfully exploiting the contradictions inherent in the old 'rule of law' and the dissatisfactions of many workers with its failures in practice – as witnessed by the level of popular support mobilized behind 'law and order' campaigns – Thompson's recipe for a purely defensive struggle in support of traditional, liberal constitutions is unlikely to stem the tide. Just as the defence of welfare requires also the democratization of its bureaucracy and the self-activity of recipients and workers, so too defence of the rule of law, if it is to require popular support, requires a level of democratization – of the courts, the judiciary, the legal profession, the police, prisons, etc. – and a level of self-activity by ordinary people which the old liberal constitution did not envisage in its appeal to the rule of law, but which was the ABC of Marx's critique. In this context it is vital that Marxists retain the independence of their critique of the limitations of liberalism, even as they join hands with liberals in a common struggle against a right-wing authoritarianism that falsely seeks to appropriate for itself the title of defender of 'the rule of law'.

## Power without people: Michel Foucault

While Pashukanis and Thompson offer critiques of private property, law and the state within the Marxist tradition, the French historian and philisopher Michel Foucault has purported to represent views that are an advance over Marxism. His approach, which rejects the categories of private property, law and the state in favour of that of power, has gained wide influence – even among Marxists – and has undoubtedly made a stimulating contribution to the modern debate. The adequacy of Foucault's critique, not only of Marxism but also of liberalism, is my focus.

Foucault describes his own critique of power as having been made possible by the May 1968 revolt in France. In his view this revolt opened the way towards a perspective on power which demands new historical concepts, new ways of theorizing and new strategic options for resistance. Foucault argued that the revolt of May 1968 made possible and necessary a radical break from all traditional theories of power and traditional conceptions of struggle, including those of Marxism.

The question posed by 1968, as he put it, was 'how can

revolutionary movements free themselves from the "Marx effect"'. Foucault presented himself as a 'post-Marxist', one who, in the words of his admirer, Gilles Deleuze, 'achieved a theoretical revolution directed not only at bourgeois theories of the state but at the Marxist conception of power and the state'. In the eyes of his followers, Foucault appears to have transcended divisions between left and right, materialism and idealism, socialism and capitalism. In reality Foucault expressed many of the themes embraced by the New Left, including many Marxists, but he was to give to them his own particular twist.

The strength of the spirit of anti-authoritarianism which invested the struggles of 1968 was that it attempted to break through the grip of Stalinism on the one hand and reformism on the other, both of which tended to idealize existing forms of power, or else to ignore them altogether by concentrating exclusively on the realm of economics. The anti-authoritarianism of 1968 represented, in its youthful way, a head-on attack against this consensus: practically every aspect of the operation of power was subjected to critical scrutiny – the state, the family, the hospital, the asylum and the prison appeared as symbols of a 'despotic' power which continues to be exercised both in the East and the West, and also as signs of the failure of the left to come to grips with the question of power. In socialist theoretical work such issues had been largely ignored and, on the practical side, the coming to power of socialist movements left these institutions solidly intact. In Foucault's eyes, a radical politics worth its salt would have to overthrow such monuments to despotism.

Equally important, he thought, was the need for a new theoretical approach capable of understanding the exercise of power in modern 'disciplinary society'. History has shown that new classes may seize control of power without altering its mode of operation. A politics exclusively oriented to the seizure of power neglects the revolutionary task of securing a transition from one form of power to another: to a form of power in which neither prisons nor asylums would have a place. Power is not centralized exclusively in the state, nor is it exclusively the property of one class; rather it is exercised in multiple centres, each with its own distinctive characteristics. It is not adequate to reduce the question of power in the asylum, the prison, the factory, the family, etc., to that of the state or ruling class; nor to assume that the despotism within these institutions will automatically disappear with the overthrow of a particular state or class.

Just as there are multiple centres of power, so too there are multiple sources of resistance: from schoolchildren, students, prisoners, psychiatric inmates, women, factory workers and so forth – each engaging in particular localized struggles; resistance does not stem from one single source, whether that source be the working class conceived as a uniform entity or the Party; but each of these struggles has its own distinctive integrity. Since power is not the exclusive possession of a particular class, it cannot be a purely rational means of securing class relations. Power is never simply 'functional' for capital; but the contradictions in its exercise inevitably lead to the constant regeneration of resistance. Nor is power something purely 'negative' or 'repressive'; it does not merely deny freedom, it also plays a 'positive' role in creating atomized servile, docile, or at least manageable individuals. The form of 'disciplinary' power emboded in prisons, asylums, factories and families is not simply given in nature, nor is it a property of every social order, but is rather a definite historical relation whose beginnings one can trace and whose end one can foresee.

Finally, the privileged position of science should not be automatically jutified; rather, knowledge and power are inextricably linked, as the close connections between 'sciences' like psychiatry and criminology and institutions like asylums and prisons clearly show. This understanding of the link between knowledge and power must be incorporated in critical theory lest it should itself become a new kind of elitism, monopolizing knowledge of the 'truth' and dismissing all other beliefs as 'false consciousness'. Foucault was not wrong to take off from themes which represented a revival of left criticism about power and the state. However, around the kernel of truth contained in these observations he built an elaborate mystical shell.

Foucault's anti-Marxism stemmed in part from a mistaken identification of some kinds of vulgar Marxism (e.g. the French Communist Party) with Marxism in general; it does not need reiterating at this stage that Marx saw revolution not merely as a transfer of power from one class to another but also as a transition from one form of power to another (in which the transformation of the asylum and the prison should be one element). He did not see seizure of the state as the solution to all oppression. Foucault's anti-Marxism was not, however, just based on a misunderstanding, it also stemmed from a real disagreement with Marx. It was basically an opposition between materialism and formalism. While Marx argued that forms of power cannot be divorced from their social content (i.e. who wields it, what functions it plays, etc.) Foucault – starting from a critique of analyses of power which ignored or idealized its forms – ended up paying exclusive attention to its forms and rejecting the very idea that there is a social content beneath them.

Slipping from the observation that power is not the exclusive property of a particular class, Foucault draws the conclusion that power is not a property of people at all; the individuals who appear to hold power are not in fact 'the *vis-à-vis* of power but rather one of its prime effects'. The question of *who* wields power is false, for power creates its own human subjects. The empirical starting point for Foucault was that the (often bureaucratic) forms of authority embodied in what he called the 'disciplines' frequently appear impersonal on their surface; they seem to be under no human control and the individuals who exercise authority (prison guards, asylum nurses, etc.) may appear to be appendages of power, rather than power being an attribute of them. Critical theory must come to terms with the depersonalization of authority in the modern world, not reduce it to an ideology obscuring class rule in the manner of vulgar Marxism. The difference between Foucault and Marx, however, lies in their respective analyses of depersonalized authority, not in their assessments of its reality.

Marxists argue that everywhere and always power is an expression of social relations between people: the form and the content of power change with time and place, but not its human foundation. People always remain the real subjects of power, even if at times they appear as no more than its predicate; if power appears impersonal, it is because relations between individuals give rise to a fetishized form. The task of theoretical criticism is to reveal the human relations which lie hidden beneath the fetish of a power abstracted from people, as a first step towards the practical task of making it possible for people to take control of power rather than for power to determine the fate of people. The fetish for power is real in modern society; individuals are subsumed under impersonal structures of law, bureaucracy and state; but the social basis of this form of subordination should be revealed in order to demystify the fetish.

Against this whole mode of criticism Foucault argued that in the past, when power was a possession of monarch and lords, it was personal. Now, however, with the advent of disciplinary power, its very substance has changed: the surface form of discipline is its reality; there is nothing beneath the surface, no 'hidden text'. For Foucault, people are the predicate of power while power is transmogrified into an impersonal subject. Between 'traditional' and 'disciplinary' forms of power, there is a historical break marking not the transfer of power from one class of people to another, nor a change in how people exercise power, but a transubstantiation of power itself from a human attribute to an impersonal entity. Thus only a formalism can capture the contemporary truth that power is an impersonal machine divorced from human agency; Foucault turns power into an independent entity that strides over the human world and moulds it according to its own will. Foucault's formalism turns the mystique of disciplinary power into the essence of power itself; it may now appear that it is power that constitutes individuals, not individuals who constitute power. This was why Foucault made a principle out of not digging beneath the surface forms of power; out of elevating what he saw as the 'politics of everyday life' into the only politics. To get at the heart of power, he insisted, we should not look for hidden social forces behind 'the great upheavals' but rather grasp power at the point where it touches the individuals, at what he calls its 'capillary forms of existence'. He offered a kind of reverse phenomenology based not on how the individual experiences the world but on how the world manifests itself to individuals. Since power makes itself felt on individuals as a suprahuman force, this indeed is the truth of power.

Foucault polemicized against what he saw as the arbitrary nature of 'interpretation'; the search beneath the text for what people 'really' mean leads, he thought, to an endless number of possible interpretations, none of which has any inherent superiority. It therefore becomes a matter of caprice or of power which interpretation is chosen as correct. The solution to this problem of authority, he argued, was to give up the illusion of a 'sub-text'. His position was that by treating others as neither meaning what they say nor knowing what they mean, the 'interpreter' acquires for him or herself a privileged status: interpretation appears to Foucault as an act of power which subordinates the discourse of others and elevates the discourse of the interpreter (as a scientist, political leader, doctor, etc.). However, the fact that some forms of interpretation are protected against criticism and public debate does not mean that all interpretation should be abandoned. Foucault himself cannot avoid 'interpretation'; this becomes particularly apparent when power relations present themselves in distinct and contradictory forms. For example, in modern capitalist society power presents itself both as a self-sufficient machine in which 'everyone is caught' and which 'no-one owns'; and juridically in terms of the rights of individuals. How does Foucault resolve the problem of dual appearances? By interpreting the juridic aspect of power to be no more than a 'mask' and its disciplinary aspect to be real.

The same problem confronted Foucault in his explanation for the development of the modern penitentiary. Its founders – the penal reformers of the late eighteenth century – campaigned under the banner of the 'rights of man' for a more humane form of punishment than that of the house of correction, public execution, torture, galley slavery and the like, and believed that the 'penitentiary' would provide a humane environment in which criminals could be reformed into good and useful citizens. At the same time, penal reformers also argued that penitentiaries would constitute a more effective, rational, complete form of control over the criminal class: a place that would induce such suffering of the soul that others would be deterred and the inmate cowed into submission. Both these images existed side by side; some reformers emphasizing the 'human' aspect of penal reforms, others their 'control' aspects, and others linking the two together (as was the case in the vivid phrase 'cords of love, chains of iron', used to describe the principle of the penitentiary and echoed in Michael Ignatieff's account of its origins). Foucault's solution to the problem of two apparently conflicting surface forms was to declare that

> The true objective of the reform movement . . . was not so much to establish a new right to punish, based on more equitable principles, as to set up a new economy of the power to punish, to assure its better distribution, to render it more

regular, effective, constant, and detailed in its effects . . . not to punish less but to punish better . . . It is this 'economic rationality' that must calculate the penalty . . . 'Humanity' is the respectable name given to this economy and to its meticulous calculation.[1]

'Humanity' appeared thus as a a mask, while 'rationality' appeared as the essence of this new apparatus of power. Foucault interpreted the utilitarian side of bourgeois ideology as the truth and its humanitarian side as an illusion. His cynical view of reform however, assumed that bourgeois humanism was an empty shell without giving any credence to the progressive character of campaigns against torture, public executions, animal-like conditions in the houses of confinement and so forth, nor to the campaigns for a form of punishment that would be reformative rather than retributive. On the other hand, he ignored the possibility that penal reformers were grossly exaggerating the effectiveness and utility of their own inventions. Foucault should not have taken at face value the hard line of rational control any more than the soft language of human rights; whereas he conveyed a scepticism concerning the humane side of bourgeois reforms, he was uncritical about their claims to rationality. This was apparent in Foucault's critique of Bentham's panopticon.

The panopticon was Bentham's utopian design for a model prison, asylum, school or workshop. He advertised it as 'a new mode of power of mind over mind, in a quantity hitherto without example, secured by whoever chooses to have it so against abuse.' He described it as 'a mill for grinding rogues honest . . . a method of becoming master of everything which might happen to men . . . a very powerful and very useful instrument which governments might apply to various objects of the utmost importance'. Parliament was not taken in by Bentham's inflated claims and rejected his design: but Foucault did little more than echo Bentham's utilitarian fantasy about creating a complete technology of power:

The panopticon made it possible to perfect the exercise of power . . . a marvellous machine which, whatever use one may wish to put it to, produces homogeneous effects of power . . . a functional mechanism that must improve the exercise of power by making it lighter, more rapid, more effective, a design of subtle coercion for a society to come.[2]

Foucault reversed the value judgement Bentham bestowed on the panopticon, presenting it as an 'extreme form' of despotism, but the substance of their analysis was the same.

Foucault's characterization of disciplinary power as 'rational', 'functional', etc. meant that, instead of examining the tensions between the form of power and its social functions, he defined the form of power in terms of its functionality, thus creating an apparent identity between the two. His formalism led him not to see the contradiction inherent in the exercise of power, as he initially hoped, but to construct an image of omnipotence.

Power appeared as a self-sufficient entity, whose only purpose is the maintenance of its own mastery. This thesis was clearly apparent in his critique of prisons, where he described the prison as an 'extreme form' of disciplinary power. However, bearing in mind the fact that prisons consistently fail to live up to their own ideals of reforming inmates into good and useful citizens, it would seem that this most functional of powers turns out not to work at all well. Foucault saved his thesis by turning to what he saw as the latent function of prison power: that of producing, in the form of 'deliquency', a politically safe form of resistance that is easy to accommodate, supervise and control. The political rationality of prisons is, however, no more assured – as is shown by their incapacity to contain collective, political revolts – than their penal rationality. It is only in periods of stability that the functionality of prisons – like that of the state in general – appears convincing. For Foucault, since the form of power is everything and power produces its own reality, there can be no obstacles to its apparent efficacy: the prison becomes the symbol of omnipotence.

Foucault's explanation for the historical development of disciplinary forms of power took off from a rejection of orthodox liberal accounts of 'progress' which explain them in terms of an advance in knowledge or in moral sensibility. He went further, however, by denying any progressive content to the penal, educational, health and other reforms and revolutions which emerged out of the Enlightenment. He also rejected the economic functionalism and reductionism which Marxists sometimes offer on the grounds that disciplinary power 'functions to reproduce capital' or 'serves the interests of the ruling class'. Foucault rejected any explanation of power in terms of social relations external to or independent of power itself. Since power, in his view, produces reality, there can exist nothing outside it to act as grounds for change; power appeared as its own premiss, explicable only in terms of its inner dynmics. Foucault's formalism led him at times to abandon the search for causal explanation altogether in favour of a synchronic morphology of power; at times to construct a theory of 'historical discontinuity' according to which the 'leap' from one historical form of power to another (e.g. 'traditional' to 'disciplinary') appears as an inexplicable fact based on 'chance', 'unpredictability' and 'invention'; at times to postpone the job of explanation to a later stage when his description of discipline is more complete.

A causal explanation for discipline nevertheless did slip into Foucault's work and coloured his conclusions in a very profound way. He located the growth of disciplinary power in the process of capital accumulation, but made no distinction between capitalist development and industrial development in general. What led to the emergence of the hierarchical non-reciprocal, top-down structures of power that make up discipline, in his view, was the growth of large-scale production irrespective of its class form: the need to organize individuals 'rationally' into a co-operative labour force, to make their work 'useful', to 'regulate their movements', to fit them into a social labour process, to 'clear up confusions' and to neutralize the effects of individual resistance – made inevitable, in Foucault's view, the parallel development of despotic apparatuses of disciplinary control.

Although Foucault referred to Marx's discussion of 'co-operative labour' in *Capital*, the contrast between their accounts is sharp. Co-operation between individuals in production appeared to Marx in itself to be positive, in respect both of the productivity of labour and to the personal well-being of individuals. Every co-operative labour process requires some form of control to 'secure the harmonious co-operation of the activities of individuals', but the particular form of control is determined by the 'social' as well as the 'technical' character of production. Thus the authoritarian character of the control exercised by the capitalist over the labour process arose not from the requirements of regulating social labour but from 'the unavoidable antagonism between the exploiter and the raw material of his exploitation'. For Marx, it was the conflict between capital and labour which led capital to exercise control in such authoritarian ways; for Foucault, it was the development of a rational, co-operative labour process that induced this authoritarianism. Foucault's view reflected his general formalism, since on the surface it appeared that it was co-operative labour itself that was despotic. Because, as Marx pointed out, the capitalist form of co-operation developed historically in opposition to peasant agriculture and petty bourgeois handicraft, it did not appear as a particular historical form of co-operation; rather, co-operation appeared as a phenomenon peculiar to capitalist production (in fact it had taken many social forms prior to capitalism). Further, because workers under capitalism are isolated from one another until they are brought together by capital, co-operation appears as an attribute of capital itself and all the authoritarian aspects of capitalist co-operation are thus projected on to co-operation itself. For this reason, Foucault's critique of disciplinary power ended up as an objection to co-operation and collectivity as such; in spite of his initial proposal that power should not be seen in terms of the repression of individual liberty, his critique was in fact based on the antagonisms between freedom of the individual and the despotism of the collective. The more socialized production becomes, the more individuals are included in co-operative labour processes, Foucault concluded, the more 'disciplinary' society will become.

The same opposition to collectivity which led Foucault to a critique of bourgeois forms of power also set him against socialist forms. Since his objection to bourgeois society was directed not at private ownership but at its tendency towards the socialization of labour, the further socialization of labour at the expense of private ownership envisaged in socialism appeared to him not as an emancipation but as a despotism. The rebirth of the prison in the grotesque form of the Gulag Archipelago in the Soviet Union thus appeared as part of the logic, not the corruption, of socialism.

In spite of his opposition to a 'repressive' view of power, Foucault believed that power itself necessarily breeds resistance regardless of who wields it, how it is exercised or what uses it is put to. However, since resistance is the product of power, he stressed the danger of its reproducing existing forms on power rather than overcoming them. On the one hand, individualized rebellion in the form of crime and delinquency is politically impotent; on the other, socialist forms of struggle – based around the collective

organization of labour – reproduce the very disciplinary mechanisms against which they are set. Foucault's whole approach did
not let him entertain the possibility that workers might develop
collective forms of organization different from, and more
democratic than, those of capital. 'Discipline' therefore appeared
endemic in socialist forms of struggle.

Foucault's alternative to socialism was not clear. He picked up
on ideas with a much broader left currency about fragmentary,
local struggles, each with its own autonomy, coming together in
temporary, spontaneous alliances without 'global' direction or
organization. He wrote vaguely about the need to replace the
'global synthesis' of struggle – epitomized in the Marxist conception
of the party – by a 'strategic codification of multiple points of
resistance'. In other words, he saw the fragmentary and spontaneous nature of the struggles of 1968 not as their limitations but as
their strength; the danger lay in their organization.

Foucault rejected the scientific elitism which he saw as endemic
in Marxist theory; to this end he advocated the replacement of
'science' by a 'genealogy' that will

> entertain the claims to attention to local, discontinuous,
> disqualified, illegitimate knowledges against the claims of a
> unitary body of theory which would filter, hierarchize and
> order them in the name of some true knowledge.[3]

In Foucault's eyes, 'science' – i.e. the search for truth and hidden
meanings – represents authoritarianism and dogma; 'genealogy'
– i.e. the reactivation of local knowledges – represents tolerance
and resistance. 'Truth' is a function of power, not of reason;
Marxism's commitment to 'truth' is a symbol of its repressiveness.
When Foucault, as a historian, examined past forms of knowledge
and unpacked them he did not assess their truth or validity; when
he examined 'local knowledges' – replete as they are with sexism,
racism and conservative prejudices as well as with the spirit of
spontaneity and revolt – he accepted them as they are for fear of
imposing an arbitrary truth. He thus rejected the Enlightenment
tradition, inherited by Marx, that the 'search for truth' is the
condition of democratic criticism and of the breakdown of
arbitrary authority. To treat other people and their view in an
egalitarian way, according to this tradition, is to engage critically
with the truth of what they say, not to abstract what they say from

any connection with truth. The elitism inherent in Foucault's view of knowledge is that it allowed him to treat all other 'knowledges' as equal only in the sense that they are all deprived of truth-value, while his own 'knowledge' transcends the many varieties of commonsense discourse.

Rather than engage with Marxism in open and rational debate about the nature and causes of disciplinary power, he invalidated it as a 'science' and so bypassed the question of which approach is closer to the truth. In fact, Foucault offered a thoroughly 'global' and 'scientific' theory of discipline, and indeed interpreted all struggles everywhere as fundamentally struggles against discipline. Foucault's laudable desire to emancipate illegitimate knowledges ended up by discounting them.

Foucault's analysis of disciplinary society was based on the supposition that law and representative democracy are empty forms – under which discipline reigns supreme. This approach tended to obscure ways in which relations between the law, parliament and the 'disciplines' are changing; to discount struggles for legal rights and democratic accountability of disciplinary apparatuses; to downplay distinctions between one kind of discipline and another (prison and school, police and welfare); and to gloss over the transition from the welfare to the police state.

The key, however, to Foucault's theory of discipline was its denial of the existence of private property, law and the state (it was in some respects like Renard's theory of institutionalism, current in the 1930s).[4] Foucault equated the state with absolutism and argued that as absolutism met its death, so too did the state in general! State sovereignty disappears for Foucault, since the state is reduced to a collection of 'institutions', whose power is 'everywhere' in society and is thus identified with the power of the organized community itself. The concept of the state implies that there are people – a group, a class, particular individuals – who exercise the sovereignty attributed to the state. While the concept of state sovereignty obscures the real, social character of those who rule, it has the merit of revealing that there are people who rule; it conceals, but it does not eliminate, the bearer of power. Foucault's 'abolition' of the state does not only conceal the social character of the bearers of power, it eliminates the bearers themselves. The categories of private property owner, legal subject and the state, for all the mystifications they engender, still point to power as an attribute of people; Foucault's rejection of these categories deepens the mystification by abstracting power from its bearers altogether. In a situation in which power is being concentrated in ever fewer hands, this approach is a dangerous delusion.

Like Foucault, Marxism rejects a liberal approach to history which idealizes existing forms of power and views the past in terms of their attainment or absence. However, Marxism also rejects a form of anti-liberalism which reduces all liberalizing reforms to no more than a mechanism of social control or means of meeting the economic needs of capital. From this standpoint, it would be as doctrinaire to discount in its entirety the progressiveness of the penal reform movement around the turn of the eighteenth or nineteenth centuries as to idealize it as the bearer of truth and light. It was a great advance to conceive of punishment as a means of turning individuals into good and useful human beings, even though from the beginning this took the abstract and oppressive form of the modern prison. On this basis, Marxism stands for the abolition of prisons, not in order to return to the old coercion but rather to construct a form of authority that would genuinely humanize those who engage in anti-social behaviour. Instead of a penal system based on a formal commitment to socialize the anti-social that it contradicts at every moment by its presuppositions – isolation, atomization, exclusion, silence, passive obedience, bureaucracy and division – Marxism stands for the 'smashing' of the prison system and its replacement by a form of regulation based on collectivity, individual rights, internal democracy, discussion and creative labour. The early liberal reformers advertised their penal inventions as models of a truly human community; so far from the truth was this that their prisons and asylums required mighty walls and iron security to keep real individuals within these supposedly human bounds. The reformers sought to construct an environment which was on the one hand more human than conditions on the outside, and on the other more painful. Thus reform was linked to deterrence, humanity to suffering. While liberalism sees a synthesis between these, Marxism sees what there in fact is: nothing but contradiction. For Foucault, humanism is nothing but a veil for despotism; for Marxism, the problem with liberal humanism is that it is abstract, incomplete, contradicted by its own premisses. A 'human' institution does not presuppose the abolition of social control and discipline, but rather a new form of social control and discipline. The point is not merely to negate liberalism abstractly – as Foucault does from the perspective of an anti-collectivism which is in fact but a one-sided expression of the very liberalism he rejects. It is rather to transcend liberalism theoretically and practically from the perspective of a more social form of collective authority. Within socialist literature we find just the beginnings of an outline of the kind of institutions which might replace prisons – such as Makarenko's *Road to Life*, an account of 'a colony' for juvenile delinquents in Russia in the 1920s. Foucault's approach allows him to offer no perspective on this question.

# Conclusion

I have tried in this book to do a number of things and would like here to review the ground I have covered. I hope that in working through the concepts of liberal jurisprudence and the various phases of Marx's critique I have been able to clarify certain areas which have hitherto been neglected or misunderstood. As well as providing pointers for future theoretical work, certain practical political conclusions also follow from the analysis I have provided.

I have argued first for a recognition and reappraisal of the achievements of liberal jurisprudence in its 'classical' phase. These lay essentially in its exposition of private property, law and the state as the fundamental categories of juridic thought; in its discovery that they are the products of human activity and not simply given in nature; in its elaboration of the historical conditions required for their emergence; in its analysis of the contradictions running through them, and in its attempts to resolve these contradictions through the institution of new forms of private property, law and state. At the same time, classical jurisprudence was by no means a homogeneous discourse: I have tried to trace some of the steps in its uneven development and some of the major differences which run through it. Nonetheless, its proponents constructed for themselves a definite historical and logical identity around the elaboration of these themes.

In one respect, however, classical jurisprudence fell short of the more radical variants of liberal thought that developed in the nineteenth century: none of the classical writers were democrats. Nonetheless, they offered a much richer foundation for the growth of a Marxist critique of jurisprudence – than did the representatives of 'vulgar jurisprudence' who followed them. This decline of liberal thought has not been the topic of my work; suffice it to say that vulgar jurisprudence lost sight of the genesis of private property, law and the state in human activity, their determinate social character which differentiated them from other forms of property and authority, their historical origins and the contradictions and antagonisms inherent in their functioning. It treated them instead as unproblematic, natural, eternal, harmonious and ideal attributes of all social organisation. In so doing, it blunted the critical edge of classical jurisprudence and subordinated scientific inquiry to the legitimation and service of bourgeois property and authority.

Marx's ongoing dialogue with the works of Smith and Hegel bears testimony to the seriousness with which he treated them. It was because he recognized the great advance in scientific and political thought achieved by classical jurisprudence that he studied and criticized its writings with such care. His object was not simply to reject liberalism – a goal which he shared with all kinds of radicals and reactionaries – but to move beyond it. It is possible, of course, to be anti-liberal without being pro-Marx and necessary to demarcate the boundaries of Marx's own critique. Marx himself warred against socialists of his time who offered an anti-liberalism which fell short of liberalism.

Marx thus applauded classical jurisprudence for reducing juridic institutions to 'man himself' and for its repudiation of traditional natural law theory; his critique was founded not on a restoration of natural law but on completing the break from it which classical jurisprudence initiated. Whilst classical jurisprudence discovered that human labour is the source of private property, law and the state, it reintroduced a concept of natural law by supposing that it is in the nature of human labour in general to express itself in these juridic forms. The question Marx posed was under what conditions – what relations of production – does the labour of individuals create private property, law and the state as its products. The point was not simply to reject the category of human labour generated within classical jurisprudence – a category which made possible the growth of juridic science – but rather to specify the definite historical relations under which it operated, such that private property, law and the state emerged as its products.

Similarly, Marx argued that the ideas of freedom and equality put forward within classical jurisprudence as both a theoretical conclusion and a political demand were themselves a product of history. They expressed the development of bourgeois relations of production in which class relations between labour and capital take the form of free and equal exchange between independent owners of private property. Marx demonstrated the formal character of freedom and equality in their abstraction from class relations of production, not in order to condemn the illusoriness of liberal ideas but to reveal the limited character of their realization within liberalism.

Marx's critique of liberal jurisprudence did not come about in a single flash of inspiration nor did it reach any final point of culmination. Rather, it was developed in stages, each one containing within itself internal tensions and limitations which Marx then sought to resolve with the growth of his theoretical and political armoury.

In the first stage, Marx appropriated the liberal concept of the rational state as a synthesis of individual liberty and the universal will of the whole, but he looked carefully at the actual state which liberals presented as the embodiment of this ideal, and found it wanting. He gave to the concept of the rational state a far more democratic content than that given to it by the liberals. The abolition of the monarchy, of bureaucratic administration, of the House of Lords, and of all legal privileges; the institution of active and passive universal suffrage; the election of officials and judges as well as deputies; strict accountability of those elected to their electors, all power to the assembly, rule through general and determinate laws impartially adjudicated and administered; the independence of the judiciary from the executive and review of executive decisions by the judiciary; popular participation in politics outside of parliament; the guarantee of substantive rights to a free press, freedom of speech, free association and free trade unionism – such, Marx argued, were the real presuppositions of a rational state which no actual state came anywhere near to embodying.

Marx's second stage was no longer to reveal the gulf between the ideal and the actual state but also to reveal the limitations of mere political emancipation. Thus he contrasted the universality and freedom inherent in the idea of the state with the egoism, inequality, alienation and dependence associated with private property. The same historical process which released the public domain from its private fetters also released the pursuit of private interest from all social obligations. Political emancipation through the construction of a rational state was not enough, for by itself it was compatible with enslavement within civil society. On the other hand, political emancipation was necessary for there could be no social emancipation without political liberty. Marx's critique was thus aimed both at those who equated political emancipation with human emancipation *tout court* and at those who counterposed socialism to political emancipation.

Marx's third stage was no longer only to contrast the rationality of the state to the irrationality of civil society, but also to reveal the alienated social character of the rational state itself. By its very nature, the state represents the alienation of power from the mass of the people and a communality that is purely formal. Even the most democratic state falls short of full democracy since the existence of the state is itself a negation of democracy. The abstract quality of the state means not only that political liberty by itself is insufficient, but also that it entails the expropriation of power from the people. The formal character of freedom and equality before the law means not only that they are by themselves insufficient, but also that they engender unfreedom and inequality as their substantive consequence. In Hegelian terms, Marx now recognized that the realization of reason required not the reconstruction but the dissolution of the state in its entirety. Rather than counterpose the universality of the state to the particularity of civil society, Marx now derived the purely formal freedom and equality inherent in the state from the purely formal freedom and equality inherent in civil society: in reality, beneath the surface, both private property and the state had enslavement and alienation as the roots of their mutual existence. Human emancipation required the withering away of the state and of law alongside that of private property; private property, law and the state no longer appeared as antagonistic social forces but as mutually complementary. It is this stage which, if taken in isolation from the texts which came before and after it, gives most support to a 'reductionist' or 'instrumentalist' view of Marx's juridic theory of law and the state.

The final stages of Marx's critique of jurisprudence have to be reconstructed from comments dispersed through his economic, political and historical writings and, most importantly, from the method which he employed in his critique of political economy. Marx's focus on political economy in his later theoretical writings can give rise to the impression that economic relations constitute the fundamental base of capitalist society, and that juridic forms are illusory, derivative or in some sense 'epiphenomenal'. This was a view which Marx never entirely abandoned, but jostling with it was another conception of the relation between jurisprudence and economics, which I have sought to bring to the surface and in some respects to develop. In this alternative account, Marx put forward the hypothesis that capitalist relations of production express themselves at one and the same time through the juridic forms of private property, law and the state *and* the economic forms of value, price, money, capital, profit, and so on. Neither sphere – juridic or economic – is logically privileged; rather their 'base', or, what Marx now referred to as their mutual 'content', is seen as comprising social relations of production which at a particular stage of their evolution necessarily give rise to both the juridic and the economic spheres. Juridic forms, like economic forms, are transitory and historical and cannot be understood in isolation from the social relations which lie concealed within them. There is no theoretical warrant for saying that economic forms are 'more real' than juridic forms; they co-exist as the mutually required ways in which definite productive relations must express themselves, and it is a one-sided Marxism which concentrates exclusively on the economic aspects.

Marx's use of the metaphor of 'form-content' rather than that of 'base-superstructure' also points to his belief that the juridic forms of productive relations are every bit as real as the productive relations themselves. The form or surface of an object is as 'material' as its inner content. From this perspective, forms of law, contract, equal exchange, etc. should not be conceived as mere masks concealing class relations but rather as real mediations. On the other hand, the form of an object cannot be separated from its content, so juridic forms should not be abstracted as timeless ideals apart from the relations between individuals which give rise to them. Bourgeois justice is neither simply a camouflage for class domination, nor an eternal truth dissociated from its class origins. Marx's critique of jurisprudence was thus based not on the substitution of one juridic theory for another but on a social critique of jurisprudence as a whole. Theoretically, Marx sought to explain the social base of juridic forms and of the categories which express them; practically, he sought the dissolution of the juridic sphere in its entirety – i.e. the abolition of private property, law and the state alongside the abolition of the law of value, money and capital – as part and parcel of what is required for the transition from capitalism to socialism.

Marx offered at this stage a more dialectical critique of the contradictions between juridic forms of freedom and equality and their class content in capitalist society than he had previously been able to do. The key to this shift lay in his investigation of private property, in which he abandoned a number of his earlier assumptions. In particular, he now saw that the concept of private property referred not to the economic base of law and the state, but was itself the simplest juridic form, and therefore had a direct connection with law and the state as more developed juridic forms. Thus the relation between private property and the law is not one between the economic and the juridic but a relation within the juridic sphere alone.

Marx resisted the tendency of some theorists to divorce private property, law and the state from one another, as if they were representative of entirely different principles (it thus makes no sense to contrast law as an unqualified human good to private property as a bourgeois evil). At the same time, he resisted the tendency of other theorists to identify private property, law and the state with one another, as if they all referred to the same basic principle, or relation (which is the assumption of those who derive private property, law and the state equally from the exchange of commodities). Rather, he saw one as a developed form of the other, just as money is a developed form of value and capital is a developed form of money. The hypothesis which Marx hinted at, and which I have here elaborated, is that simple commodity production gives rise to private property, the generalization of commodity production gives rise to law, and the transformation of commodity into capitalist production gives rise to the state. Within the general context of capitalist productive relations, changing relations between labour and capital give rise to quite distinct forms of the state and distinct relationships between private property, the law, the state executive and parliament. Further, in the socialist transition, new and more democratic forms of private property, law and the state should emerge, leading eventually to their dissolution under communist relations of production. With the development of higher forms of juridic life, the lower forms do not cease to exist but acquire new functions.

At the same time, Marx's approach reveals the inherently contradictory character of these forms. The emergence of law may serve to resolve some of the antagonisms associated with the pursuit of private property, and the emergence of the state may serve to resolve some of the contradictions associated with the law; but in each case new contradictions necessarily emerge. The question of the emergence of definite juridic forms and that of their functions and uses once they have emerged are distinct, and no symmetry can be presupposed between them. Thus the generalization of commodity production creates a need for new forms of regulation to sustain 'free and equal exchange' in the face of inevitable divisions between rich and poor; at the same time it creates the means for meeting this need in the form of law. But there can be no guarantee concerning the adequacy of this form for fulfilling this function. Marx's method entails a rejection both of functionalism (that is, the reduction of juridic forms to their functions) and of formalism (the reduction of juridic functions to their forms); in their place, he urges us to examine the necessarily contradictory ways in which private property, law and the state serve to reproduce capitalist relations of production.

Marx abandoned the one-sidedness of his earlier critique of private property, in which he had revealed its alienated and exploitative social content, but dismissed its formal qualities of free will, equality and universality as fictions concealing enslavement and mere egoism. He now combined a critique of the alien social content of private property with an appreciation of the real significance of its formal attributes. He now explained – though there were tensions in his position which he never resolved – that while the freedom, equality and universality associated with wage labour are compatible with class subordination they are nonetheless material factors which give capitalism its emancipatory potential. Under capitalism, he now argued, workers are not commodities at all but the owners of commodities 'with their own need for development'.

The derivation of juridic forms from relations of commodity exchange led either to their idealization as embodiments of freedom, equality and justice or to their dismissal as embodiments of egoism, conflict and mutual indifference, depending on one's view of the exchange relation. Marx now argued that both were partial truths: both equally abstract exchange from the relations of production which engender exchange. Thus the different content of private property under commodity, capitalist and socialist relations of production is obscured as long as analysis remains on the surface of exchange relations. So too, while equality before the law always entails inequality in fact – because individuals are treated according to one set of dimensions alone and not according to their needs – nevertheless the degree and nature of this inequality undergoes radical shifts between and within commodity, capitalist and socialist societies. Thus the general inequality existing between capital and labour in no way obviates the fact that the relation between capital and labour is not fixed once and for all but is one in which labour may acquire more or less influence, recognition and share of wealth. One cannot speak of the legal form in the singular, if this is taken to mean that all legal forms are essentially the same. Private property, law and the state take quite different forms under different relations of production and one form may be far preferable to another from the perspective of democracy, individual liberty, social equality and the production of wealth. The fact that, in general, private property, law, and the state represent a restrictive freedom, a restrictive equality and a restrictive fraternity, and that the contradictions associated with them cannot finally be resolved within a juridic framework, does not mean that we can ignore the differences between their various forms and contents.

Marx sought to transcend private property, law and the state not because he was sceptical of democracy, but because of the limits which juridic forms impose upon it. At the same time as he recognized its progressiveness as a means of expressing what Hegel had called a synthesis between the universal will of all and the particular will of the individual, he also exposed the limits of the synthesis possible within the narrow horizons of jurisprudence. Thus when Marx referred to the withering away of private property, law and the state, he had in mind not merely their abolition but also their replacement by *more* democracy and *more* individual liberty than is possible within their confines. Ripped out of context, the concept of 'withering away' does not rule out the possibility that private property may be dissolved in favour of state property, that law may be dissolved in favour of bureaucracy or that the state may be dissolved – as various fascist thinkers put it – in favour of the Community and the Leader. For Marx, the withering away of juridic forms signified a process of democratization and extension of individual rights to the point of the dissolution of the juridic sphere in its entirety; rather than counterposing its democratization to its withering away, Marx saw one as the culmination of the other.

Where does this leave us today? Workers value their liberties and are right to do so. They value the right to think and act for themselves as individuals, the civil liberties which protect them from arbitrary authority, the economic freedom to join a trade union and to withdraw their labour, the political liberty to elect a government, protest against bad laws and remove from power those who oppress them. Thus it is no part of working class politics to reduce private property, law and the state to mere instruments of the ruling class or mere functions for the reproduction of class relations. A socialist politics which debases the coinage of individual liberty and political democracy – or which presents private property, law and the state as mere negations of these values – is unlikely to win favour among those it would champion: not because workers are bedevilled by false consciousness but because they understand what is important to them. The task of Marxism is not to negate this working class consciousness but to encourage its growth by giving it theoretical expression.

Those who tell workers that democracy is a bourgeois illusion or that individual liberty is a bourgeois vice may see themselves as very radical and the workers who ignore them as very backward, but on such occasions the workers may well be more advanced than those who would lead them. We are sometimes told, for example, that socialist democracy transcends free elections; that workers' rights to strike are narrow and selfish; that individual freedom is no more than an illusion or a bourgeois vice; that workers' own organizations can express the will of the working class regardless of the extent to which workers themselves have a say in their running; that state property is socialist even though workers have no control over its use and are punished for interfering with it. A form of socialism has developed that reflects in a grotesque way the formalism which Marx detected in Hegel whereby the people are treated with obsequious courtesy as long as they silently haunt the ante-chambers of power but find the doors to the inner chambers barred and a notice up saying: 'Reserved for public business; no admission to the public.' What may have originated as a temporary measure subordinating democracy to the class struggle has turned into a general disregard for democracy in the name of the class struggle. For example, the suppression of workers' rights to organize independently of the state is no more acceptable because the state declares itself socialist than it is in a capitalist state. This is why Lenin was right to argue in 1920 and 1921 – against those who wished to subordinate trade unions to the socialist state – that trade unions should retain their rights to defend 'the material and spiritual interests' of the workers against the workers' state: not merely, as he put it, because the 'workers' state' was actually a 'workers' and peasants' state' and because it suffered from bureaucreatic distortions, but because the state is in its essence a power alien to labour. A working class politics, such as that enunciated by Marx, declares the stubborn refusal of workers to surrender their rights, whether they are asked to do so in the name of a democracy conceived of as something apart from the real will of individuals or in the name of a socialism viewed as something apart from the people who constitute it.

# Notes

## 1. Classical jurisprudence

*The defeat of traditional natural law theory*
1. Cited in I. Hont and M. Ignatieff, 'Needs and Justice in *The Wealth of Nations*: an Introductory Essay', in *Wealth and Virtue: The Shaping of Political Economy in the Scottish Enlightenment*, Cambridge University Press 1984, p. 27.
2. Cited in J. Tully, *A Discourse on Property: John Locke and his Adversaries*, Cambridge University Press 1982, p. 71.
3. Cited in Hont and Ignatieff, 'Needs and Justice', p.34.
4. J. Locke, *Two Treatises of Government*, Cambridge University Press 1963, 2.5.48.
5. J. Locke, *Two Treatises*, p. 332.
6. O. Gierke, *Political Theories of the Middle Ages*, Boston: Beacon 1958.
7. C. Hill, *The Century of Revolution*, Nelson 1980.

*Hobbes*
1. T. Hobbes, *Leviathan*, Penguin 1968, p. 217.
2. O. Gierke, *Natural Law and the Theory of Society*, Cambridge University Press, 1934.
3. T. Hobbes, *Elements of Law*, Cambridge University Press, 1928, II.1.19.
4. T. Hobbes, *Leviathan*, p. 316.
5. *Ibid.,* p. 232.
6. *Ibid.,* p. 318.
7. *Ibid.,* p. 321.
8. *Ibid.,* p. 314.

*Rousseau*
1. L. Colletti, *From Rousseau to Lenin*, London: New Left Books 1972, p. 174.
2. J–J. Rousseau, *The Social Contract and Other Discourses*, Dent & Sons 1973, p. 107.
3. *Ibid.*
4. *Ibid.,* p. 89.

5. *Ibid.*, p. 101.
6. *Ibid.*, p. 113.
7. *Ibid.*, p. 160.
8. *Ibid.*, p. 159.
9. *Ibid.*, p. 184.
10. *Ibid.*, p. 176.
11. *Ibid.*, p. 177.
12. L. Colletti, *From Rousseau to Lenin*, p. 181.
13. O. Gierke, *Natural Law and the Theory of Society*, Cambridge University Press 1934, p. 150.
14. L. Colletti, *From Rousseau to Lenin*, p. 185.
15. J-J. Rousseau, *The Social Contract*, p. 124.
16. *Ibid.*, p. 182.
17. *Ibid.*, p. 134.
18. *Ibid.*, p. 138.
19. *Ibid.*
20. *Ibid.*, p. 178.
21. *Ibid.*, p. 129.
22. *Ibid.*, p. 195.
23. *Ibid.*, p. 209.
24. *Ibid.*, p. 212.
25. *Ibid.*
26. *Ibid.*, p. 213.
27. *Ibid.*, p. 208.
28. *Ibid.*, p. 193.
29. *Ibid.*
30. *Ibid.*, p. 250.
31. *Ibid.*, p. 240.
32. *Ibid.*
33. *Ibid.*, p. 241.
34. *Ibid.*, p. 203.
35. L. Colletti, *From Rousseau to Lenin*, p. 183.
36. *Ibid.*, p. 145.
37. *Ibid.*, p. 147.
38. *Ibid.*, p. 180.
39. *Ibid.*

Smith
1. Adam Smith, *The Wealth of Nations* (abridged), Pelican 1978, p. 111.
2. *Ibid.*, p. 118.
3. *Ibid.*, p. 119.
4. *Ibid.*, p. 121.

5. *Ibid.,* p. 109.
6. Cited in I. Rubin, *A History of Economic Thought*, Ink Links 1979, p. 169.
7. A. Smith, *The Wealth of Nations*, Routledge & Kegan Paul, undated, V.II.715.
8. A. Smith, *The Wealth of Nations* (abridged), p. 117.
9. L. Colletti, *From Rousseau to Lenin*, New Left Books 1972, p. 156.
10. A. Smith, *The Wealth of Nations* (abridged), p.357.
11. *Ibid.*
12. *Ibid.,* p. 358.
13. A. Smith, *The Wealth of Nations*, IV. IX 540
14. *Ibid.*
15. *Ibid.,* p. 556.
16. *Ibid.,* p. 546.
17. *Ibid.,* p. 613.
18. *Ibid.,* p. 615.
19. *Ibid.,* p. 618.
20. *Ibid.*
21. *Ibid.,* p. 313.
22. *Ibid.,* p. 315.
23. *Ibid.,* p. 317.
24. Cited in K. Haakonssen, *The Science of a Legislator*, Cambridge University Press 1981, p. 6.
25. *Ibid.,* p. 57.
26. Smith, *The Wealth of Nations*, p. 556.
27. Thompson, *Writing by Candlelight*, Merlin Press 1980, p. 178.

*Hegel*
1. K. Löwith, *From Hegel to Nietzsche*, New York: Doubleday Anchor 1967, p. 240.
2. G. Hegel, *Philosophy of Right*, Oxford University Press 1973, para. 194.
3. *Ibid.,* para. 244.
4. Cited in S. Avineri, *Hegel's Theory of the Modern State*, Cambridge University Press 1972, p. 97.
5. *Ibid.,* p. 74.
6. Hegel, *Philosophy of Right*, para. 40.
7. *Ibid.,* para. 215.
8. *Ibid.,* para. 224.
9. *Ibid.,* para. 228.
10. *Ibid.,* para. 214.
11. *Ibid.*
12. *Ibid.,* addition 211.

13. *Ibid.*, addition 213.
14. *Ibid.*, addition 217.
15. *Ibid.*, para. 278.
16. *Ibid.*, para. 317.
17. *Ibid.*, addition 180.
18. *ibid.*, para. 308.
19. *Ibid.*, para. 273.
20. *Ibid.*, para. 273.
21. *Ibid.*, para 309.
22. *Ibid.*
23. *Ibid.*, para. 311.
24. *Ibid.*, para. 303.
25. *Ibid.*, para. 252.
26. *Ibid.*, para. 294.
27. *Ibid.*, para. 297.
28. *Ibid.*, para. 301.
29. *Ibid.*, addition 300.
30. *Ibid.*, para. 273.
31. *Ibid.*, para. 279.
32. *Ibid.*, para. 100.

## 2. Marx's critique of classical jurisprudence

1. K. Marx, 'Debates on Freedom of the Press', 1842.
2. Cited in H. Draper, *Karl Marx's Theory of Revolution*, Vol. 1, New York: Monthly Review Press.
3. K. Marx, *Contribution to a Critique of Hegel's Philosophy of Law*, 1843, in *Marx's Early Writings*, ed., L. Colletti, Pelican 1975.
4. *Ibid.*, p. 67.
5. *Ibid.*, p. 127.
6. *Ibid.*, p. 166.
7. *Ibid.*, p. 182.
8. *Ibid.*, p. 125.
9. *Ibid.*, p. 107.
10. *Ibid.*, p. 108.
11. *Ibid.*, p. 109.
12. *Ibid.*, p. 112.
13. *Ibid.*, p. 112.
14. *Ibid.*, p. 188.
15. *Ibid.*, p. 189.
16. *Ibid.*, p. 195.
17. *Ibid.*, p. 87.

18. Cited in H. Draper, *Karl Marx's Theory* . . ., p. 101.
19. *Ibid.,* p. 96.
20. K. Marx, 'Contribution . . .', p. 120.
21. *Ibid.,* p. 190.
22. K. Marx, *On the Jewish Question*, 1843, in *Marx's Early Writings.*
23. *Ibid.,* pp. 212-26.
24. *Ibid.,* p. 219.
25. *Ibid.*
26. *Ibid.,* p. 220.
27. *Ibid.*
28. *Ibid.,* p. 226.
29. *Ibid.,* p. 223.
30. *Ibid.*
31. *Ibid.,* p. 229.
32. *Ibid.,* p. 219.
33. *Ibid.,* p. 231.
34. *Ibid.,* p. 222.
35. K. Marx, *Economic and Philosophical Manuscripts*, 1844 in *Marx's Early Writings.*
36. *Ibid.,* p. 330.

## 3. The genesis of Marx's class theory of law and the state

1. H. Draper, *Karl Marx's Theory* . . .
2. K. Marx, *Economic and Philosophical Manuscripts.*
3. Marx and Engels, *The German Ideology*, 1846, Moscow: Progress Publishers 1964.
4. *Ibid.*
5. *Ibid.*, p. 99.
6. *Ibid.*
7. *Ibid.,* p. 348.
8. *Ibid.*
9. *Ibid.,* p. 52.
10. *Ibid.,* p. 53.
11. *Ibid.*
12. *Ibid.*
13. *Ibid.,* p. 99.
14. *Ibid.,* p. 87.
15. *Ibid.,* p. 100.
16. *Ibid.*
17. Cited in H. Draper, *Karl Marx's Theory* . . ., p. 217.
18. *The German Ideology*, p. 52.

## 4. Law, state and capital

1. Marx, *Economical and Philosophical Manuscripts*, p. 281.
2. Marx, *The Poverty of Philosophy*, 1847, Moscow: Progress Publishers, p. 170.
3. Marx, *Capital* Vol. 1, Penguin 1976 p. 178.
4. Marx, *Critique of Political Economy*, 1859, Moscow: Progress Publishers, p. 207.
5. Marx, *Economic and Philosophical Manuscripts*, p. 351.
6. *Ibid.,* p. 361.
7. *Ibid.,* p. 342.
8. *Ibid.,* p. 178.
9. Marx, *Critique of Political Economy*, p. 192.
10. Marx, *Grundrisse*, 1858, Penguin 1973 p. 472.
11. *Ibid.,* p. 475.
12. *Ibid.,* p. 484.
13. *Ibid.,* p. 485.
14. *Ibid.,* p. 489.
15. Marx, *Capital 1*, p. 303.
16. Marx, *Grundrisse*, p. 488.
17. *Ibid.*
18. Marx, *Capital 1*, p. 152.
19. Marx, *Grundrisse*, p. 251.
20. *Ibid.,* p. 243.
21. Marx, *Capital 1*, p. 178.
22. Marx, *Grundrisse*, p. 245.
23. *Ibid.,* p. 156.
24. *Ibid.,* p. 83.
25. Marx, *Capital 1*, p. 132.
26. Marx, *Grundrisse*, p. 156.
27. *Ibid.,* p. 161.
28. *Ibid.,* p. 163.
29. *Ibid.,* p. 157.
30. Marx, *Critique of the Gotha Programme*, 1875, in *Selected Works of Marx and Engels*, Lawrence & Wishart 1968, p. 320.
31. *Ibid.,* p. 319.
32. Marx, *Critique of Political Economy*, p. 193.
33. Marx, *Grundrisse*, p. 247.
34. Marx, *Capital 1*, p. 280.
35. Marx, *Grundrisse*, p. 251.
36. Cited in Simon Clarke, *Marx, Marginalism and Modern Sociology*, Macmillan 1982, p. 86.

37. Marx, *Capital 1*, p. 680.
38. *Ibid.,* p. 713.
39. *Ibid.* p. 729.
40. Marx, *Grundrisse*, p. 514.
41. Marx, *Capital 1*, p. 344.
42. Marx, *Grundrisse*, p. 507.
43. *Ibid.,* pp. 283ff.
44. R. Rosdolsky, *The Making of Marx's Capital*, Pluto Press 1977, ch. 12.

## 5. Bourgeois and socialist democracy

1. Marx, *18th Brumaire of Louis Bonaparte*, 1852, in D. Fernbach ed., *Surveys from Exile*, Penguin 1973.
2. Cited in Draper, *Karl Marx's Theory* . . . 1, p. 300.
3. *Ibid.,* p. 301.
4. See Draper, *Karl Marx's Theory* . . ., Vol. 2.
5. Cited in Draper, *Karl Marx's Theory* . . ., Vol. 1, p. 183.
6. Marx, *Critique of the Gotha Programme,* 1875, in *Selected Works*, p. 320.
7. *Ibid.*
8. *Ibid.*
9. *Ibid.,* p. 317.
10. Marx, *First Draft of the Civil War in France*, 1871, in D. Fernbach ed., *The First International and After*, Penguin 1974, p. 246.
11. Marx, *Economical and Philosophical Manuscripts*, p. 346.
12. Marx and Engels, *The German Ideology*, p. 95.
13. *Ibid.,* p. 97.
14. Marx, *The Civil War in France*, 1871, in *Selected Works*, p. 291.
15. *Ibid.,* p. 296.
16. *Ibid.,* p. 289.
17. Marx, *Critique of the Gotha Programme*, p. 320.
18. Marx, 'Letter to Kugelman', 12.4.1871, in *Selected Correspondence*, Moscow: Progress Publishers.
19. Marx, *The Civil War in France*, p. 295.

## 6. The contradictory foundation of law and the state

1. Cited in E.P. Thompson, *Poverty of Theory*, Merlin 1978, p. 259; Engels, 'Letter to Mehring', 1893.
2. Rosdolsky, *The Making of Marx's Capital*, pp. 129–30.
3. Marx, *Grundrisse*, p. 177.
4. Marx, *Capital 1*, p. 165.
5. *Ibid.,* p. 163.

6. *Ibid.,* p. 189.

7. Pankhurst, S. *The Suffragette Movement*, Virago 1977, p. 37.

8. Marx, *Grundrisse*, p. 123.

9. *Ibid.,* p. 251.

10. Marx, *Capital* Vol. III, Penguin 1981, p. 794.

11. *Ibid.*

12. Marx, *Grundrisse*, p. 254.

13. See first four chapters of Marx, *Capital*, Vol. II, Penguin 1978.

14. Marx, *First Draft of the Civil War in France*, in Fernbach, *The First International*, p. 285.

## 7. Twentieth-century theories

### Pashukanis

1. Evgeny Pashukanis, *Law and Marxism*, Pluto Press 1983, p. 81. (I have also used some translations from the Academic Press edition, ed. Beirne & Sharlet, 1980).

2. Marx, *Capital* Vol. III.

3. Marx, *Grundrisse*, p. 156.

4. Pashukanis, *Law and Marxism*, p. 119.

5. Marx, *Capital* Vol. I, p. 448.

6. *Ibid.,* p. 450.

7. Pashukanis, *Law and Marxism*, p. 134.

### Thompson

1. E.P. Thompson, *Writing by Candlelight*, Merlin 1980.

2. Thompson, *Poverty of Theory*, p. 5.

3. *Ibid.,* p. 288.

4. *Ibid.,* p. 289.

5. Thompson, *Whigs and Hunters*, Penguin 1977, p. 260.

6. Thompson, *Poverty of Theory*, Merlin 1978, p. 288.

7. Thompson, *Whigs and Hunters*, p. 268.

8. *Ibid.,* p. 268.

9. Thompson, '18th Century English Society – class struggle without class?' *Social History* 2, 1978.

10. D. Hay in Hay *et al., Albion's Fatal Tree*, Penguin 1977, p. 246.

11. C. Hill, *Reformation to Industrial Revolution*, Penguin 1979.

12. A. Smith, *The Wealth of Nations*.

### Foucault

1. M. Foucault, *Discipline and Punish*, Allen Lane, 1975 p. 80.

2. *Ibid.,* p. 202.

3. Foucault, *Power/Knowledge*, Harvester Press 1980, p. 83.

4. See F. Neumann, *Behemoth*, Gollancz 1942.

# Bibliography

**Classical jurisprudence (Chapter 1)**

*Place of publication of books is London unless otherwise indicated.*

Atiyah, P.S., *The Rise and Fall of Freedom of Contract*, Oxford University Press 1979.

Avineri, S., *Hegel's Theory of the Modern State*, Cambridge University Press 1972.

Colletti, L., *From Rousseau to Lenin*, New Left Books 1972.

Colletti, L., *Marxism and Hegel*, Verso 1979.

D'Entreves, A.P., *Natural Law: An Introduction to Legal Philosophy*, Hutchinson 1977.

Elshtain, J. B., *Public Man, Private Woman: Women in Social and Political Thought*, Martin Robertson, Oxford University Press 1981.

Forbes, D., *Hume's Philosophical Politics*, Cambridge University Press, 1975.

Forbes, D., *Hume's Philosophical Politics*, Cambridge University Press, 1975.

Gierke, O., *Political Theories of the Middle Ages*, Boston: Beacon 1958.

Gierke, O., *Natural Law and the Theory of Society*, Cambridge University Press 1934.

Gramsci, A., *History, Philosophy and Culture in the Young Gramsci* P. Cavalcanti, and P. Piccone, eds, St. Louis: Telos 1975. 1958.

Grotius, H., *Of the Law of War and Peace*, 1927 tr. F.W. Kelsey.

Haakonssen, K., *The Science of a Legislator*, Cambridge University Press 1981.

Habermas, J., *Theory and Practice*, Heinemann 1974.

Hegel, G., *Philosophy of Right*, Oxford University Press 1973.

Hill, C., *The Century of Revolution*, Nelson 1980.

Hobbes, T., *Leviathan*, Penguin 1968.

Hobbes, T., *Elements of Law*, Cambridge University Press 1928.

Hont, I. and Ignatieff, M., 'Needs and Justice in *The Wealth of Nations:* an

Introductory Essay', in *Wealth and Virtue: the Shaping of Political Economy in the Scottish Enlightenment*, Cambridge University Press 1984.

Laski, H., *An Introduction of Politics*, George Allen & Unwin 1934.

Laski, H., *Political Thought in England: Locke to Bentham*, Oxford University Press 1948.

Locke, J.. *Essays on the Laws of Nature*, W. von Leyden, ed., Oxford University Press 1954.

Locke, J., *Two Treatises of Government*, Cambridge University Press 1963.

Löwith, K., *From Hegel to Nietzsche*, New York: Doubleday Anchor 1967.

Macpherson, C.B., *The Political Theory of Possessive Individualism*, Oxford University Press 1962.

Marcuse, H., *Reason and Revolution: Hegel and the Rise of Social Theory*, Boston: Beacon 1960.

Meek, R., *Smith, Marx and After*, Chapman 1977.

Meek, R., *Studies in the Labour Theory of Value*, Lawrence & Wishart 1973.

Montesquieu, *The Spirit of Laws*, Berkeley: University of California 1977.

Pufendorf, S., *Of the Law of Nature and Nations*, 1729. Tr. Basil Kennett.

Rousseau, J-J., *The Social Contract and Other Discourses*, Dent & Sons 1973.

Rubin, I.I., *A History of Economic Thought*, Ink Links 1979.

Skillen, A., *Ruling Illusions*, Harvester, 1977.

Smith, A., *Lectures in Jurisprudence*, Oxford University Press 1978.

Smith, A., *Theory of Moral Sentiments*, Oxford University Press 1978.

Smith, A., *The Wealth of Nations*, George Routledge, undated.

Smith, A., *The Wealth of Nations* (abridged), Penguin 1978.

Thompson, E.P., 'The Moral Economy of the English Crowd', *Past and Present* 50, 1971.

Tribe, K., *Land, Labour and Economic Discourse*, Routledge & Kegan Paul 1978.

Tuck, R., *Natural Rights Theories*, Cambridge University Press 1979.

Tully, J., *A Discourse on Property: John Locke and his Adversaries*, Cambridge University Press 1982.

Warrender, H., *The Political Philosophy of Hobbes*, Oxford University Press 1957.

Willey, B., *The Seventeenth Century Background*, Penguin 1972.

## Classical Marxism (Chapters 2 — 6)

Althusser, L., *Lenin and Philosophy*, New Left Books 1971.

Cain, M and Hunt, A., eds, *Marx and Engels on Law*, Academic Press 1979.

Clarke, S., *Marx, Marginalism and Modern Sociology*, Macmillan 1982.

Cohen, G., *Karl Marx's Theory of History*, Clarendon, Oxford 1978.

Cohen, M. *et. al.*, eds., *Marx, Justice and History*, Princeton University Press 1980.

Colletti, L., *Introduction to Marx's Early Writings*, Penguin 1975.

Draper, H., 'Karl Marx's Theory of Revolution, Vols. 1 and 2', New York: Monthly Review 1977, 1978.

Engels, F., *The Condition of England: The English Constitution*, (1844) in *Marx and Engles Collected Works 3*, Lawrence & Wishart, 1975.

Engels, F., *The Condition of the Working Class in England 1844*, Panther 1972.

Engels, F., *Anti-Dühring* (1885), Lawrence & Wishart 1943.

Engels, F., *Germany: Revolution and Counter-Revolution*, Lawrence & Wishart, 1969.

Engels, F., 'Letter to Schmidt' (1890) in *Selected Correspondence*, Lawrence & Wishart, 1975.

Engels F., *The Origin of the Family, Private Property and the State*, in *Selected Works of Marx and Engels*, Lawrence & Wishart, 1968.

Engels F., *Outlines of a Critique of Political Economy* (1843) in *Marx and Engels Collected Works* 3, Lawrence & Wishart 1975.

Fine, B. *et. al.*, eds., *Capitalism and the Rule of Law*, Hutchinson 1979.

Holloway, J. and Picciotto, S. (eds), *State and Capital*, Edward Arnold 1978.

Marx, K., *Capital: I* (1866), Penguin 1976.

Marx, K., *Capital: II* (1885), Penguin 1978.

Marx, K., *Capital: III* (1894), Penguin 1981.

Marx, K., *The Civil War in France* (1871), in *Selected Works of Marx and Engels*, Lawrence & Wishart 1968.

Marx, K., *The Class Struggle in France* (1850) in D. Fernbach, ed., *Surveys from Exile*, Pengn 1973.

Marx, K., *Comments on the Latest Prussian Censorship Laws*, (1842), in *Marx and Engels Collected Works* I, Lawrence & Wishart 1975.

Marx, K., *Contribution to a Critique of Hegel's Philosophy of Right*, (1843), in *Marx's Early Writings*, Pelican 1975.

Marx, K., *Contribution to the Critique of Political Economy* (1859), Moscow: Progress Publishers 1977.

Marx, K., *Critique of the Gotha Programme* (1875), in *Selected Works of Marx and Engels*, Lawrence & Wishart 1968.

Marx, K., *Debates on Freedom of the Press* (1842) *Marx and Engels Collected Works* I, Lawrence & Wishart 1975.

Marx, K., *Debates on the Law of Thefts of Wood*, (1843), *Marx and Engels Collected Works* I, Lawrence & Wishart 1975.

Marx, K., *Economic and Philosophical Manuscripts* (1844) in *Marx's Early Writings*, Pelican 1975.

Marx, K., *18th Brumaire of Louis Bonaparte* (1852), in D. Fernbach, ed., *Surveys from Exile*, Penguin 1973.

Marx, K., *First Draft of the Civil War in France* (1871), in D. Fernbach, ed., *The First International and After*, Penguin 1974.

Marx, K. and Engels, F., *The German Ideology* (1846), Moscow: Progress Publishers 1964.

Marx, K., *Grundrisse*, Penguin 1973.

Marx, K., 'Letter to Annenkov 28.12.1846' *Marx and Engels Selected Works*, Lawrence & Wishart 1968.

Marx, K., 'Letter to Kugelman, 12.4.1871 *Marx and Engels Selected Works*, Lawrence & Wishart 1968.

Marx, K., 'Letter to Schweitzer 24.1.1865', *Marx and Engels Selected Correspondence*, Lawrence & Wishart 1975.

Marx, K., *On the Jewish Question* (1843) in *Marx's Early Writings*, Pelican 1975.

Marx, K., *The Poverty of Philosophy* (1847), Moscow: Progress Publishers 1967.

Marx, K., 'Critique of Hegel's Doctrine of the State' (1843) in *Marx's Early Writings*, Penguin 1975.

Meszaros, I., *Marx's Theory of Alienation*, Merlin, 1970.

Picciotto, S., 'The Theory of the State, Class Struggle and the Rule of Law', in B. Fine *et. al.*, *Capitalism and the Rule of Law*, Hutchinson 1979.

Rosdolsky, R., *The Making of Marx's Capital*, Pluto Press 1977.

Rubin, I. I., *Essay on Marx's Theory of Value*, Detroit: Black & Red 1972.

Sumner, C., *Reading Ideologies: An Investigation into the Marxist Theory of Ideology and Law*, Academic Press, 1979.

Young, G., 'Justice and Capitalist Production: Marx and Bourgeois Ideology', *Canadian Journal of Philosophy* 8, 3, September 1978.

Young, G., 'Marx's Theory of Bourgeois Law' in S. Spitzer, *Research in Law and Sociology, Vol. 2*, Greenwich, Connecticut: JAI Press 1978.

**Twentieth-century theorists (Chapter 7)**

**E. Pashukanis**

Arthur, C. J., 'Towards a Materialist Theory of Law', in Critique 7, Winter 1976–7.

Arthur, C.J., 'Editor's Introduction' to E. Pashukanis, *Law and Marxism*, Pluto Press 1983.

Balbus, I., 'The commodity form and the legal form', *Law and Society Review* II, 3, 1977.

Binns, P., 'Law and Marxism', *Capital and Class* 10.

Carr, E.H., *Foundations of a Planned Economy*; Vol. 2, pp. 348–81: 'The Rule of Law'.

Carr, E.H., *Socialism in One Country*; Vol. 1, Macmillan 1958. pp. 66–88: 'The Law'.

Collard, D., *Soviet Justice*, Gollancz 1937.

Dobvin, S., 'Soviet jurisprudence and socialism', *Law Quarterly* 52, 1936, pp. 402–24.

Edelman, B., *Ownership of the Image*, Routledge & Kegan Paul 1979.

Fuller, L., 'Pashukanis and Vyshinski', *Michigan Law Review* XLVII, 1949, p. 1157.

Hazard, J., 'The abortive codes of the Pashukanis school' in D.D. Barry, F.J.M. Feldbrugge and D. Lasok eds., *Codification in the Communist World*, Leyden 1975, pp. 158–67.

Hazard, J., 'Housecleaning in Soviet Law', *American Quarterly on the Soviet Union* I, 1, 1938.

Hazard, J., 'Pashukanis is no traitor', *American Journal of International Law* L1, 385, April 1957.

Hazard, J., ed., *Soviet Legal Philosophy*, Harvard University Press 1951.

Hirst, P., *On Law and Ideology*, Macmillan, 1979.

Jessop, B., 'On recent Marxist theories of law, the State and juridico-political ideology', *International Journal of the Sociology of Law* Vol. 8, 4, November 1980.

Kamenka, E. and Tay, A.E.S., 'The life and afterlife of a Bolshevik Jurist', *Problems of Communism*, January/February 1970.

Kelsen, H., *The Communist Theory of Law*, Stevens and Sons 1955.

Laski, H., *Law and Justice in Soviet Russia*, L. & V. Woolf 1935.

Lenin, V.I., *State and Revolution* (1917) Moscow: Progress Publishers 1961.

Norrie, A., 'Pashukanis and Commodity Form Theory: A Report to Warrington', International Journal of Sociology of Law, 10, 4, November 1982.

Pashukanis, E., *Law and Marxism*, Pluto Press 1983.

Pashukanis, E., eds. P. Beirne and R. Sharlet, *Selected Writings on Marxism and Law*, Academic Press 1980.

Redhead, S., 'The discreet charm of bourgeois law: a note on Pashukanis', *Critique* 9, 1978.

Renner, K., *The Institutions of Private Law and Their Functions*, Routledge & Kegan Paul, 1949.

Schlesinger, R., *Soviet Legal Theory*, Kegan Paul, Trench, Trubner & Co. 1946.

Sharlet, R., 'Pashukanis and the rise of Soviet Marxist jurisprudence 1924–30' *Soviet Union* Vol. 1, 2, 1974.

Sharlet, R., 'Pashukanis and the withering away of law in USSR' in Sheila Fitzpatrick, ed., *Cultural Revolution in Russia 1928-31*, Indiana University Press 1974.

Trotsky, L., *The Revolution Betrayed*, Pathfinder Press, 1973.

Vyshinksy, A., *The Law and the Soviet State*, Macmillan 1948.

Warrington, W., 'Pashukanis and the commodity form theory', *International Journal of the Sociology of Law*, 9, 1, February 1981.

Zelitch, J., *Soviet Administration of Criminal Law*, University of Pennysylvania Press 1931.

Zile, Z., ed., *Ideas and Forces in Soviet Legal History*, Wisconsin University Press 1970.

### E. P. Thompson

Anderson, P., *Arguments Within English Marxism*, Verso 1980.

Brewer, J. and Styles, J., eds., *An Ungovernable People*, Hutchinson 1980.

Clarke, S., 'Socialism, humanism and the critique of economism', *History Workshop* 8, Autumn 1979.

Cockburn, J.S., ed., *Crime in England 1550-1800*, Methuen 1977.

Hay, D. *et. al.*, *Albion's Fatal Tree*, Penguin 1977.

Hall, S., *et. al.*, (eds) *Policing the Crisis*, Macmillan 1978.

Hill, C., *Reformation to Industrial Revolution*, Penguin 1979.

Hilton, R., Introduction to *The Transition from Feudalism to Capitalism*, New Left Books 1976.

Hobsbawm, E., *Bandits*, Penguin 1972.

Hobsbawm, E., 'The Machine Breakers' in *Labouring Men*, Weidenfeld & Nicolson 1964.

Hobsbawm, E., *Primitive Rebels*, Manchester University Press 1959.

Horowitz, M., 'The rule of law: an unqualified human good?' *Yale Law Journal*, Volume 86 (1977).

Johnson, R., 'Edward Thompson, Eugene Genovese and socialist humanist history' *History Workshop* 6, 1978.

Linebaugh, P., 'Eighteenth century crime, popular movements and social control', *Bulletin for the Study of Labour History*, 1972.

Linebaugh, P., 'Karl Marx, the theft of wood and working class composition. A contribution to the current debate', in *Crime and Social Justice*, Fall/Winter 1976.

Merri, H.A., 'The nature and function of law: A criticism of E.P. Thompson's "Whigs and Hunters" ', *British Journal of Law and Society* 7, 2, 1980, pp. 194–214.

Neumann, F., *The Democratic and Authoritarian State* Collier-Macmillan 1957.

Philips, D., 'The revisionist history of crime in Britain' in S. Cohen, and A. Scull, eds., *Social Control and the State*, Oxford: Martin Robertson 1983.

Rudé, G., *London and Paris in the Eighteenth Century: Studies in Popular Protest*, Fontana 1970.

Thompson, E.P., 'Eighteenth-century England: class society without class', *Social History* 2, 1978, pp. 133–66.

Sugerman, D., *et. al.*, 'Crime, law and authority in nineteenth century Britain', Middlesex Polytechnic History Journal, Spring/Autumn 1982.

Thompson, E.P., *The Making of the English Working Class*, Penguin 1976.

Thompson, E.P., 'The moral economy of the English crowd in the eighteenth century', *Past and Present* 50, February 1971, pp. 76–136.

Thompson, E.P., 'Patrician society, plebian culture', *Journal of Social History* 7, 1974, pp. 382–405.

Thompson, E.P., *Poverty of Theory*, Merlin 1978.

Thompson, E.P., *Whigs and Hunters*, Penguin 1977.

Thompson, E.P., *Writing by Candlelight*, Merlin 1980.

Trotsky, L., *The Struggle Against Fascism in Germany*, Pathfinder 1971.

**M. Foucault**

Dews, P., 'The "Nouvelle Philosophie" and Foucault' *Economy and Society* 8, 2, 1979.

Fine B., 'The Bourgeois Prison', *Crime and Social Justice* 13, Summer 1980.

Fine B., 'Objectification on and the contradictions of bourgeois power', *Economy and Society* 6, 4, 1977.

Fine B., 'Struggles against discipline: The theory and politics of Michel Foucault', *Capital and Class* 9, 1979.

Foucault M., *The Archeology of Knowledge*, Tavistock 1972.

Foucault M., *Discipline and Punish*, Allen Lane 1975.

Foucault M., *The History of Sexuality*, Allen Lane 1979.

Foucault M., *Madness and Civilisation*, Mentor 1967.

Foucault M., 'On Attica', *Telos*, Spring 1974.

Foucault M., *Power/Knowledge*, Brighton: Harvester Press 1980.

Foucault M., 'Prison talk', *Radical Philosophy* 16, 1977.

Gordon C., 'Birth of the subject', *Radical Philosophy* 17, Summer 1977.

Ignatieff, M., *A Just Measure of Pain*, Macmillan 1978.

Ignatieff, M., 'State, civil society and total institutions: a critique of recent social histories of punishment' in S. Cohen and A. Scull eds., *Social Control and the State*, Oxford: Martin Robertson 1983.

Makarenko, A., *The Road to Life*, Progress 1973.

Melossi, D., and Pavarini, M., *The Prison and the Factory*, trans. G. Cousin, Macmillan 1981.

Morris M. and Patton P., eds., *Michel Foucault, Power, Truth, Strategy*, Feral, Sydney 1979.

Neumann F., *Behemoth*, Gollancz 1942.

Poulantzas, N., *State, Power, Socialism*, Verso, 1978.

Renard, *L'Institution*, Paris 1931.

Rusche, G., and Kirchheimer, O., *Punishment and Social Structure*, Russell and Russell, New York, 1968.

# Index